Women and Family Life in Early Modern German Literature

Writers of sixteenth-century German popular literature took great interest in describing, debating, commenting on, and prescribing gender roles, and discourses of gender can be traced in texts of all kinds from this period. This book focuses on popular works by Georg Wickram, Jakob Frey, Martin Montanus, and Johann Fischart, all of whom published novels, joke books, plays and/or moral treatises on marriage and family life in Strasbourg in the sixteenth century. Their works express not only their own ideas on women's roles as wives and mothers, but also societal values at a time of religious, political, and cultural change. The view of gender issues provided by these writers is not a simple one, as they ascribed widely varying characteristics to "woman" and her relationship to "man." The book thus analyzes the social and cultural construction of the concept of "woman" as indicated not only by the narrators' comments, but also by the relationships and roles of men and women characters in the narratives. Overall, the focus is on the disparities that persisted in the sixteenth-century discourse of gender, confusing all attempts to arrive at definitive gender roles. In the end, the study argues for something that can best be described as a "flowing continuity" or a "continuous flow" in the discourses that form the sixteenth-century concepts of "woman" and "man."

Elisabeth Wåghäll Nivre is associate professor of German at Växjö University, Sweden.

Studies in German Literature, Linguistics, and Culture

Edited by James Hardin
(*South Carolina*)

Women and Family Life in Early Modern German Literature

Elisabeth Wåghäll Nivre

CAMDEN HOUSE

Copyright © 2004 Elisabeth Wåghäll Nivre

All Rights Reserved. Except as permitted under current legislation, no part of this work may be photocopied, stored in a retrieval system, published, performed in public, adapted, broadcast, transmitted, recorded, or reproduced in any form or by any means, without the prior permission of the copyright owner.

First published 2004
by Camden House

Camden House is an imprint of Boydell & Brewer Inc.
668 Mt. Hope Avenue, Rochester, NY 14620, USA
and of Boydell & Brewer Limited
PO Box 9, Woodbridge, Suffolk IP12 3DF, UK

ISBN: 1–57113–197–3

Library of Congress Cataloging-in-Publication Data

Nivre, Elisabeth Waghall
  Women and family life in early modern German literature / Elisabeth Waghall Nivre
    p. cm. — (Studies in German Literature, Linguistics, and Culture)
  Includes bibliographical references and index.
  ISBN 1–57113–197–3 (hardcover: alk. paper)
  1. German literature — Early modern, 1500–1700 — History and Criticism. 2. Women in literature — History — 16th Century.
  3. Family in literature — History —16th century. I. Title. II. Series.

PT241.N58 2003
830.9'3522—dc21

2003016001

A catalogue record for this title is available from the British Library.

This publication is printed on acid-free paper.
Printed in the United States of America.

To Joakim and Fredrik

Contents

Acknowledgments ix

Introduction 1

1: Chapbooks — Popular Texts for a Large Audience 27

2: The Novels of Georg Wickram 95

3: Woman, Wife, Witch?: The Representation of Woman in Johann Fischart's *Geschichtklitterung* 131

4: Polizeiordnungen: Taming the Shrew with Common Sense and the Law 157

Conclusion 191

Works Cited 199

Index 217

Acknowledgments

THIS BOOK IS THE RESULT of a long process that started at Davidson College in 1993, when I received a generous travel grant enabling me to spend a summer in Strasbourg and to start a new project after the completion of my dissertation. The stay in Strasbourg was of immense importance to me: I was able to browse through the library catalogues at the university library (BNUS) and acquaint myself with the municipal archives as well as with the holdings of the Collegium Wilhelmitanum of the St. Thomas seminary in my search for texts dealing with the construction of the early modern woman. Anthony Steinhoff and Elizabeth Sage, then graduate students in history, now friends and colleagues, helped me both to find my way in the archives and libraries and to make myself understood when my poor conversational skills in French proved to be of little or no use.

The research I started in Strasbourg resulted in a number of papers that have been presented at conferences, but my scholarly work was put on hold because of my decision to leave Davidson College and my inspiring and helpful colleagues there (a special thanks to my mentor at the college, Robin Barnes), and to return to my native country of Sweden. I was offered a position at Växjö University, which I had attended as an undergraduate in 1995. I was kindly granted a research sabbatical, and the time this provided allowed me to apply for a grant from the Council for Research in Humanities and the Social Sciences (Humanistisk-Samhällsvetenskapliga Forskningsrådet, HSFR). Without this grant it would have been almost impossible for me to finish this book, since Swedish institutions of higher education are largely dependent on external funding for research projects (their own funds usually cover only graduate programs). The grant has been crucial for my scholarly work, and I am deeply grateful for having been given this opportunity.

The grant has also paid for several conference trips and a second visit to the archives in Strasbourg. The friendly assistance of the employees at the municipal archives was of tremendous importance to me. I would especially like to thank François Schwickert, who very kindly let me use his annotated list of contents of the first four volumes of the Mandats et Reglements (known as R/1–4).[1] The list was still in preparation in 2001 but will be of great help to scholars of Strasbourg history when published. My husband, a linguist fluent in French, helped me find the right person to talk to at the BNUS, and the desired texts were promptly made available to me.

I want to express my gratitude to Gerhild S. Williams, my mentor, colleague, and friend, who has always encouraged me to believe in what I am doing while also acting as a discussion partner and critical reader of my scholarly work. Special thanks go to Lynne Tatlock, who helped me write my project proposal in English, and to Tom Brady, who gave me all the information I could possibly need before going to Strasbourg to plan my new project. There are also a number of other colleagues in the United States who have inspired me to work on this book — my thanks go to each and every one of you.

Sweden is a small country, and the field of sixteenth-century studies is even smaller here. However, I have the privilege and pleasure of working with colleagues in the history department at Växjö University who have provided me with food for thought in numerous great discussions. I am particularly grateful to Malin Lennartsson who has taken her time to read the complete manuscript. I also want to thank Roddy Nilsson for reading the introduction, especially in regard to Foucault, and my colleague in the German department, Bärbel Westphal, for reading parts of the manuscript and discussing theoretical questions. I would also like to thank my student assistants Nina Johansson and Maria Gårdmo, who helped me with everything from checking quotations to checking the spellchecker, and my doctoral student Anna Callenholm, who gave me ideas for making the text more readable. Toril Moi once said: "I also speak as a Norwegian teaching French literature in England, as a stranger both to France and to the English-speaking world, and thus a woman writing in a foreign language about matters to which in many ways she remains marginal."[2] As a native Swede working with early modern German texts and often writing in English, I know exactly what Moi is referring to. I am forever indebted to Cheryl Jones Fur and Deborah Anne Bowen, who corrected my English and proofread the manuscript.

Finally I would like to express my gratitude to Professor James Hardin and Camden House, who have believed in my capacity to finish this project successfully. I also want to thank my husband for his patience and for having promised to not write a book at the same time as I as long as there is a small child in the family. This leads me to the last person I would like to mention: my son Fredrik, who is now three and a half years old and loves life as much as one could wish for, but whose answer when asked in daycare what his mother loves most of all in life was: books. Fortunately, this is not true.

E. W. N.
Växjö October 2002

Notes

[1] The Mandats et Reglements consist of city ordinances issued by the magistrates of Strasbourg, many of them dealing with the social standing of women, restrictions surrounding marriage, and the moral aspects of the relationship between men and women.

[2] Toril Moi, *Sexual/Textual Politics: Feminist Literary Theory* (London, New York: Methuen, 1985), xiv.

Illustration from Georg Wickram's *Vom guten und bösen Nachbarn*.

Introduction

"Du sagst mir ein ding"/ sprach Lucia / "so mir mein liebste Cassandra gantz rhaw und onbewißt ist / mocht aber (wo dirs nit vertrüßlich were) gern semliche Histori von gedachten weibern vernemmen." Darauff antwort Cassandra / "ich sag dir mein liebste Lucia / das ich dise Histori / nit einmal / sunder zum offtern mal gelesen hab / Darzu mich dann nit wenig geursacht hat / der nutz und schaden so daraus erfolgt ist."[1]

IN *VON GUTEN UND BÖSEN NACHBARN* the German author Georg Wickram has two female characters, Cassandra and Lucia, talk about historical and mythological figures, using them as examples of what they — or rather Wickram — consider correct and incorrect female behavior. By referring to past events, age-old thoughts and ideas, and something that can best be described as convention or "traditional behavior," the manners of women from the growing urban middle class of the sixteenth century are commented upon. By generalizing and by using well-known stories from the past the author is thus able to justify or condemn what he considers typical female behavior.

It was originally my intention to focus on the construction of "woman"[2] in the early modern period by investigating the representation of woman primarily in a number of texts that generally are regarded as fictional as well as in some legal documents from the same period.[3] It has, however, proven impossible without taking "man" into account. The main problem to be dealt with is thus the seemingly various characteristics ascribed to (inscribed in) "woman" and her relationship to "man" as depicted in literary texts of different kinds, texts whose primary function — according to their authors — is to tell a "good story." I will therefore analyze not only the social and cultural construction of "woman" but also the relationship between characters described as "men" and "women" in the narrative. All texts discussed below are written by male authors, but most of them address men and women alike. What implications does this have for the depiction of male and female characters in the text? The need to look at the position of the male author and narrator as well as the male characters in the text in order to investigate relationships between men and women rather than to simply search for stereotypes necessitates a widening of the concept "women's studies."[4] The study can be called feminist in that it has special interest in the female characters in the texts — but only in their relationships to the male characters. The goal is to avoid readings of the text that by definition reduce the interpretation to a pinning down of misogynist comments made by the male author/narrator. It seems more important to look for the functions men and women are given, for the roles they play in the text, and for the possible reversal of roles — the play with sex as well as gender — that can be found, especially in some of the chapbook texts discussed here. Joan Wallach Scott's analysis of how sexual difference per se is articulated in various discourses and by various institutions by asking the question what makes man into man and woman into woman can easily be adapted for the analysis of early modern texts and is therefore crucial for this study.[5]

The analyses presented in this book will give neither a true and complete picture of gender roles in early modern Germany nor a survey of all changes in literature and society.[6] My aim, rather, is to map discursive fields that are part of the larger discourse of gender. The study hopes to offer the reader some parts of the jigsaw puzzle concerning the relationship between women and men in sixteenth-century German literature, a time sometimes referred to as late medieval, sometimes as early modern in scholarly texts.[7] It will analyze the role literature plays in constructing, disseminating, circulating, revising, and preserving myths of cultural identity of which gender is one of many aspects. The scholarship on women and gender in sixteenth-century English texts is vast and includes scholars from all disciplines, and a great deal is written on Italian texts, but there is considerably less on German literature, even with the increase in publications in the 1990s.[8] This book should be seen as one of a growing number of publications that tries to work for a change.

Sixteenth-century authors of vernacular literature took great interest in discussing, commenting on, describing, and prescribing gender roles — intentionally or not. Something subsumed under a "discourse of gender" can be found in texts of very different types. By "discourse" I understand a system or set of textual — written and oral — statements or utterances as well as institutionalized or conventional mental patterns shaped by and shaping the institutions they are part of.[9] It includes the study of the rules generating discourse and the cultural and social setting in which a discourse is realized. An important question to ask is whether the interest in matters regarding one's sex or one's gender marks a change in discourse or even a paradigmatic shift — assuming that social changes influence the way we perceive ourselves — or if we need to search for other answers. This study focuses on the disparity that seems to break all barriers of this discourse, confusing all attempts to clear answers. It will therefore try to argue for something that can best be described as a "flowing continuity" or a "continuous flow" in the discourses that form "woman" and "man."

The introduction will present some thoughts on different theoretical aspects of importance for my discussion as well as a presentation of the authors and the texts. Chapter 1 focuses on a discussion of early modern chapbooks — "Schwanksammlungen" — by Georg Wickram (ca. 1505–ca. 1560), Jakob Frey (ca. 1520–ca. 1562), and Martin Montanus (ca. 1530–after 1566). All wrote books consisting of "Schwänke," short humorous stories on human weaknesses, mocking men and women, old and young. The second chapter will analyze significant prose novels by Wickram, whose great productivity and interest in portraying relationships between men and women make his texts an interesting source for analysis. In chapter 3 I will turn to a text by Johann Fischart (1546–ca. 1590), whose literary work can in some respects be regarded as the opposite pole to Wickram's more modest texts. Fischart's grotesque picture of the world in the *Geschichtklitterung* is, stylistically in particular, as far away from Wickram's straightforward prose and quiet characters as one can possibly come. Chapter 4 investigates non-fictional prose, specifically, a number of city ordinances from sixteenth-century Strasbourg. It will question whether these documents express a different approach to gender matters if compared with fictional texts, even though they have a common interest in drawing up limits for male and female agency. The concluding chapter should be regarded as an attempt to summarize and to make sense of the disparate images of women and men circulating in the various texts. The whole study is based on doubt, doubt that coherence can be found at all, but I hope to find some parts that will fit into the jigsaw puzzle of gender relations in early modern texts.

Theoretical Backdrop: Gender, Culture, Literature

The interest in explaining and justifying the present by comparing it with the past remains vivid even though the ways we look at the connections between the past, the present, and the future have changed.[10] The fascination with the encounter with past times and cultures is still strong in a world known as postmodern, questioning what was long known as "facts"; the loss of belief in a unified world does not seem to keep us from searching for meaning and coherence in order to expand our knowledge of the world and of ourselves. This can help explain the growing number of scholarly texts on a time often regarded as a threshold to the modern world.[11] Most of these texts agree that the encounter with new lands and continents, scientific progress, the establishment of nation-states, and the reformation movements within the Western Church led to immense structural, political, cultural, and religious changes throughout Europe. The debate as to when these changes occurred, how they are related to each other, how they can best be described, and what impact they had on the common man has been intense, however, and will not come to an end unless we lose interest in what preceded us. The so-called cultural turn experienced in literary and historical research in the past two decades has offered new insight into the early modern period; the cultural dimension of the social has opened up for a critical discussion and revaluation of previous work.[12] The result is a notion of cultural expressions and representations as fluid and variable. They are seen as taking different forms over time and space as well as within a certain time frame. It is thus no longer problematic that gender or class identities take different expressions in different discourses within a certain society. This recognition makes possible a reading of popular texts in the vernacular — like *Von guten und bösen Nachbarn* — that does not regard them as simple mimesis of the early modern middle class or as less important cultural artifacts compared with the learned texts in Latin.

If used with care this openness when looking at "culture" and "discourse" does not have to end in complete relativism, but rather allows for an interdisciplinary approach that can be very fruitful for the analysis of early modern literature. Even though the value of literary texts for the study of what is commonly called real life and real events remains in debate one cannot forget that literary works are historical documents: they have come down to us in written form, they provide firsthand information, not just information about the literary production at a given time, as interesting as this might be. But they do not merely reflect "the reality," the world we live, work, and act in, nor do they work as mirrors of the time they depict, nor of the time in which they were written. Like any text of the past they offer only glimpses of their time. The themes and topics they present therefore only partly correspond to real life events while other parts appear in a different way; ideals, visions, and prejudices take on a different appearance than they would have in the material reality.[13] This is probably as close as we can get in our knowledge — or rather perception — of the past. Some of those histories we will despise, some of them we will reject, some of them we will not understand, and with some of them we will identify. No single image will be accepted by everyone, but taken together they will show a cluster made up of "history" as we perceive it.

Catherine Belsey has pointed out the importance of not seeing the past as more homogenous than the present, to accept the coexistence of continuation and change, to respect the simultaneous existence of various discourses also in the past.[14] Writing on early modern England Belsey says:

> We do the period an injustice, I increasingly believe, if we try to make meanings and values fit together to form an internally consistent totality, expect physiological knowledge to "explain" Shakespearean comedy, for instance, especially if to explain is to efface or resolve the discordant elements within the texts.[15]

Belsey's plea for writing history "at the level of the signifier" excludes complete arbitrariness by emphasizing its dependence on the text and its value as signifier.[16] The emphasis on representation, value, and meaning further explains the differences — the dissent — between lived reality and the kind of life depicted in literary texts. Life is not presented "as it is" but as it could or should be. This then implies that there is no direct correspondence between representation and the lived reality. Although closely interrelated, material and textual reality should not be regarded as binary opposites but rather as different sides of the same coin that ask and answer different questions differently.

Most recent scholarship agrees that there is little or no change in the medieval perception of "man" and "woman" — they are created by God and thus belong to the "Heilsgeschichte" (salvation history) — in the late medieval period, but there is no consensus beyond this assumption. Some scholars have regarded the Reformation as representing a positive change in the status of women owing to the new importance attached to married life.[17] Celibacy was no longer the best way to reach salvation; marriage became the preferred state, and man and woman were equal before God.[18] Others claim this to be a chimera: women enjoyed more freedom before the Reformation and became even more dependent on man when no options were left outside of marriage.[19] If one adds the problematic relations surrounding the lived reality and written documents to the discussion, the picture becomes even more confused. This controversy only shows the complexity of early modern society and does little to prove the position of women in the literature and society of that time.[20] It would be wrong to claim that negative portrayals of women were exclusive to the early modern period; the misogynist tradition in European literature dates back to ancient Greece and Rome and is implicit not only in the Christian tradition with the antithesis of Eve and Mary but also in other cultures.[21] It can further be argued that many positive portrayals of women can be found in ancient and medieval history, mythology, and literature. The intense debates as to whether there were changes or not does, however, indicate uneasiness about gender matters that cannot simply be dismissed and that need further investigation.

It is commonly stated that the acceptance of innovations of any kind was slow in the pre-modern, pre-industrial Western European society, but literary texts and historical documents of the time nevertheless often express an uncertainty, a fear of innovation and change, a feeling of alienation, and a loss of order that indicate changing circumstances.[22] It can be seen in the descriptions of anything foreign to the early modern European, of the persecution of dissidents of all kinds, of the growing number of witch tracts and witch trials, and in the religious wars of the sixteenth and seventeenth centuries. This fear of the "other" has always resulted in a desire to assimilate, to tame, and to control,[23] and it often focuses on the other sex, usually on male power over women (and children).[24] Concern regarding one's gender identity seems to be a crucial part of a century that found a solution to the gender problem in accusing women — but also men and children — of witchcraft and sentencing them to death.[25] The need for scapegoats at times characterized by cultural, political, scientific, and religious conflicts was not a new phenomenon in the early modern period, but rarely have so many been accused and prosecuted because of their sex — or rather because of the gender stereotypes ascribed to "woman."[26]

A discussion of gender in early modern texts is thus intriguing and challenging as well as important for our understanding of them. When looking at questions regarding the construction of gender, one is, however, immediately struck by the problem of defining the word "gender" and phrases like "gender analysis" and "gender criticism." While "gender" is commonly used for the social and cultural representation of biological sex, more recent studies tend to also regard sex as socially or culturally constructed, especially as argued by Judith Butler.[27] The terminology in the field of gender studies and women's studies in my view has become an obstacle in itself in contemporary research focusing on male-female relationships — hence my hesitance to label this study feminist. "Gender studies" is often used interchangeably with "women's studies" but this is too narrow a definition. In my opinion the use of the word gender denotes inclusion rather than exclusion; various roles and relationships of men and women must be implicit in the definition of the term.[28] A further problem is that gender first needs to be constructed before it can be used as a category to define identity. It is important to see the construction of gender not as something imposed on a person from a diffuse "above" but rather as an interaction between a person and the surrounding community or society. Using the theories developed by Michel Foucault as well as contemporary gender theory, I will base this study on the assumption that men and women are active in shaping their own identity — consciously and unconsciously. They further project their notion of gender identity onto people they see, know, or meet. This implies that gender roles and images can never be seen as fixed entities but should be regarded as changing cultural interpretations of the body. Hence, I agree with the thesis of gender being "done": one is not passively born into gender, we act and react in accordance with the expectations and prejudices we meet in everyday life. Gender thus generally needs to be understood or defined in a larger social context, as, for example, Joan Wallach Scott does. Here I will use the term gender as defined by Barbara Becker-Cantarino, "as a system of relationships, constructed self-identifications and ascriptions of 'the other.'"[29] Gender is clearly a social, cultural, and historical construct that changes over time and within time.

The texts discussed below all indicate distinctions between men and women, between what is considered male and female, but this does not necessarily mean that the characters in the texts are given an identity that is based on their gender only. A person's gender identity is but one of several important factors in the construction of personal identity. Aspects such as class, social status, race, or religious affiliation can be equally important.[30] Moreover, individuality — one of the most important personal characteristics in the postmodern era — was of less importance and had a different meaning to early modern men and women, who largely identified themselves as part of a larger whole.[31]

In the following I will look at a variety of texts in order to find not only one, but several patterns that constitute the discursive fields surrounding "man" and "woman."[32] Depending on author, genre, use, tradition, expected readership, and so on, different texts take a different focus with a different intention (explicitly formulated or implicit in the text). An example is that Wickram never is as blunt in his depictions of love relationships as are Frey and Montanus, while Fischart's authorship is confusing and at times strikes the modern reader as paradoxical. Yet, they all write on the relationship between man and woman with the aim to reach an audience they do not know. Hence the feeling of complexity, multiplicity, and contradiction when trying to formulate a discourse of gender in many sixteenth-century texts. It is of course possible to cover only a few texts in a study like this, but it is obvious that texts of different kinds — as far as they can be defined — have in common that they move within the same discursive fields and practices even if they make use of them in different ways. Once the parameters for the investigation are set they should thus be applicable to many texts.

It is important to follow two paths when reading early modern German texts: one focusing on the deployment of alliance with its focal point on family and kinship ties, one on the deployment of sexuality, taking partially different directions.[33] This makes even greater sense if we regard marriage as binding family/kinship and sexuality together, something commonly done in texts written at the time of the Reformation. When reading the texts discussed here it will become clear that gender roles and male-female relationships cannot be reduced to dichotomies like husband vs. wife, marriage vs. adultery, as is commonly done in feminist scholarship. Below I will argue that all texts investigated move within at least three different discursive fields inherent in a larger gender discourse: sexuality, marriage, and family life. Together they form what is commonly conceived of as gender roles and to which are connected various rights, duties, obligations, restrictions, and prohibitions.[34] If defined as acts carried out to satisfy sexual desire or lust as well as to procreate, sexuality can be seen as a prerequisite for marriage and family life,[35] but sexuality is often suppressed in popular texts when marriage and family life are introduced — as odd as it might seem to the modern reader.[36] Marriage was said to bind a discussion of sexuality and family life together.[37] It presents various sides of the relationship between husband and wife (and possible lovers). Sexuality is often introduced by the author to involve men and women that do not or need not have any closer ties to each other; with few exceptions it excludes any mention of children. The reverse can be seen in depictions of the family that include relationships between the father, the mother, and the children. Common for all interpersonal relationships as presented in the texts is the circulation of knowledge and power: the will to know correct and incorrect behavior, the will to gain control, and the will to find order.

The Authors and the Texts

Works by Johann Fischart, Jakob Frey, Martin Montanus, and Georg Wickram, and Some City Ordinances from Strasbourg

It is not easy to detect genres or to differentiate between texts that were written at a time when the literary market was far less organized than the one we are familiar with. The market was developing quickly and therefore not yet well structured, neither with regard to recipients and distribution, nor with regard to genre. Latin remained the language of preference among the learned, but popular texts were written in or translated into the vernacular, and the national languages were increasingly used for a wide array of texts.[38] Genres like sermons, fables, and parables — to mention only a few — were well established in the sixteenth century, but many popular works written in the vernacular cannot be as easily labeled. These were products of the growing print industry, relying heavily on older works but taking advantage of the new medium.[39] They reached new readers when more people became literate, with the result that the audience was more diverse than before the invention of paper and the printing press — before the spread of the printed word. Even though one pays great attention to the categorization of medieval and early modern texts, and emphasizes the audience and the reception of the text, the problem remains: there is no easy labeling of these texts, even if that were desirable. We might have to look for additional methods of inquiry.

As opposed to a scholar like Rüdiger Schnell, who has focused on non-fictional prose in his research, on religious texts dealing with marriage, I will examine secular texts written in the vernacular,[40] and whose authors were not trained theologians. The texts often explicitly address a large audience, men as well as women and sometimes children or young adults. Even though the differences between the texts seem vast at times, they do have certain features in common and there are several factors indicating that perceived differences should be regarded as variations rather than opposites on a scale. One can also expect several topics to appear in different kinds of texts, but the way they are used will probably differ from text to text. The danger of not comparing like with like is obvious, but if we stay at the level of the signifier — as suggested by Belsey — and try to examine representations without falling prey to a discussion of mimesis, then it should be possible to detect discursively produced genre specific as well as non genre-specific practices.

The so-called *Spiegelliteratur* — manuals for various purposes but mostly advising on proper behavior — was immensely popular, judging by the number of titles that can be found in archives and libraries. Also considering texts such as *exempla,* fables, and other moralizing stories warning the reader and setting good examples, the list of works dealing with human behavior becomes almost endless. I have chosen to focus on texts that reached large groups of the population — at least in the cities. The texts have certain features in common: (1) they are all written for an educated but not necessarily learned readership; (2) with one exception discussed below their primary aim is to entertain, even though many of them also claim a desire to teach by good and bad examples — the double argument defending the reason for the publication of the text; (3) the texts are not primarily or exclusively focused on love, marriage, or family life, but rather on interpersonal relationships; and (4) all texts can be categorized as pro-Protestant, even though they do not explicitly take up a definite position. It will be the task of a further study to investigate Catholic texts and to search for similarities and dissimilarities. My aim is to investigate how the relationship between men and women is depicted, how gender roles are perceived, presented, and portrayed in texts that pay great attention to the relationships between women and men and that seem to find an abiding interest in defining gender identities and forcing them on the reader. The study will thus be descriptive; it will focus on discursive practices as perceived by a person reading the texts 450 years after their first publication.[41]

I have chosen to include one type of text that does not fit into the pattern of "popular literature" — a selection of city ordinances from Strasbourg where matters such as prostitution, marriage, and extramarital relationships are explicitly discussed and regulated. These texts are interesting for reasons of comparison because they offer insight into the work of the city authorities: how they tried to come to terms with problems commonly discussed in literary texts through legislation. The ordinances should thus be regarded as a source of reference and not as constituting a foreground or background to the fictional texts. It is easy to be blinded by chauvinist men and misogynist pictures of women in fictional texts, and the dangers are obvious: stereotypes are established that make further scrutiny of the text superfluous. Other legal documents could have been used for the same purpose, but I found it important to choose texts that were likely to have been widely known and hence texts that presumedly could have been familiar to the authors as well as to the readers (and listeners) of vernacular literature — not necessarily word-by-word but as to content. The city ordinances may or may not show proof of correspondence with the fictional texts in their representation of sex, marriage, and family life. The category nonfiction prose is no more true, representative, or "natural" than fictional writing; it is further almost impossible to make a correct distinction between fiction and nonfiction. Legislative texts do, however, depict the intention of those in power. It will thus be the task of the discussion below to show the limits and limitations of the discourses presented above.

The choice of Strasbourg as the center of my study is due to the cultural importance of the city at the time of the Reformation and its flowering literary market. Praised by Erasmus of Rotterdam, Strasbourg was known for its relative tolerance towards dissidents,[42] and the city fought with success for its independence as a free imperial city. When consulting Miriam Usher Chrisman's excellent inventory of imprints in Strasbourg between 1480 and 1599, one is struck by the number of printers as well as works printed.[43] The city could no doubt offer a thriving climate for many authors trying to publish their texts. Johann Fischart, Jakob Frey, Martin Montanus, and Georg Wickram are only a few of those who had their work printed and published in Strasbourg. Frey's chapbook the *Gartengesellschaft* (Garden Society, 1557) was widely known, but we know of few other texts by him; Montanus wrote two chapbooks — *Der Wegkürtzer* (The Road Entertainer, 1557) and *Das ander theyl der Gartengesellschaft* (Part Two of the Garden Society, date unknown) — and some adaptations of stories out of Boccaccio's *Decamerone*. Very little is known about Montanus[44] and close to nothing about Frey.[45] Their lives remain in the dark while we know more about the life and work of Wickram[46] and Fischart.[47] Fischart was — as far as we know — the only "officially" learned man among the four. He held a doctorate in law while Wickram had a limited formal education, and Montanus wandered about southern Germany, perhaps as a student.

All four authors had in common the fact that they published works that reached large audiences. Wickram's *Rollwagenbüchlein* (Carriage Booklet, 1555), *Der jungen Knaben Spiegel* (Manual for Young Boys, 1554), and *Der Goldtfaden* (The Golden Thread, 1557) were reprinted on several occasions while *Von guten und bösen Nachbarn* (Of Good and Bad Neighbors, 1556) — the first prose novel to deal exclusively with merchants, tradesmen, and craftsmen and with a growing middle class in the cities — was less successful and published in only two editions.[48] Wickram wrote texts in prose as well as in verse. Most of his work relied heavily on traditional themes, topics, and genres but especially in his prose novels he shows innovative signs that point toward the early novel. Frey and Montanus both claimed Wickram to be their role model, which is hard to understand for anyone familiar with their work — the only common thread to be found in their texts is the interest in telling a good story. Most scholars agree on Wickram's peculiar position as an author: he does not have any predecessors nor does anyone follow in his footsteps, but some of his texts were repeatedly reprinted.

Fischart was, however, far more outstanding in his production than was Wickram. His work is enormous and comprises more than eighty known titles, a strange mixture of popular and learned literature of all imaginable kinds. Having studied at several schools and traveled extensively in his youth, Fischart's sources of influence were clearly not only numerically larger but also more varied than those of Wickram, who is known to have been on only one long journey outside of Alsace[49] and who — because of a limited formal education — had less knowledge of languages and literature. Fischart wrote his own original works, and translated and reworked older texts into Latin and German. His "adaptation" of Rabelais' *Gargantua* — known as *Affentheuerlich Naupengeheuerlichen Geschichtsklitterung [. . .]* (Adventuresome Narrative Scribbling, 1582) — grew into a completely new text, far longer than the original. It has become famous for its virtuoso play with the German language, its stylistic inventiveness and remarkable verve and energy. It was first published in Strasbourg in 1575 and then again in 1582 and 1590, each time reworked, becoming more elaborate and extensive. Fischart also translated one of the most famous witch tracts of the early modern period into German, Jean Bodin's *De Démonomanie de Sorcieres* (Of the Demonomania of Witches, 1581) and edited a new German version of the *Malleus maleficarum* (1486) by Heinrich Institoris. It is known as *Hexenhammer* (Hammer of Witches, 1582). He is the only author among these four who published texts on witches and witchcraft. This can be explained in part by the fact that he lived at a time when the witch persecutions were steadily increasing in some areas of Germany, and in part by his profession: as a trained lawyer he was likely to have had firsthand experience with witch trials. As a lawyer he must also have had interest in the legal practices surrounding marriage; he published the marriage tract *Ehezuchtbüchlein* (Philosophical Treatment on Marital Discipline, 1578), a compilation of well-known tracts on marriage by pagan as well as Christian authors, and he wrote a satire on women, *Flöh, Hatz, Weiber Tratz* (Hunting of Fleas, Defiance of Women, 1573–7?).

Wickram is interesting because his works with few exceptions seem to offer a positive view of women and of the relationship between men and women, and thus differ from many sixteenth-century texts. Warnings and bad examples are always present, but in several works Wickram tries to keep order in society by describing ideal living conditions. This idealization of women and married life changes greatly in Frey's and Montanus's work, where women are shown as evil, unfaithful, and often stupid, and marriages are doomed to fail due to wicked women and weak men. In comparison with Wickram their texts are much more explicit in their descriptions of controversial topics, many focusing on sex and dirty jokes. Fischart on the other hand was familiar with the academic discourse of his time and the only one with the ability to read texts in Latin. His works probably circulated mostly among the educated, but the German texts can be assumed to have had a more varied readership than his works in Latin. A friend of the reformed Church with often radical ideas in matters concerning politics and religion, he worked on two of the most important texts written on witchcraft, two of the most misogynist texts printed in the fifteenth and sixteenth centuries. It can be argued that he needed them as a practicing lawyer, but is this necessarily true? Without genuine interest in the topic he would hardly have been preoccupied with such elaborate work.[50] Ambivalent portrayals of women and their relation to men may not be new in literary texts but the appearance of the female witch, the pact with the devil, and the witch Sabbath add a new perspective to gender matters as discussed in sixteenth-century documents.

It is once again important to emphasize that Wickram, Frey, and Montanus published their works at a time relatively free from witch persecutions — as opposed to Fischart. According to Gerhild S. Williams, among others, the witchcraft debate was slumbering in the years between approximately 1520 and 1560, even though there was an increasing interest in the matter in the 1550s.[51] Since longer discussions always precede actual action — *Hexenhammer* was published at a time when few witches were prosecuted — it is likely that Frey, Montanus, and Wickram were aware of the witch problem without consciously taking it into account in their works. It should furthermore be noted that the geographical distribution of trials and persecutions was very uneven; the Southwest of the German lands saw several outbreaks of the witchcraze while the city of Strasbourg was less engaged in the witch-hunts.[52] It would therefore be dangerous to relate the awareness of gender roles and stereotypes to this phenomenon only.

I hope the discussion above makes clear that I am seeking what Barbara Becker-Cantarino has called "an acute awareness of one's gender, gender role, and its limitations" in sixteenth-century literature.[53] What roles are conveyed to the reader/listener? This takes us back to the quotation at the beginning of this introduction, to the women Lucia and Cassandra, to the female characters with no voice of their own. The male author-narrator, who is only able to produce or reproduce an imagined "female discourse," communicates their thoughts, ideas, and moral values. The objection can be raised that all literary characters speak through the author and that they are only narrated, they are pure text. However, this does not solve the problem at stake here. The voice of the author-narrator manipulates the way the characters are perceived as gendered subjects: Lucia and Cassandra speak through a man, through the other sex.[54] The male characters in the texts are no more "authentic" than the female — they are products of discourse just like the women — but there is no discrepancy in sex between author, narrator, and figure.

The question to ask is what influence this has on the representation of gender in early modern texts. For reasons of space I have chosen not to include texts written by women in this study. Scholars of English literature and history have mainly carried out research on women writers in the early modern period. In the field of German studies the research has been less extensive, even though scholars like Barbara Becker-Cantarino, Lyndal Roper, Erika Rummel, Merry Wiesner-Hanks, Heide Wunder, and several others have emphasized the work of early modern women. Still, more manuscripts need to be made accessible in reprints or scholarly editions, more texts need to be examined in libraries and archives, more texts need to be found so that they can give early women a voice of their own.

Notes

[1] Georg Wickram, *Sämtliche Werke*, ed. Hans-Gert Roloff, vol. 4, *Von guten und bösen Nachbarn* (Berlin: Walter de Gruyter, 1969), 133. All quotations in German correspond with the original text, except that diacritical marks other than the umlaut have been omitted.

[2] In the following I will use "woman" and "man" in quotation marks to indicate that I am referring to the categories that include all individuals commonly regarded as women and men.

[3] The problems surrounding terms like fact, fiction, and nonfiction, especially in regard to early modern texts, have yet to be solved satisfactorily. A discussion also including literature and "nonliterature" risks ending in complete relativism, but it is nevertheless very important. It is, however beyond the scope of this book to engage in this discussion. Even though well aware of the changing character of genre, I have here chosen to go by the classification made by the author or the otherwise most commonly found specification in secondary sources. In a forthcoming publication I am discussing the concept of "fictionality" in Wickram's work. See further, Natalie Zemon Davis, *Fiction in the Archives: Pardon Tales and Their Tellers in Sixteenth-Century France* (Stanford: Stanford UP, 1987); Lawrence Stone, *The Past and the Present* (Boston: Routledge & Kegan, 1981); Hayden White, *The Content of the Form: Narrative Discourse and Historical Representation* (Baltimore: Johns Hopkins UP, 1987); and Hayden White, *Figural Realism. Studies in the Mimesis Effect* (Baltimore: Johns Hopkins UP, 1999).

[4] Ulrike Gaebel has pointed out the complicated relationship between author and narrator in Marquart's *Ritter vom Turm*. I agree with her that there is a tendency to regard author and narrator as interchangeable in medieval and early modern literature, even though many texts have a more complex narrative structure. Ulrike Gaebel, "Erzähler und Erzählkonzepte in Marquarts Vom Stein *Der Ritter vom Turm*," in *Erzählungen in Erzählungen: Phänomene der Narration in Mittelalter und Früher Neuzeit*, ed. Harald Haferland and Michael Mecklenburg (Munich: Wilhelm Fink, 1996), 346.

⁵ See the essays in Joan Wallach Scott, *Gender and the Politics of History: Revised Edition* (New York: Columbia UP, 1999). The differences and similarities between men and women, between different men and different women, have been topics of great concern in Western culture and society since Antiquity. Useful texts on the topic gender and history are Joan Wallach Scott, "Feminism and History: Introduction," in *Feminism and History*, ed. Joan Wallach Scott (Oxford: Oxford UP, 1999), 1–13, and Merry Wiesner, *Gender in History* (Oxford: Blackwell, 2001).

⁶ The publication on sixteenth-century Germany is vast and only a few titles in English that I have found useful can be mentioned here: Thomas A. Brady, *The Protestant Reformation in German History* (Washington, DC: German Historical Institute, 1998); Thomas A. Brady, Heiko Augustinus Oberman, and James D. Tracy, *Handbook of European History, 1400–1600: Late Middle Ages, Renaissance, and Reformation* (Grand Rapids, MI: W. B. Eerdmans, 1996); Peter Burke, *The European Renaissance: Centres and Peripheries*, Making of Europe (Oxford: Blackwell Publishers, 1998); Euan Cameron, *The European Reformation* (Oxford: Clarendon Press, 1991); G. R. Elton, *Renaissance and Reformation, 1300–1648*, Ideas and Institutions in Western Civilization (New York: Macmillan, 1976); Mark Greengrass, *The French Reformation* (Oxford: Blackwell, 1987); R. Po-chia Hsia, *The German People and the Reformation* (Ithaca, NY: Cornell UP, 1991); Carter Lindberg, *The European Reformations* (Oxford: Blackwell, 1996); Steven E. Ozment, *The Age of Reform, 1250–1550: An Intellectual and Religious History of Late Medieval and Reformation Europe* (New Haven: Yale UP, 1980); Robert W. Scribner and Trevor. Johnson, *Popular Religion in Germany and Central Europe, 1400–1800*, Themes in Focus (Basingstoke, Hampshire: Macmillan, 1996). See also Merry Wiesner-Hanks's thoughtful comments on writing survey books, "The Hubris of Writing Surveys, or A Feminist Confronts the Textbook," in *Attending to Early Modern Women*, ed. Susan D. Amussen and Adele Seeff (Newark: U of Delaware P, 1998), 297–307.

⁷ The research in this field is growing quickly: for a discussion on Germany see: *Das Berliner Modell der Mittleren Deutschen Literatur. Beiträge zur Tagung Kloster Zinna 29.9–01.10.1997*, ed. Christiane Caemmerer, et al. (Amsterdam: Rodopi, 2000). The "Berlin model" suggests the use of the term "middle German" (mittlere deutsche) instead of "early modern" when discussing German literature, since "early modern" originates in historic research and thus includes connotations that are irrelevant to literary research. I have chosen to use "early modern" without any political or ideological intentions because it is commonly used in English and not because I have a preference as to which expression to use. For sixteenth-century Germany I believe that "late medieval" and "early modern" can be used interchangeably. Both terms have an advantage over other terms often used in scholarly works, such as "humanism," "Renaissance," or "Reformation" since they are less exclusive and primarily refer to a specific time in history.

⁸ The topic "feminist (German) literary studies in Germany" has been presented in a critical article by Barbara Becker-Cantarino, "Feministische Germanistik in Deutschland: Rückblick und sechs Thesen," in *Women in German Yearbook 8* (Lincoln, London: U of Nebraska P, 1993), 219–34. Almost ten years have passed since the article was published, but the differences in tradition between German-speaking and Anglo-Saxon countries seem to remain. Cf. Barbara Becker-Cantarino, "(Sozial)

Geschichte der Frau in Deutschland, 1500–1800: Ein Forschungsbericht," in *Die Frau von der Reformation zur Romantik*, ed. Barbara Becker-Cantarino (Bonn: Bouvier Verlag Herbert Grundmann, 1980), 243–81. Jutta Osinski has pointed out differences and similarities in her introductory textbook to feminist literary studies aimed at a German readership in *Einführung in die feministische Literaturwissenschaft* (Munich: Erich Schmidt, 1998). A critical comment of some publications on early modern women can be found in: Barbara Becker-Cantarino, "Dames des Lettres und die Ordnung der Geschlechter: Neue Forschung zu Frauen und Geschlecht in der Frühen Neuzeit," *Daphnis* 23 (1994): 469–81. See also Natalie Zemon Davis, "Displacing and Displeasing: Writing About Women in the Early Modern Period," in *Attending to Early Modern Women*, ed. Susan D. Amussen and Adele Seeff (Newark: U of Delaware P, 1998), 25–37.

[9] The literature on "discourse" is immense, from Michel Foucault's *L'ordre du discours* (Orders of Discourse, 1971) and *Les mots et les choses: une archéologie des sciences humaines* (Paris: Gallimard, 1966), in English: Michel Foucault, *The Order of Things: An Archaeology of the Human Sciences* (London: Routledge, 2001), to comments on Foucault's work, encyclopedic entries, vast discussions on the Internet, and endless definitions in theoretical works. In *The History of Sexuality: An Introduction*, vol. 1 (1976), Foucault briefly defines discourse: "We must conceive discourse as a series of discontinuous segments whose tactical function is neither uniform nor stable. To be more precise, we must not imagine a world of discourse divided between accepted discourse and excluded discourse, or between dominant discourse and dominated one; but as a multiplicity of discursive elements that can come into play in various strategies. It is this distribution that we must reconstruct. . . ." Here I am using the English translation by Robert Hurley: Michel Foucault, *The History of Sexuality I–III*. (New York: Vintage Books/ Random House, 1990), 100. For an introduction, see: Klaus-Michael Bogdal, *Historische Diskursanalyse der Literatur* (Opladen: Westdeutscher Verlag, 1999). For a discussion on German scholarship on the topic, see: Rüdiger Schnell, *Frauendiskurs, Männerdiskurs, Ehediskurs. Textsorten und Geschlechterkonzepte in Mittelalter und Früher Neuzeit* (Frankfurt am Main: Campus Verlag, 1998), 29–38 and Rüdiger Schnell, "Geschlechtergeschichte, Diskursgeschichte und Literaturgeschichte. Eine Studie zu konkurrierenden Männerbildern in Mittelalter und Früher Neuzeit," *Frühmittelalterliche Studien* 32 (1998): 310, especially footnote 8. See also Gerhild S. Williams, "On Finding Words: Witchcraft and Discourses of Dissidence and Discovery," in *The Graph of Sex and the German Text: Gendered Culture in Early Modern Germany 1500–1700*, ed. Lynne Tatlock (Amsterdam: Rodopi, 1994), 48.

[10] Stephen Greenblatt's well-known but paradoxical "desire to speak with the dead" is shared by many scholars in the humanities even if they do not otherwise agree with New Historicism or Greenblatt's "poetics of culture." Stephen Greenblatt, "Towards a Poetics of Culture," in *The New Historicism*, ed. H. Aram Veeser (New York: Routledge, 1989), 1–14. For a critique of Greenblatt's use of "desire," see Jürgen Pieters, "Facing History, or the Anxiety of Reading: Holbein's *The Ambassadors* According to Greenblatt and Loytard," in *Reading the Past Literature and History*, ed. Tamsin Spargo (Basingstoke: Palgrave, 2000), 88–102. especially 92 and 180.

[11] Hans Blumenberg's work on "Epochenschwellen" is of immense importance for the concept of early modern society as in the process of change: Hans Blumenberg, *Die Genesis der kopernikanischen Welt,* 3 vols., 3rd ed. (Frankfurt am Main: Suhrkamp, 1996) and Hans Blumenberg, *Die Legitimität der Neuzeit,* 2nd ed. (Frankfurt am Main: Suhrkamp, 1999). See also Gerhild S. Williams on Blumenberg in: Gerhild S. Williams, "Provokation und Antwort. Hans Blumenbergs Frühe Neuzeit," in *"Der Buchstab Tödt — der Geist macht lebendig." Festschrift Zum 60. Geburtstag von Hans-Gert Roloff von Freunden, Schülern und Kollegen. Band I.,* ed. James Hardin and Jörg Jungmayr (Bern: Peter Lang, 1992), 109–26, and Gerhild S. Williams, *Defining Dominion: The Discourses of Magic and Witchcraft in Early Modern France and Germany* (Ann Arbor: U of Michigan P, 1995), 9–10.

[12] The complexity of the word and the values often related to it makes it very hard to define. As long as one regards "culture" mainly as a homogenous and closed entity or as something reserved for the upper classes, the definition remains narrow, but culture has come to be regarded as much more multiform than that and it has been the object of intense scrutiny during the past ten years. One should therefore meet the use of the term in current research with great caution, since it often is used without being clearly defined, though a definition does not have to be so narrow that it excludes the openness mentioned above. Gady Algazi's very dynamic concept of "culture" as a "system of productive options," or patterns that necessitate human action as well as make it possible, therefore seems useful for this study. Gadi Algazi, "Kulturkult und Rekonstruktion von Handlungsrepertoires," *L'homme. Zeitschrift für Feministische Geschichtswissenschaft* 1, no. 11 (2000): 105–19. If culture is understood as "how to do what" (113), as different interacting systems, one is not confined to one form in which culture can find its expression. Rather, one opens up for a study of material and semiotic-symbolic structures found in a given society at a given time. Culture, according to Algazi, is not pure interpretation or a matter of giving "the world" meaning; it offers "repertoires" for action and should thus be based on models instead of products. Algazi claims: "Kultur ist nicht als Garant von Identität und Einheit zu untersuchen, sondern als heterogenes Medium für Handlungen und Konflikte" (119). Algazi sums up: Dies sieht anders aus, wenn Kultur als ein offenes System aufeinander bezogener, stets miteinander konkurrierender Repertoires verstanden wird, die je nach sozialer Lage und Akkulturation unterschiedlich zugänglich sind. Beobachtbare Differenzen werden somit nicht auf homogene Kulturen zurückgeführt, sondern als praxisbezogene Spielarten, als situationsgebundene Gebrauchsweisen heterogener, unterschiedlich zugänglicher Repertoires gesehen" (119). See also Gadi Algazi, "Ein gelehrter Blick ins lebendige Archiv: Umgangsweisen mit der Vergangenheit im 15. Jahrhundert," *Historische Zeitschrift* 266 (1998): 317–57. In the last few years the term culture has experienced a renewed interest among German scholars as a result of international influences, the growing importance of "cultural studies" and "new historicism" in German literary theory. For an interesting discussion of "gender" and "culture," see Andrea Griesebner and Christina Lutter, "Geschlecht und Kultur. Ein Definitionsversuch zweier umstrittener Kategorien," *Geschlecht und Kultur. Beiträge zur historischen Sozialkunde* Sondernummer (2000): 58–64. For a study of identity and culture in the early modern period, see Hans-Georg Gadamer's philosophical hermeneutics in *Wahrheit und Methode* (Truth and Method) with its interest in how the individual perceives the

world surrounding him or her (Verständnishorizont, Gesamthorizont): Hans-Georg Gadamer, *Truth and Method*, 2nd ed. (New York: Continuum, 1994).

[13] Cf. Catherine Belsey, *Shakespeare and the Loss of Eden: The Construction of Family Values in Early Modern Culture* (Houndmills: Palgrave, 2001), preface. The introduction has also been published *Reading the Past Literature and History*, ed. Tamsin Spargo (Basingstoke: Palgrave, 2000), 1–17, an interesting collection of articles on the topic history and literature. See also Rüdiger Schnell, "Geschlechterbeziehungen und Textfunktionen. Probleme und Perspektiven eines Forschungsansatzes," in *Geschlechterbeziehungen und Textfunktionen. Studien zu Eheschriften der Frühen Neuzeit*, ed. Rüdiger Schnell (Tübingen: Niemeyer, 1998), 7–11.

[14] Belsey, *Shakespeare and the Loss of Eden*, 15–16.

[15] Belsey, *Shakespeare and the Loss of Eden*, 16.

[16] See Belsey, *Shakespeare and the Loss of Eden*, 5–6. By pursuing history at the level of the signifier she wants to avoid speculations as to "how it really was" or "what people really thought" and to instead focus on the reading of the text, on representation, since "representational priorities change as values change, and history at the level of the signifier records these shifts of value" (6). Without denying that culture within a given society is also "lived" she shifts her focus to the side of culture that is learned, to the side that has come down to us in written form.

[17] For Germany, see among others the works by Steven Ozment, *When Fathers Ruled: Family Life in Reformation Europe* (Cambridge, MA: Harvard UP, 1983), *Flesh and Spirit: Private Life in Early Modern Germany* (New York: Viking, 1999), and Heide Wunder, *He Is the Sun, She Is the Moon: Women in Early Modern Germany* (Cambridge: Harvard UP, 1998).

[18] Rüdiger Schnell and others would not agree with this but argue that the equality of man and woman before God can be found in much older texts and that Luther only emphasized this in his teachings.

[19] See the works by Merry Wiesner: *Working Women in Renaissance Germany* (New Brunswick, NJ: Rutgers UP, 1986), *Women and Gender in Early Modern Europe* (Cambridge: Cambridge UP, 1993), *Gender, Church and State in Early Modern Germany* (Harlow: Longman, 1998), and *Christianity and Sexuality in the Early Modern World: Regulating Desire, Reforming Practise* (London: Routledge, 1999); Lyndal Roper, *The Holy Household*; Elisabeth Koch, *Maior dignitas est in sexu virili: Das weibliche Geschlecht im Normensystem des 16. Jahrhunderts* (Frankfurt am Main: Vittorio Klostermann, 1991). Joan Kelly Gadol's "Did women have a Renaissance" from 1977 is often regarded as a pioneering work in the reevaluation of Renaissance women. Kelly turns against the long-lasting hypothesis presented by Jacob Burkhardt in 1860 that men and women alike enjoyed greater freedom after the Middle Ages: Joan Kelly Gadol, *Becoming Visible: Women in European History*, ed. Reante Bridenthal, Claudia Koonz, and Susan Stuard (Boston: Houghton Mifflin, 1987), 175–201.

[20] See Schnell, "Geschlechterbeziehungen und Textfunktionen." Rüdiger Schnell represents the standpoint that the opposing views on the rights of early modern women can not only be referred to contradictions within sixteenth-century society but should also be traced back to the difference in focus and interpretation in different scholarly disciplines such as literary studies, cultural and social history, and relig-

ion or theology (1–6) and to the intermixing of "reality" and "discourse" (7–9). Clashing interests thus blur the common goal — the Renaissance or Reformation notion of woman. Schnell's critical standpoint towards past and contemporary scholarship is just as obvious as his wide reading of the research in this field — the footnotes in his article refer to a vast number of titles, most of them commented upon. Schnell's discussion of the necessity of good knowledge in the field of medieval *and* early modern studies is, however, unnecessary because of its obviousness (11).

[21] Robert Scribner talks of a change in the image of Eve that adds strong erotic connotations to the image of her as evil — as is also the case with the witch — in the course of the sixteenth century: R. W. Scribner, *Religion and Culture in Germany (1400–1800)*, ed. Lyndal Roper (Leiden: Brill, 2001), 138–40. See Helmut Brackert, "Zur Sexualisierung des Hexenmusters in der Frühen Neuzeit," in *Ordnung und Lust: Bilder von Liebe, Ehe und Sexualität in Spätmittelalter und Früher Neuzeit*, ed. Hans-Jürgen Bachorski (Trier: Wissenschaftlicher Verlag, 1991), 337–57, on the sexualization of the witch.

[22] Jean Delumeau's pioneering work on fear, *La peur en Occident (XIVe–XVIIIe siècles): une cité assiégée*, 1978; *Le péché et la peur: la culpabilisation en Occident: (XIIIe–XVIIIe siècles)*, 1983, is by now almost thirty years old but has found more followers than can be accounted for here. English translation: Jean Delumeau, *Sin and Fear: The Emergence of a Western Guilt Culture, 13th–18th Centuries* (New York: St. Martin's Press, 1990).

[23] Gerhild S. Williams identifies three different discourses that are important to the increasing fear of change in early modern Europe: "the discourse of religious diversity and dissidence, the discourse of discovery, and the discourse of magic and witchcraft." Williams, "On Finding Words," 47. See further, Williams, *Defining Dominion*, 126. See also Allison P. Coudert, "The Myth of the Impovered Status of Protestant Women; The Case of the Witchcraze," in *The Politics of Gender in Early Modern Europe*, ed. Jean R. Brink, Allison P. Coudert, and Maryanne C. Horowitz (Kirksville, MO: Sixteenth-Century Essays & Studies, 1987), 65: "To establish a context for the witchcraze, it is important to recognize that the Reformation and Counter-Reformation periods witnessed a new and unparalleled concern with order and orthodoxy. The breakdown of social, political, and religious consensus was paralleled by the collapse of traditional, intellectual and scientific systems."

[24] Merry Wiesner claims in an article that discusses the Reformation of women: ". . . at the heart of the issue was the control of female sexuality and the maintenance of a moral order in which women were subservient. These factors will emerge in nearly all the religious conflicts involving women in the Reformation period, even when the participants did not articulate them." Wiesner, *Gender, Church and State*, 64.

[25] Cf. Roper, *The Holy Household*, 5.

[26] Allison Coudert comments: "The politics, economics and intense religious conflicts of the Reformation period, together with changes in the law, combined to focus misogyny in the image of the witch in this relatively short period." Coudert, "Myth of the Impovered Status of Protestant Women," 63; for a discussion of Protestantism and patriarchy, 70. See also Williams, *Defining Dominion*, 83, and Wiesner, *Gender, Church and State*, 85: "Academic jurists found justification in both Roman and German law for excluding women from a wide variety of legal functions. Roman law

stressed women's alleged physical and mental weakness, . . . Germanic law based women's secondary status on their ability to reform vassal service and duty to obey their husbands . . . ." Cf. Koch, *Maior dignitas,* 179–90 on the inferiority of women according to humanistic legal thought.

[27] For further reading, see Judith Butler, *Gender Trouble: Feminism and the Subversion of Identity* (London: Routledge, 1990) and Judith Butler, *Bodies That Matter: On the Discursive Limits of "Sex"* (London: Routledge, 1993).

[28] This means that I regard women's studies as a part of gender studies. Both approaches can be "feminist," then including a political or ideological standpoint. The term "women's studies" to me is too narrow in that there is no natural connection to "men."

[29] Barbara Becker-Cantarino, "Dr. Faustus and Runagate Courage: Theorizing Gender in Early Modern German Literature," in *The Graph of Sex and the German Text: Gendered Culture in Early Modern Germany 1500–1700,* ed. Lynne Tatlock (Amsterdam: Rodopi, 1994), 30–31. See also Brauner, "Gender and Its Subversion," 179. "The term gender denotes foremost the social construction of men and women into masculine and feminine identities and must be differentiated from biological sex." Cf. Williams, "On Finding Words," 46–47. See the fall issue of *differences* 9 (1997) for different aspects of the relationship between women's and gender studies.

[30] Joy Wiltenburg emphasizes the importance of gender to the social order or disorder in her article on female crime in early modern society: "Family Murders: Gender, Reproduction, and the Discourse of Crime in Early Modern Germany," *Colloquia Germanica* 3–4 (1995): 371. See also her study of the concept of woman in early modern English and German cheap prints, *Disorderly Women and Female Power in the Street Literature of Early Modern England and Germany* (Charlottesville, VA: UP of Virginia, 1992). Natalie Zemon Davis in an article on the writing of "women's history" comments on the changes in scholarly work that have resulted in new ways of reading and writing of the past and of understanding the lives of those who lived before us. She states: "Our goal is to understand the significance of the *sexes,* of gender groups in the historical past. Our goal is to discover the range in sex roles and in sexual symbolism in different societies and periods, to find out what meaning they had and how they functioned to maintain the social order or to promote its change. Our goal is to explain why sex roles were sometimes tightly prescribed and sometimes fluid, sometimes markedly asymmetrical and sometimes more even": Natalie Zemon Davis, "'Women's History' in Transition: The European Case," in *Feminism and History,* ed. Joan Wallach Scott (Oxford: Oxford UP, 1999), 88. This important statement can be used for the study of literature by adding that we then try to understand the significance of the sexes and of gender groups as produced by discourse in the narrative.

[31] Heide Wunder has written an important article on the significance of "gender" in regard to identity among early modern women and men: "Geschlechtsidentitäten: Frauen und Männer im späten Mittelalter und am Beginn der Neuzeit," in *Frauengeschichte — Geschlechtergeschichte,* ed. Karin Hausen and Heide Wunder (Frankfurt/New York: Campus, 1992), 131–36. On male honor as an integral part of male identity, see Lyndal Roper, "Männlichkeit und männliche Ehre," in *Frauengeschich-*

te — Geschlechtergeschichte, ed. Karin Hausen and Heide Wunder (Frankfurt/New York: Campus, 1992), 154–72.

[32] Foucault in the first part of *The History of Sexuality* links a shift in the discourse of sexuality to changes in seventeenth-century society: Foucault, *History of Sexuality,* 27. The sixteenth-century is mentioned only in passing a few times. I would argue, however, that this merely shows the arbitrariness of periodization. Scholars of the sixteenth century have already proved that much of what Foucault claims typical for the seventeenth century and the Enlightenment has its roots in the sixteenth century and even earlier. It therefore seems wrong to talk about a paradigmatic shift (in discourse) and better to regard this as transitions within existing discourses. Cf. Gerhild S. William's discussion of the discourses of magic and witchcraft and the application of Foucault's use of episteme and archive in *Defining Dominion,* 9.

[33] Foucault, *History of Sexuality,* 106–7. Foucault seems to regard the deployment of sexuality as completely different from the deployment of alliance, but this does not exclude their interdependence on each other.

[34] Hans-Jürgen Bachorski talks of the discursive field of marriage instead of a marriage discourse and is thus able to widen the discussion to cover related areas of discourse, but he looks at the genre of the text as well as at the (imagined) readership much like Schnell. Hans-Jürgen Bachorski, "Diskursfeld Ehe: Schreibweisen und thematische Setzungen," in *Ordnung und Lust: Bilder von Liebe, Ehe und Sexualität in Spätmittelalter und Früher Neuzeit,* ed. Hans-Jürgen Bachorski (Trier: Wissenschaftlicher Verlag, 1991), 511–45. Rüdiger Schnell has conducted very interesting research in this field, but here I have for two reasons chosen not to follow Schnell's division of discourses into a discourse of men, a discourse of women, and a discourse of marriage: First, Schnell is working on texts that deal specifically with marriage; this justifies the position the discourse of marriage takes in his research but not in my study. Second, I find it hard to talk about one discourse of men and one of women, not only because there always are several discourses on both sexes but also because they often unite into a larger discourse of gender. See Schnell, *Frauendiskurs, Männerdiskurs, Ehediskurs,* 29–38.

[35] Tilmann Walter similarly defines sexuality as "Handlungen von Personen, die an sich selbst oder an anderen zum Zwecke des sexuellen Lustgewinns vollzogen werden," in his study of sexuality in early modern texts, *Unkeuschheit und Werk der Liebe. Diskurse über Sexualität am Beginn der Neuzeit in Deutschland* (Berlin: De Gruyter, 1998), 30.

[36] Foucault discusses the separation of marriage and sex in *History of Sexuality,* 4. This will be of great relevance when looking at the prose texts by Georg Wickram.

[37] There are of course overlaps, as there are in most scholarly texts discussing marriage or sexuality; Wolfgang Beutin's extensive psychoanalytical study of sexuality and the obscene includes a chapter on marriage: *Sexualität und Obszönität. Eine literaturpsychologische Studie über epische Dichtungen des Mittelalters und der Renaissance* (Würzburg: Königshausen & Neumann, 1990), 329–93. Walter's study of the discourse of sexuality in early modern texts contains several parts on marriage: *Unkeuschheit und Werk der Liebe.* See also the anthologies: *Ordnung und Lust. Bilder von Liebe, Ehe und Sexualität in Spätmittelalter und Früher Neuzeit,* ed. Hans-Jürgen Bachorski (Trier: Wissenschaftlicher Verlag, 1991) and *Desire and Discipline: Sex and Sexuality*

in the Premodern West, ed. Jacqueline Murray and Konrad Eisenbichler (Toronto: U of Toronto P, 1991).

[38] Strasbourg was one of the leading centers of print culture in the Empire. Erich Kleinschmidt stresses the importance of the growing middle class for publications in German in an article on Johann Fischart's role for the print culture in the city: "Gelehrtentum und Volkssprache in der Frühneuzeitlichen Stadt: Zur Literaturgesellschaftlichen Funktion Johann Fischarts in Strassburg," *Zeitschrift für Literaturwissenschaft und Linguistik: Eine Zeitschrift der Universität Gesamthochschule Siegen* 37 (1980): 128–51. See further, Erich Kleinschmidt, *Literatur und Leben. Stadt und Literatur in der Frühen Neuzeit* (Cologne: Böhlau, 1982) for a comprehensive study of the culture of reading and print in the southwestern German cities at the time of the Reformation. Ursula Peters has studied the time before the Reformation and the printing press in *Literatur in der Stadt. Studien zu den sozialen Voraussetzungen und kulturellen Organisationsformen städtischer Literatur im 13. und 14. Jahrhundert* (Tübingen: Niemeyer, 1983). See also Rolf Engelsing, *Analphabetentum und Lektüre: Zur Sozialgeschichte des Lesens in Deutschland zwischen feudaler und industrieller Gesellschaft* (Stuttgart: Metzler, 1973); Rolf Engelsing, *Der Bürger als Leser. Lesergeschichte in Deutschland 1500–1800* (Stuttgart: Metzler, 1974); Rob A. Houston, *Literacy in Early Modern Europe: Culture and Education 1500–1800* (London: Longman, 1988).

[39] There are numerous publications on early modern literary genres and the impact of the print industry. See among others anthologies like *Intertextualität in der Frühen Neuzeit,* ed. Wilhelm Kühlmann and Wolfgang Neuber (Frankfurt am Main: Peter Lang, 1994); *Erzählungen in Erzählungen. Phänomene der Narration in Mittelalter und Früher Neuzeit,* ed. Harald Haferland and Michael Mecklenburg (Munich: Wilhelm Fink, 1996); *"Aufführung" und "Schrift" in Mittelalter und Früher Neuzeit,* ed. Jan-Dirk Müller (Stuttgart: Metzler, 1996); *Text im Kontext: Anleitung zur Lektüre deutscher Texte der Frühen Neuzeit,* ed. Alexander Schwarz and Laure Abplanalp (Bern: Peter Lang, 1997); *Das Berliner Modell der Mittleren Deutschen Literatur. Beiträge zur Tagung Kloster Zinna 29.9–01.10.1997,* ed. Christiane Caemmerer, et al. (Amsterdam: Rodopi, 2000).

[40] Schnell, among others, supports the idea that texts of different kinds should not be compared with each other and that a diachronic study is useful only when investigating texts of the same kind. Schnell claims that "woman" and "man" have different functions depending on the type of text or literary genre; genre thus generates different images of gender. He argues convincingly in his research, but the definition of genre can be difficult. Cf. Schnell, *Frauendiskurs, Männerdiskurs, Ehediskurs,* especially 11–21, 282–87; see also Rüdiger Schnell, "Text und Geschlecht. Eine Einleitung," in *Text und Geschlecht. Mann und Frau in Eheschriften der frühen Neuzeit,* ed. Rüdiger Schnell (Frankfurt am Main: Suhrkamp, 1997), 9–46, as well as Schnell's two articles "Geschlechterbeziehungen und Textfunktionen" and "Die Frau als Gefährtin (Socia) des Mannes. Eine Studie zur Interdependenz von Textsorte, Adressat und Aussage," in *Geschlechterbeziehungen und Textfunktionen. Studien zu Eheschriften der Frühen Neuzeit,* ed. Rüdiger Schnell (Tübingen: Niemeyer, 1998), 119–70. See also Ursula Peters, *Text und Kontext: Die Mittelalterliche Philologie zwischen Gesellschaftsgeschichte und Kulturanthropologie* (Wiesbaden: Westdeut-

scher Verlag, 2000), 27 on the importance of looking at texts of the same kind in the search for discursive patterns.

[41] I have chosen to discuss genre when found important for the analysis and to connect it with the discussion of single texts.

[42] Cf. Lorna Jane Abray, *The People's Reformation: Magistrates, Clergy, and Commons in Strasbourg, 1500–1598* (Ithaca, NY: Cornell UP, 1985), 174. Abray stresses that toleration mainly was a matter concerning the individual and that confessional toleration was very limited. As long as people lived in accordance with the religious and secular legislation they were free to have their own faith, but they were not allowed to join in sects or other organizations.

[43] Miriam Usher Chrisman, *Bibliography of Strasbourg Imprints 1480–1599* (New Haven: Yale UP, 1982).

[44] There is not much published on Martin Montanus, either on his life or his work. See *Martin Montanus Schwankbücher (1557–1566)*, ed. Johannes Bolte (Tübingen: Der literarische Verein in Stuttgart, 1899), VII–KL; Walther Killy, *Literaturlexikon. Autoren und Werke deutscher Sprache* (Berlin: Directmedia, 1998, CD-ROM), 14219–20, Jean Deutinger, *L'age de la Littérature en Alsace* (Mundolsheim: Deutinger Verlag, 1986), 189–90.

[45] Also Frey is an author of whom little is written. See the introduction to Jakob Frey, *Jakob Freys Gartengesellschaft (1556)*, ed. Johannes Bolte (Tübingen: Literarischer Verein, 1896), vii–xix; Walther Killy, *Literaturlexikon. Autoren und Werke deutscher Sprache* (Berlin: Directmedia, 1998, CD-ROM), 5752–54, Deutinger, *L'age de la Littérature*, 187–88.

[46] See Elisabeth Wåghäll, "Georg Wickram — Stand der Forschung," *Dapnis* 24, no. 2–3 (1995): 491–540; Elisabeth Wåghäll, *Dargestellte Welt — Reale Welt: Freundschaft: Liebe und Familie in den Prosawerken Georg Wickrams* (Bern: Peter Lang, 1996); Elisabeth Wåghäll, "Georg Wickram," in *German Writers in the Late Middle Ages, Humanism, and Reformation: 1280–1580*, ed. James Hardin and Max Reinhart (Columbia, SC: Bruccoli Clark Layman and Gale Publishers, 1997), 309–16. See also: Erich Kleinschmidt, "Jörg Wickram," in *Deutsche Dichter der Frühen Neuzeit (1450–1600): Ihr Leben und Werk*, ed. Stephan Füssel (Berlin: Erich Schmidt, 1993), 494–511; Walther Killy, *Literaturlexikon. Autoren und Werke deutscher Sprache* (Berlin: Directmedia, 1998, CD-ROM), 22417–23.

[47] Wilhelm Kühlmann, "Johann Fischart," in *Deutsche Dichter der Frühen Neuzeit (1450–1600): Ihr Leben und Werk*, ed. Stephan Füssel (Berlin: Erich Schmidt, 1993), 589–612; Stephen L. Wailes, "Johann Fischart," *German Writers*, 55–62; Walther Killy, *Literaturlexikon. Autoren und Werke deutscher Sprache* (Berlin: Directmedia, 1998, CD-ROM), 5321–5329; Deutinger, *L'age de la Littérature*, 191–200.

[48] See Roloff in his epilogue to *Von guten und bösen Nachbarn*, in Wickram, *Von guten und bösen Nachbarn*, 193.

[49] See Erich Schmidt, "Wickram," *Allgemeine Deutsche Biographie* 42 (1897): 329. Wickram went to the book fairs in Frankfurt am Main and Speyer as the representative of the city of Colmar, according to Schmidt.

[50] Cf. Williams, "Der Teufel und die Frau," 290, footnote 11.

[51] Gerhild S. Williams, *Defining Dominion*, 76. See also 135 on the periodization of the witch hunts.

[52] See H. C. Erik Midelfort, *Witch Hunting in Southwestern Germany 1562–1684: The Social and Intellectual Foundations* (Stanford: Stanford UP, 1972).

[53] Barbara Becker-Cantarino, "Dames des Lettres," 43.

[54] Diane Wolfthal discusses how male figures are portrayed as spying on women in early modern woodcuts, prints, or paintings. They at times appear as narrators — often a text accompanies the picture — and the female voice is then moderated through them: "Women's Community and Male Spies: Erhard Schön's *How Seven Women Complain About Their Worthless Husbands*," in *Attending to Early Modern Women*, ed. Susan D. Amussen and Adele Seeff (Newark: U of Delaware P, 1998), 140–45. See also Berit Wagner, "Kultur, Geschlecht, Erzählen," *Geschlecht und Kultur. Beiträge zur historischen Sozialkunde* Sondernummer (2000).

Illustration from *Das Rollwagenbüchlein,* by Georg Wickram.

1: Chapbooks — Popular Texts for a Large Audience

Der Schwank

CHAPBOOKS, "SCHWÄNKE" OR "Schwanksammlungen," were immensely popular and relatively inexpensive publications in the vernacular that were often reprinted over and over again in the sixteenth, seventeenth, and eighteenth centuries. In no way a new genre, it seems that the compilations of often humorous short stories of the kind that were found in Germany in the sixteenth century — starting with Johannes Pauli's *Schimpf und Ernst*[1] in 1522 — have certain characteristics in common. They have often been accused of crudeness and lack of stylistic elegance, as well as stereotypical and prejudiced portrayals of different occupations and social groups, and a rather extreme misogyny. It is nevertheless dangerous to exaggerate the similarities of these texts; the stories vary in length, language, and style, as well as in their use of stereotypes. Hence, it is impossible to find the typical "Schwank," a text that can be regarded as representative for all texts included in the compilations, especially since texts defined as "Schwänke" are normally of different origin. They are often based on the learned Latin *facetiae* but they can also be translations from French or Italian into German, or they might originate in the oral tradition.[2] They sometimes present current topics and events or sensational occurrences that were likely to attract a large readership.[3] It is, however, not my intention to once more try to find a definition for texts as different as the ones found in the "Schwanksammlungen." I agree rather with Peter C. M. Dieckow that the word "Prosaerzählsammlungen," used in analogy with the term "Prosaromane," is a better term for these very heterogenic texts.[4] The expression "Prosaerzählsammlungen" does not imply moral or aesthetic values and is general enough to include all shorter texts that can be found in the sixteenth-century compilations that were often defined as "Schwänke" by their authors. It is not, however, generally accepted or used. For lack of a better term in English I therefore use the common term "chapbook" for compilations, and the German "Schwank" or "Schwänke" when discussing the different stories.

In this chapter I intend to look closer at the chapbooks *Rollwagenbüchlein* (1555) by Georg Wickram, *Gartengesellschaft* (1556) by Jakob Frey, *Der Wegkürzer* and *Das ander theyl der Garten gesellschafft* (1557?) by Martin Montanus — this last a book the author in the preface claims to be a continuation of Frey's text.[5] Even though Frey and Montanus are both said to have modeled their texts on Wickram's *Rollwagenbüchlein*, their works differ a great deal. All authors draw on the same tradition and use the same or similar sources for their stories,[6] but they use well-known texts, such as the *Decamerone*, freely for their own purposes and turn them into their own works of literature.[7] Due to the popularity of these texts I find it incorrect to simply disregard them when discussing matters regarding gender in the sixteenth century as is often done in scholarly studies.[8] Chapbooks are cultural artifacts even if they are generally known for preserving a social system based on traditionally male values and the repression of woman.[9] We must understand them as representations of culture, and as such they were widely told and read at a time when the printing press had made the mass publication of texts possible.[10] Always exaggerating human depravity, they were likely to create as well as preserve stereotypical behavior while claiming to tell "the truth" about human behavior. The chapbooks thus have much in common with the woodcuts found in the popular literature of the sixteenth century of which the art historian Keith Moxey has said, "we need to understand their cultural significance for those who produced and acquired them and thus demonstrate the ways these images actively articulated the structure of social relations."[11] Drawing on the research of Erwin Panofsky, Moxey sees art as "wholly determined and shaped by the culture in which it has currency."[12] The same can be claimed for literary texts. Moxey's analysis of the woodcuts is therefore interesting when investigating "Schwänke" since he — like Panofsky — "considers visual themes in light of the way analogous themes were used in the written culture of the sixteenth century."[13] Woodcuts were furthermore often used as illustrations in chapbooks, and as such they became part of the popular culture.[14]

Moxey's discussion makes clear that the text as well as the image can be treated as projections of cultural consciousness, but he further concludes that "all analysis constitutes a cultural representation that is determined by the interests and attitudes of the culture to which the author belongs."[15] The danger of an interpretation that sees the text or visual sign as mere reflection is obvious, but important in a study of gender relations if the narrative in the chapbooks is taken as an ideological sign system.[16] The text should not be regarded as a mirror showing "reality" but rather as "Vermittler von Werten und Meinungen, in diesem Fall der massiven Bestätigung der Herrschaftsansprüche des Mannes," to quote Elfriede Moser-Rath in her study of seventeenth- and eighteenth-century chapbooks.[17] Again turning to the visual arts, Moxey points out that "satirical imagery that regarded marriage as spiritually inferior to celibacy, had different implications in a context that regarded marriage as the most desirable form of social life."[18] This is of great importance for the interpretation of the chapbooks since the themes they present in no way are new, but their social and cultural context changes and gives them a different meaning after the introduction of the Reformation in northern Europe.[19] Since the topics were well known to the readers and listeners the difference from other types of texts of this time is not so much what the Schwänke discuss but how they do it. Instead of prescribing immaculate behavior they describe the opposite: instead of prescribing sexual abstinence they describe adultery and fornication, the lust and desire inherent in every human being — especially the female. It is therefore not surprising that the chapbooks were regarded as dangerous to read among those who claimed to be guarding good morals, divine and secular law, and social order.

The matter discussed below is the representation of gender relations in texts that are normally said to be highly stereotypical in their portrayals of men and women. Even though most texts describe the relationship between man and woman and between husband and wife as highly problematical, marriage is described as a natural and almost necessary estate. An unmarried adult thus appears as unnatural, almost suspicious.[20] Gender and sexuality become biological givens in the world of the chapbook.[21] Deviations from the heterosexual relationship between adult men and women seem to be experiments of thought intended to show the problems related to any change in gender relations. When it comes to the attention paid to sexuality however, the difference among the texts is striking. Relationships between men and women in Wickram's Schwänke are clearly subordinate problems common to all mankind, while Frey and Montanus devote a greater part of their stories to the problems caused by women and aimed at men. There is of course no rule without an exception, and a few of the stories in *Rollwagenbüchlein* are similar to the ones told by Frey and Montanus, but they are strikingly few.[22]

Deviations From a Common Pattern?

Das Rollwagenbüchlein by Georg Wickram

> Es ist von alter har / freündtlicher und gütiger Leser / ein sprichwort under vilen gewesen / wenn man etwan schampere und schandtliche wort geredt / hat man gesagt / Stilla mutz / diß gehört auff den Rollwagen oder ins Schiff / welches meines beduncken nit seer wol gesprochen gewesen / dieweil sich zu vil malen zu tregt / dass züchtige erbare weiber / ja auch Jungfrauwen auff wagen oder zu schiff faren / deren man gar wenig verschonen thut.[23]

Wickram dedicates *Rollwagenbüchlein* to his friend Martin Neuen — burgher of the city of Colmar and one of the innkeepers in town — and assures Neuen that the booklet (büchlein) is written to entertain the reader without any intention of lecturing or insulting anyone.[24] He has tried to write a book that will satisfy all needs and tastes and is careful to point out that it can be read "on allen anstoß" (without causing offense, 5). He signs the dedication "Jörg Wickram, town clerk of Burckheim," which indicates that before the book was published he had left his position as a lower clerk in Colmar for a more honorable assignment in the town of Burgheim on the eastern shore of the Rhine. In the preface Wickram turns to a wider audience and again signs with his name. This time the person he addresses is clearly a fictional or imagined reader, but he does not himself consciously enter the text as a fictitious author or anonymous narrator.[25] He takes the opportunity here to make clear his intentions with the book. His outspoken aim is to write stories for people of all kinds on long journeys and to entertain them so that time passes quickly. Considering the means of transportation available in the sixteenth century, traveling was not only slow and physically strenuous but also dangerous. The appearance of some kind of travel literature comprising stories short enough to also be told orally must have been welcomed by many. Since women also traveled at times, Wickram is very cautious to make clear to "the kind reader" (zum gütigen Leser, 7) that his selection of stories suits women well. By doing so he takes the moralizing stand he claims to avoid, but he also makes clear that his stories are written for women and men alike and that everyone will find something to laugh about without having to feel shame or guilt. This can be seen as a rhetoric strategy to avoid offending the censors, but one can also regard Wickram's brief introduction preceding the actual Schwänke as a smart way of defining an unknown audience and thus gaining readers.

Even though partially using the same sources as Frey and Montanus, Wickram shows less interest in the anal and obscene. Only four of his stories — numbers 4, 20, 45, and 79 — contain any kind of sexual allusions. Number 20 is the only story including an unmarried woman: the daughter of an old and wealthy farmer's wife. The mother is probably widowed, since a father or husband is not mentioned and she seems to run the household by herself. The daughter has hurt her foot by stepping on a thorn and has to stay in bed. One day a friar, who is a well-known guest in the house, comes to beg for cheese. When he is told about the daughter he promises that he will try to help her, but instead of pulling out the thorn he seems to abuse her sexually. What happens to the daughter is only mentioned indirectly in the text. The reader is told that the friar grabs her foot, that she dislikes this and that she screams out loud. The mother yells to the daughter from downstairs to keep quiet: she will have to stand some pain in order to be cured.[26] Wickram then describes how the friar quickly leaves the house after having finished the "treatment" ("Alß aber der Münch fertig war," 41), afraid of being caught by the mother. He has obviously done something more to the daughter than pull out a thorn from her foot; he has committed a sinful act that has hurt her. Did he try to suck the thorn out with his mouth instead of using his hand or did he actually rape the woman? The text leaves the answer to the reader's own imagination but there are clear sexual insinuations. The daughter tells the mother what has happened, but the reader is not told exactly what she says. The text only states: "und alß die Muter zu der tochter kam / befand sie daß er anders mit ir gehandlet hett dann den dorn betraff."[27] In addition, the friar has violated a virgin, because in bed she is completely defenseless, vulnerable, and exposed to male desires. The mother has no reason not to believe the daughter and quickly goes after the friar who has run off and never returns to the village.

In this story an innocent woman's body has been sexually violated, and no blame is put on her; she is described as highly unwilling rather than as seductive. Male desire and physical power dominate the discourse of sexuality.[28] All the blame is put on the man, but he is not a respectable (working) man. He is a friar, one of the most common figures scrutinized and criticized in the chapbooks. Often characterized as sexually possessed, the friar or the Catholic priest transgresses all moral boundaries and violates all rules. The sexual lust inherent in women can thus be downplayed for the sake of anti-Catholic propaganda. The discourse of sexuality focuses on male lust rather than female and the woman appears as almost asexual. Because of her probable virginity — she is still living at home with the mother — she is still untouched and hence the counterpart to the friar who has broken his monastic vows. He should live under the rule of celibacy just like the unmarried woman, but instead he takes the position of the moral outcast. This allows the farmer's wife to act on behalf of the daughter and to look for revenge for her lost honor, but the story ends with the friar running away before being caught. Without expressing it clearly the sympathy of the narrator rests entirely with the old woman and her daughter. One could ask if the outcome of the story had been the same had the husband and father been present. Does the friar take advantage of the fact that the household consists of women only? In the world of the chapbooks monks and priests often fool faithful husbands, who then appear weak and foolish. Here the sexuality of the women is downplayed to stress the immoral behavior of the friar. The women are fooled but are no fools, they are vulnerable and yet strong, they are allowed to react and to act in an attempt to save the family honor.

In story number 45 the reader finds a cunning wife who has sex with the parish priest when her faithful husband is out working on the fields. One day he returns home to pick up a tool he has forgotten, but he is in too much of a hurry to look twice towards the bed, even though he believes to have seen two heads on the pillow. The priest immediately leaves the house in great fear, but the wife is able to make up a story when bringing the husband lunch: she acts as if she sees two men out on the fields and makes her husband believe that he had the same problem with his eyesight that same morning. The story ends with the couple having lunch together, happily talking and joking. Since no one besides the woman knows about her affair with the priest, the honor of husband and wife is never threatened. Wickram here refrains from openly criticizing the man or the woman even though the woman no doubt has committed adultery: She has sex with a friend of the family who also happens to be the parish priest. He runs off ashamed and scared while she is able to make a plan that saves her marriage and the shame the husband would feel, had he known the true facts. Her shrewdness is part of female stereotypes as portrayed in many chapbooks, but Wickram does not make her evil. He is more concerned with saving the marriage from breaking up. This includes a portrayal of the happy couple at the end of the story. Neither wife nor husband is punished for inappropriate behavior — the woman for transgressing the rules of matrimony nor the husband for not having controlled his wife more thoroughly. It may be that Wickram thinks that they deserve each other; it may be that he wants to harmonize the world portrayed. The discourse of sexuality, since it is never made public, does not interfere with the discourse of marriage.

Sexual problems of various kinds constitute a great part of the Schwänke that deals with the relationship between men and women. The discourse of sexuality does not, however, only include adulterous relationships but it also takes its expression in the opposite, in childlessness. Schwank number 4 tells a story of a wealthy childless couple that has been longing for a child for fifteen years. The wife blames her husband for not being able to reproduce, but this only makes him wonder whose "fault" it actually is ("ob die schuld mein sey oder nit," 17) and he manages to talk the new maid into sleeping with him so that he can test his virility. She promptly becomes pregnant and the man has proven that he is sexually superior to his wife. Instead of being happy, the husband has to deal with a serious problem: as a member of the city council he will be deprived of his honor ("von allen eeren gesetzt," 17) if he is discovered committing adultery. The man shows great concern about his public reputation, but thinks little of the reaction that can be expected when the wife finds out about what has happened. The family physician promises to help the husband save his honorable reputation. He tells the wife that the husband has become pregnant and that he will need to sleep with the maid in order for the child to be transferred to the female body. No wonder that the woman is astounded and unlikely to accept the arguments presented by the doctor, but the social standing granted a physician makes it hard for the wife to question his arguments no matter how ridiculous they may seem. She manages to convince the maid of the importance of saving the husband from the disease — the pregnancy — and promises to raise the child as her own.

The maid does not have to worry about the anger of the wife or about leaving the house, the wife does not find out about her own inability to become pregnant, and the husband can continue his life as respectable burgher of the city. Order has been reestablished and the honor of the household remains intact: "und bliben all bey eeren" (and they did not lose their honor, 18). The doubts of the husband provoked the affair with the maid. The sex act between the husband and the maid appears to emanate from the husband's despair at his inability to reproduce, and it can thus be explained and excused. The man needs to find out if his virility or masculinity is threatened. By having a baby with the maid the husband manages to make his own marriage complete — a child is born into the family, a kind of early modern in vitro fertilization — while proving to himself that he is a complete man. Little is said about the women who have to accept what is presented to them, but the smiles encountering the wife every time she meets the doctor tell her that something awkward has happened. She is neither stupid nor helpless, but has definitely been fooled. At the same time her future is secured. She will have a child and her marriage is not threatened. The order is upheld despite the transgression of norms. By making a male pregnancy appear as a disease, gender roles are further enhanced; a woman should bear children while this condition would make the man sick.

Several of the female characters in *Rollwagenbüchlein* are married and hence part of a relationship that needs to be preserved according to customs and legal regulations. The interest among the authorities in keeping marriages from breaking apart is expressed in secular and religious texts of the sixteenth century and is also a hot topic in the popular literature. In Schwank 17 the wife of a tailor is verbally as well as physically abused by her husband "wiewol sy frumm unnd treüw was" (although she was pious and faithful, 35). He has to spend time in jail, and the wife takes him to court on several occasions. At the end the husband has to promise good behavior so that the wife "kein klag mer über in furt" (does not accuse him of any more things, 36) or he will be in great trouble. Story 84 describes a similar case: a man who is constantly plagued by jealousy without having any reason for his feelings. He decides to move to another place so that he can better keep an eye on the wife and keep all men away from her but does not tell her about his plans. When she finally discovers the reason for moving she is able to make him understand his own stupidity. In this story, too, Wickram puts the blame on the husband. He argues against (male) jealousy since it can encourage women to take a lover. Women tend to want what is forbidden to them, he claims, but it is clearly the man who is the fool in the story. He needs to be in control of his feelings and in charge of the household so that the wife does not yield to the desire inherent in her.[29] Wickram does not question the common claim that women are incapable of controlling themselves, nor does he question male authority over women. He nevertheless allows the women in his Schwänke to be active parties in the marriage and does not make them responsible for all problems within the relationship only because of their sex.[30] Wickram rather uses his female characters to help preserve the patriarchal society that they are subjected to. He does this without reducing them to mere objects that are completely controlled by their husbands or by making them the target of evil powers as is the case with witch-like figures in Frey's and Montanus's works.

Schwank 84 starts with a reference to Sebastian Brandt's *Narrenschiff* and the difficulty of controlling a wife, but Wickram manages to turn the story into a dissemination of male jealousy, thereby criticizing the man instead of the woman. In the text a jealous husband does his best to ruin his marriage to a pretty woman by seeing every male person in the village who talks to her as a possible threat to their marriage. The husband tries to keep the wife away from all social gatherings out of fear that "sie wurd im lebendig gefressen" (she would be eaten alive, 161). As a result of his behavior the neighbors make fun of him and the wife — who has long been aware of what is wrong — "ließ sichs aber ye langer ye weniger bekümmern" (cared less and less, 161). The husband is described as trapped in his own stupidity, always suspecting that "was man den Weibern understehet zu layden / darnach verlanget sie erst" (women desire what is forbidden to them, 161). The jealous husband has no trust in his wife and presents his view of women as unreliable and always longing for the forbidden. The thought appears almost as a leitmotif in the early modern chapbook, but here it seems out of place. The woman is depicted as tired of being constantly distrusted, and her growing thoughtlessness when meeting other men is a result of male stupidity not female lust. The husband is given various names such as "Fantast," "Stockfisch," and "Tüppel," all alluding to his foolish behavior. Only the wisdom of his wife saves the relationship and makes the husband understand his own silliness: "Die gut fraw so mehr witz hatt dann ihr Mann . . ." (The good wife was wiser than her husband, 161–62). The moral of the Schwank is apparent: Possessiveness within marriage only results in what it tries to get away from: adulterous wives and unhappiness.[31]

Wickram's story ends happily — the wife is able to make the husband realize his own foolhardiness and the marriage can be saved, but this also means that order is reestablished and the man can reclaim his position in the family hierarchy. The wife here helps the husband to become a righteous head of the family ("ein rechtgeschafner Hawßman," 162). The similarity with the opening quotation of this book is striking: Wickram once again leaves it to a female figure to explain the order within marriage and in the family, thus stressing her virtue and the value of submissiveness among women. This might seem peculiar, but by returning to what is depicted as the natural order, the woman is made a winner too. Her husband will again be a respected part of the community and she will be his respected wife. She will no longer be the target of sexual insinuations from the male villagers; her weakness as a woman — to desire what is forbidden to her — will not be challenged. The wife is thus given the power to help her husband so that he can reestablish his position within their marriage and regain his lost masculinity. In Wickram's stories this is no goal in itself; the fear of an order lost is the fear of the loss of harmony at all levels of society. A "proper" order thus equals a happy life, and in the works of Wickram men as well as women are made responsible for realizing a life lived in accordance with secular and religious regulations.

Some of the Schwänke in *Rollwagenbüchlein* demonstrate that a good wife helps her husband in all matters regarding their married life. Difference in temper hence appears as a positive factor within marriage. Differences in age and class were on the other hand commonly regarded as a problem for a happy marriage in sixteenth-century literature, and were often a target of ridicule in popular texts as well as in art.[32] In the lived reality it was not uncommon that the widow of a craftsman married one of his apprentices in order to keep the business running.[33] One also often comes across marriages between older men and younger women for different reasons. The need to find a stepmother for small children should not be underestimated at a time when public or private child-care was unheard of. Court records and other documents rarely give enough information for scholars to draw any conclusions regarding real-life marriages, but literary texts often stress that differences of various kinds make for unhappy marriages. A common attitude is that one spouse necessarily benefits more from a marriage than the other and that this is the source of conflict. Most often this is made evident in the lack of experience among young people or the attraction of old people to youth and beauty that make them forget more important matters, such as class. The danger most commonly expressed can be traced to the fear of female power over men.[34] It should, however, be noted that gender undoubtedly is of less importance than the social standing of the person. Older people held a different position in society than did young adults and women of a fertile age. The desire to pair equals with equals thus included age and social class. The world of the chapbooks is therefore full of stories of vain widows and widowers and shrewish young men and women.

In *Rollwagenbüchlein* Wickram demonstrates how a young cunning woman tries to fool her much older husband and thus reverse the household order.[35] Her disrespect for the older man does not, however, result in anything but beatings. Her plans are discovered by the husband who reestablishes the order that was temporarily lost. He resumes command over the household and the woman never tries to hoodwink him again.[36] As in Schwank number 17 the wife is beaten, but the sixteenth story justifies male violence, something very uncommon in Wickram's work. The difference between the stories is clear; number 17 portrays a man who is always violent, number 16 a man who at first lets his wife get by with a lie, only to later see her try the same trick over and over again. If he wants to keep his position as head of the household he has to act quickly and react strongly. In this case the violence towards the wife is depicted as necessary. She has to respect and to obey her parsimonious husband even if this means that she can never buy anything for herself.

The forty-fourth story brings up a similar topic. An old widow is courted by a young soldier who is able to appeal to her vanity and make her marry him. He wants her money and she wants a young man who can take care of an aging woman.[37] The marriage is doomed to fail: the young husband starts spending his wife's money as soon as the wedding is over, and does nothing to help his old wife in her daily work at home. He sees his friends and spends a great deal of time in the tavern while she wants to stay home. When he brings guests home she decides to pretend that she is sick, but the husband no longer accepts any excuse from her side. Instead of showing her sympathy he starts beating her on her head, telling her that she has enough servants to run the house and that she should be able to sit at the table and keep the guests company. The beating does not end until the woman promises to never have another headache: "laß dein zorn ab gegen meinen kopff / er thut mir nimmer wee" (let go of your anger towards my head, it will never hurt again, 84). But instead of ending the story with the subservience of the woman, Wickram goes on to tell the reader that her submissiveness results in a more compromising attitude on the part of the husband: "Als sy nun zeletst von irem kiflen abließ / und den mann nicht mer also frettet / stund er selbs von seiner weyß eins theils ab."[38] The husband is here allowed to beat his wife, but in Wickram's texts there is always a need to find "a plausible explanation" for violence within the family. Domination by violence is in itself no solution to marital problems in his texts. In this story the husband has failed in his role as respectable head of the household and he has to reach an agreement with the wife. The marriage can thus be saved, but it seems to be a forced agreement. The violence directed at the woman is only justified if the marriage itself is more important than the actual relationship between the spouses.

Two of the Schwänke deviate from what is commonly regarded as typical for these kinds of texts, numbers 55 and 75; they are neither humorous nor satirical and they are clearly moralizing. Number 55 is often used as an example of a story that will not fit into any formal, structural, or other definition of a Schwank.[39] Based on a true story it describes how two men gamble and lose everything they own to each other, with the result that they have to trade homes and businesses. The wives are not informed until facing the facts. The men are too involved in what they consider their own business. The result is disastrous; one of the women loudly argues with her husband throughout the night, but in the morning the servants start worrying. Neither husband nor wife comes down for breakfast and no sound can be heard from the master bedroom. Later in the day the room is opened and husband and wife are found stabbed to death. It becomes evident that the man has murdered his wife and then killed himself, and also that he has killed his own child since his wife was pregnant: "so dann sein eigen fleysch unnd blut inn muter leib sampt seinem Ehgemahel lesterlichen ermordet hat" (so that he had savagely killed his own flesh and blood in its mother's womb as well as his wife, 112). The claim found in the preface to the book that it does not want to moralize is long forgotten. The moral of the story is as clear as it is surprising: it is not what could be expected, namely that women should remain silent, do what their husbands tell them, and avoid arguments, but rather that gambling is a deadly sin. One could further have assumed that the blame would be put on the woman for being quarrelsome, but Wickram does not write a word about it. He seems to give the wife the right to speak up in order to make her husband change his mind and prevent a tragedy that, after all, might not have happened had she agreed to move and yet for which Wickram does not hold her to blame. He thus emphasizes the role of the woman as a respected authority within the household.

Schwank number 75 can be regarded as the opposite to number 55 because of its happy ending, but the similarity in the function of the female characters is striking. The story begins when two young noble people fall in love with each other and secretly meet at night. Nothing is said about what happens between the young man and woman, but the reader is assured of their innocence: "es mag ein yeder wol gedencken / wie trewlich sy einander gemeinet haben" (anyone should understand, how honest they had been about each other, 142). Frey or Montanus would probably both have emphasized this part of the story with intimate details, had they been telling it in their chapbooks.[40] In Wickram's text it seems sufficient that the count has already forbidden his daughter to become involved with the young man (who is serving the count at the court) and threatened her with severe punishment if she does not obey him. Yet the young woman does not listen to her father and he does not keep his threats. After discovering the couple in the garden he recognizes their love and decides to arrange a wedding for them. Even though he can be blamed for telling neither his daughter nor his wife about his plans, this story ends happily. The young lovers do not have to hide their love after their relationship has been legalized and the family honor has been saved. The daughter is never punished for disobeying her father, and Wickram praises him: "Dann zu geschechnen dingen sol man allzeit das best radten" (for regarding things that have already occurred one should always give the best advice, 143). No one is hurt, no harm has been done. There is nothing to laugh at, nothing to joke about, there are no misogynist utterances, no sex. The world has not been turned upside down even though the woman initiates the secret meeting and disobeys male authority. The father uses his authority as head of the household to make the relationship legal, but in this case he only fulfills what the daughter dreams of. This is in a way perfect Reformation propaganda — the young people marry out of love with parental consent and the woman is allowed to take active part in the relationship without punishment — but it seems to be an ideal with little connection with the lived reality or other chapbook texts.

It is noteworthy however that women rarely appear cunning in an evil way in Wickram's Schwänke. They are more likely to make use of tricks as a defense against unwanted male company. When a young soldier tries to spend the night at the house of a widow and her daughter, the women let him share his supper with them, but when the night comes they want him out of the house.[41] The cunning women arrange a bet about who can jump the farthest from the front door, and when the soldier has jumped out the women close the door so that he has to spend the night in the pig pen. The strong man — the soldier — sees himself fooled by the women. The strength that helped him to jump far is of no help in this situation. The women have used their mental instead of physical powers to play a practical joke on the soldier. They furthermore manage to keep their virtue even though they did nothing to hide their interest in his company, a free supper, and free wine in the evening. Not until bedtime do they act like the virtuous women in Wickram's prose novels, women who never seem to consume alcohol or enjoy the company of foreigners. The behavior of the women shows that there is sometimes greater room for female agency, without its conflicting with male superiority, than Wickram depicts in his idealistic prose novels.

A complete stranger, especially a soldier, was no doubt a danger to single women who had little chance of defending themselves because of the difference in physical strength. If we read the Schwank with feminist eyes the women are true winners, but considering the bad reputation of soldiers traveling the countryside in the search for food and a place to stay in sixteenth-century Germany, it is dangerous to read too much into the text. Landowning women certainly had a higher position in society than did the soldiers.[42] As an integrated member of a farming community the widow must guard her own reputation and that of her daughter, while the soldier, looking for a place to settle down, has nothing to loose. The text thus sends out signals to the reader that the soldier is stupid enough to be fooled by women. Because of their higher social standing the women in this story can be allowed the power to defend themselves and their home. They are not given physical strength that is considered "male," but rather an artfulness that is considered "female" and only dangerous if directed towards a man of good reputation.

Wickram does not, however, always deviate from the common Schwank. Story number 91 is one of very few in which he stays completely within the realm of convention. It describes how a young painter/artist in love with life marries the widow of a farmer, a woman with little interest in changing her habits. Every day she sweeps the floors without using any water, so that the dust swirls about the house and sticks to the husband's oil paint. She does not listen to his complaints but just asks him to leave the house until the dust has settled. The husband — fed up with her behavior — uses the opportunity to drink with his friends in the local tavern. After eight days on a drinking spree he brings his friends home and watches how his wife has "learned her lesson." She has come to realize the danger of asking her husband to stay away from home, for he now comes home drunk every night. The conclusion drawn is that women should not tell their men to leave while they are cleaning because it is a part of male nature to want to get away from home: "Dann in sonst von natur angeboren ist / daß sie nit gern daheym bleyben" (173). The stereotypes are clear: women belong in the house and are responsible for making it appealing to the men so that they desire to stay home. Men, restless by birth, need women who make marriage attractive enough for them to want to stay within the boundaries of matrimony.

In Wickram's texts the men seem as weak or strong as the women who are left in charge of making marriage work, of making the men understand that they need to take responsibility for their families in order to be "real" men, active heads of the household with the power to rule successfully. Thus a message is conveyed to the reader that both men and women should work towards compromise and understanding, and that the man should avoid acting on behalf of the wife without her consent. This does not imply that men and women are equals in the sense that they have the same legal rights and obligations, but *Rollwagenbüchlein* allows women a great deal of responsibility and freedom to act within marriage. The women are undoubtedly shown greater respect than the female characters in other chapbooks, and are given the power at times to manage the household. However, as soon as these wise women have reestablished order they return the right to rule to the men. The men do to a certain extent acquire wisdom, honesty, and the will to compromise through their wives. They are not allowed to rule because of their sex exclusively, but rather they need the proper skills. Being a woman in Wickram's work does not exclude the right to be heard or the right to initiate changes in the household that are intended to save the reputation of the family. But a woman does not have access to any of the functions outside of this realm. Despite these positive aspects, one has to conclude that a woman in Wickram's Schwänke is only given her positive features so that she can serve the man well. By taming the violent sides ascribed to "man" in these texts, by helping him to a virtuous life, the "woman" finds her justified place in the world. Here, "woman" does not equal "wife"; unmarried women and widows can also function as a kind of human pacifier that is used to comfort "man" on his way to salvation. That also seems to be her way to salvation. They can join as equals before God.

Having said this, it should be emphasized that Wickram does not altogether avoid insulting jokes or sexual insinuations in his stories. The Schwank genre seems to have allowed for great freedom in the description of human weaknesses, and Wickram takes advantage of this lack of restrictions in a way that one cannot find in his longer prose texts. He also dedicates relatively little space to the relationship between man and woman in his Schwänke compared with his other prose texts or with chapbooks by other authors. Of the 110 stories ascribed to Wickram in *Rollwagenbüchlein*, only seventeen involve topics immediately related to women or the relationship between men and women.[43] They vary thematically but generally seem to turn against any change of what could traditionally be perceived as a natural social order. All other stories focus almost entirely on male protagonists, despite the explicit address to female readers in the preface. What effect does this have on the construction of gender and the distribution of power in matters regarding gender? Looking at the discourses of sexuality, marriage, and family life, we find that Wickram's stories do not necessarily fit into the common pattern of gender hierarchies as presented in many Schwänke. Despite the lack of female protagonists in the *Rollwagenbüchlein*, Wickram seems to be aware of the complex relationship between author and readership. It is not likely that anyone was interested in hearing about his or her own stupidity in a highly insulting way and Wickram tries to juggle coarseness and rudeness with the will to believe in humankind in a way other authors of chapbooks do not, but he in no way is omnipresent as narrator. In the various stories he steps back and reduces his involvement in the text to brief comments and moralizing summaries, but he no longer speaks straight to the reader as in the introduction. One is tempted to ask if he succeeded in satisfying all tastes. The immense popularity of *Rollwagenbüchlein* might be the answer.

Disharmony in the Garden

Jakob Frey's *Gartengesellschaft*

> Ich hab auch nichts, so ungeschicklichs oder ungebürlichs vor erbaren frawen oder junckfrawen zureden were, hieher setzen noch anziehen wöllen. Dann ye frawen und junckfrawen alle ehr, zucht und erbarkeit in alle weg zu erbieten ist und auch erbotten werden solle, wiewol ich von etlichen, doch nit vilen, die eben des selben gleichen volcks, kleine schimpfliche meldung allein zu guter warnung gethon haben.[44]

Despite his claim to follow Wickram, Frey in his *Gartengesellschaft* pictures a world partly different from the world found in the *Rollwagenbüchlein*. In Frey's Schwänke there are very few good women but there are not many good men either. Frey seems to have lost his faith in humankind and most of his stories involving men and women deal with adultery, fornication, disagreements, fights, physical and sexual abuse — problematic topics common to the chapbook reader. The danger is a world turned upside down, a world with the woman on top.[45] This fear of the reversal of conventional gender rules as expressed in Frey's stories can be an indication of ruptures in the sex/gender system. The sex/gender roles might appear biologically established once and for all with the subordination of the woman in focus in the Schwänke, but the play with sex/gender conventions sends out signs of change. Misogynist comments and frequent calls for the subordination of woman are mixed with long accounts of men failing in their roles as head of the family. Even though addressing male and female readers in the preface, Frey gives little evidence of communication between men and women in the Schwänke. They talk to each other, not with each other, and there seems to be an invisible wall — similar to the one described in Marlen Haushofer's book with the same name from a much later date (*Die Wand*, 1963) — built between the sexes. Just like Wickram, Frey opens the book with a dedication that does not mention women. It is followed by a more general preface addressing the "gütigen Leser" (friendly reader, 5). Already the title explains the purpose of the book: Frey's intention is to entertain honest people when they gather outdoors for pleasant company. It is supposed to fight melancholy, a dangerous disease in the eyes of many sixteenth-century men and women.[46] The author defends his choice of texts by claiming the importance of jokes and fun; one sometimes needs to make space for the fool: "Man muß zu weilen auch dem narren platz geben" (4). Frey chooses freely among Latin texts by Heinrich Bebel, Francesco Poggio, and Johann Adelphus; he adds and changes various parts and rewrites the text to suit his own purpose.[47] Johannes Bolte, in his critical edition of Frey's *Gartengesellschaft*, speculates on the possibility that some of the Schwänke might be Frey's own texts, but it has been difficult to find proof for this claim since it is hard to trace the original source of the stories in the *Geschichtsklitterung* and thus also to tell if any of them were published for the first time or simply adaptations of older stories.[48]

An imagined audience is defined: In the dedication only men are addressed — Reinbolten von Kageneck, a man belonging to the magistrate of Lor and his "honorable friends" — but in the preface Frey makes clear that his book is written to suit virtuous women and virgins as well as men (6) and that he does not want to offend anyone with his stories. By his closing remarks it does, however, become evident that he understands the repulsive character of some of the texts in the book. He emphasizes that he only wants to entertain and make jokes — a good laugh is thus a better reaction than anger (7). The inclusion of women as possible readers of his stories might therefore be a strategic choice and not necessarily something he seriously considered. Texts described as suitable for women — the weaker sex — were less likely to appear offensive to the censors. The brief statement that some of the texts are included as warnings and bad examples must be another way to justify their crudeness;[49] the vocabulary is at times close to pornographic and he does not shy away from nudity or graphic descriptions of sexual intercourse. Does this strategy to justify the publication of the book prove successful? Frey signs his real name rather than a pen name[50] and the book was reprinted on several occasions, an indication that it passed the censors. Its emphasis on female desire and sexuality might be more offensive to the reader of the twenty-first century than to Frey's own time, but there are nevertheless clear differences from Wickram's Schwänke. We do not know if Frey and Wickram had the same readership, but they address the same audience — everyone! If one assumes that they were aware of the limited number of readers due to illiteracy, everyone has to be understood as meaning every literate person. To this group could be added an audience listening to texts read aloud, but it is almost impossible to find accurate literacy rates.[51]

Frey's interest in human — particularly female — sexuality sets the tone for the Schwänke. Few of them depict women in situations where their sex or gender is irrelevant and where they act and react less because of their sex or gender than because of their personal characteristics. One very short text portrays a woman of weak understanding who loves the sound of the organ in the cathedral of Strasbourg so much that she wants the instrument "to come to her house."[52] She calls herself "gaffelstirne," thereby indicating her own foolishness,[53] but there is no further comment made by the author-narrator, concerning either her sex or her stupidity. The story is unique for Frey in that, though it depicts a woman, it might just as well have had a male protagonist. The topic — human foolishness — is not related to the sex of the protagonist and not used by the author-narrator to indicate specific female stupidity. There is only one more story in *Gartengesellschaft* with a female protagonist that can be considered similarly "gender neutral": a widow tries to please a guest who is dissatisfied with her wine. She finally decides to play a joke on him: having served him all her best wines without any recognition, she brings him a glass of her own urine after having let it cool off.[54] Too caught up with his own excellent taste in grapes and wines the guest does not even notice the change of beverage; he comes to the conclusion that the glass was poorly washed and that it had previously contained vermouth. The story ends with the guest leaving the house pleased with the hospitality and in good spirits and the woman being paid for her wine! The sympathy is on the side of the woman; the guest has been unfriendly and demanding for no reason.

Both these stories include male and female characters, but the scatological jokes are not gender or sex specific and the role of the insulted innkeeper could have just as well been played by a character like Till Eulenspiegel — one of the most infamous figures in early modern literature. The absence of a discourse of marriage, family life, or sexuality seems to stabilize the male-female relationship; the woman is not first and foremost a temptress or a wife with rights and obligations, the man is neither tried by his own desires, nor is his manliness as such threatened. When the woman has a function that does not reduce her to her sex/gender only, when Frey refrains from exclusively focusing on stereotypical male-female dichotomies and instead brings up problems of relevance for men and women alike, the characters might appear foolish, but only in their roles as human beings. As soon as female sexuality — inside or outside of marriage — is mentioned, male self-control and thus power is at risk.

Another short story portraying women (number 26) makes an interesting comparison. One woman blames another for having stolen her wool and starts an argument that neither of them can win: they are equally blameworthy and unlikely to give in. So far the plot is comparable with stories with male protagonists. The difference from the story with the "gaffelstirne" is that it not only portrays stupid or evil people but that it has a clear sexual undertone. The women call each other whores, a word intimately related to the female sex and thus representing woman. Tilman Walter, in his excellent work on sexuality in the early modern period, has pointed out that the word "whore" was ambiguous, referring to inappropriate behavior both social and religious, and that the connotation of the word was wider than its original meaning.[55] This makes the transfer to a more general meaning of the word easier. All bad women turn into whores; since almost all women are bad in Frey's text, "woman" thus equals "whore." Trying to outdo each other, the women in the Schwank start the argument with the plain word "whore" and continue with expressions like "a priest's whore" and "a monk's whore" and the fight ends with whole sentences of invectives.[56] The women use the worst words they can think of for their own sex, words clearly and purely sexual. They use language instead of their fists, and Frey thereby reinforces the conventional view of woman as unable to keep her mouth shut.[57] The consequence is paradoxical in that the two women help create what they despise — the image of the cunning and shrewish woman. This further strengthens the representation of woman as obsessed with her own sexuality. The women in this text not only act like whores themselves, they also blame others for being whores, thus leaving little room for any other type of female behavior. It is no longer possible to substitute men for women in this story. What at first seemed to be the theme of the story — theft — is only used as the backdrop to sexual insinuations. The fight ends even and the author-narrator concludes that one is as good as the other.[58] This implies that both women are whores, women who are unable to control themselves and who commit adultery and fornication, thus breaking the law — not just local order — by their loud dispute. By generalizing and making the behavior of the women stereotypical, the image of woman as always driven by her instinct is reinforced.

One further aspect of the shrewish woman touched upon in *Gartengesellschaft* is her relationship to the devil. Only one story goes as far as calling a woman a witch (number 103) but sexual allusions are missing and the short text makes little of what could have been a hot topic. Frey seems more interested in scatological jokes than possible connections between an old woman and evil powers. The young people surrounding her make her an outsider — old and ugly — and when she bends over to pick up a spindle and at the same time farts, she tries to excuse herself by referring to her age without any success. A young man makes fun of her and chases her out of the house with the explanation that she must be a witch since the devil took possession of her rear with such noise. There is little evidence that the term witch is meant very seriously — Frey tells the story of a happy gathering filled with jokes and entertainment — but here it is used for a woman whom it no longer suits to gather with young people. The title of the story only mentions an old woman, an "alt weib," and the image of the witch is used to illustrate what is considered her poor behavior. The woman does not belong to the group; she represents a diffuse other. Her behavior does not justify the fact that she is referred to as "witch," but it leaves the narrator with a plausible explanation for the reaction of the younger people in the group. Her position as a weak but threatening outcast is underlined by the use of a young, strong man as her opponent. Even though "young daughters" are present, one of the young men is speaking for the group. This is hardly a coincidence but rather seems like a conscious choice made by the author. The contrast is striking and the sex/gender hierarchy obvious despite the lack of sexual allusions.

The Schwank brings the difference between the sexes to its point. The young, virile man who talks in the name of God accuses the old woman — no longer of childbearing age — of being possessed by the devil. The discourse of sexuality is thus expressed indirectly in the argument between the old woman and the young man. The man believes he is taking responsibility for his friends and clears the house of unwanted guests. His quick reaction saves the party. The "witch" is in no position to explain or defend herself and she is chased out of the house, out of sight.

The majority of the stories in *Gartengesellschaft* that include male as well as female characters focus on what they represent as members of the group "men" and "women" and on their relationship with each other. They concentrate on the lack of communication between the sexes, on what could or should be considered male and female. The fear of an order lost, the fear of change, is not always explicitly expressed but is implicit in discourse, especially in the representation of woman and her position to man. The engendering of male and female stereotypes, produced by discourse, preserves a hierarchic system that is only reversed in the world turned upside down. The effect of this is vividly described in Schwank number 20 where a man suggests that his quarrelsome wife should take on his duties while he stays at home to take care of the household.[59] Frey focuses his story on the husband, who cannot do anything correctly. Besides being completely incapable of even the simplest housekeeping he accidentally kills his own child and is finally bitten by the little foal in the barn — thereby losing his most important male organ, his penis.[60] He no doubt deeply regrets the suggestion he made his wife and fears her return: He asks himself: "Warumb binn ich nit man bliben!" (Why did I not remain a man, 31).[61] The wife at first seems to forgive her husband for what he has (not) done, but when finding out that the foal "erwüscht . . . den knabenbuben" (caught the little boy, 32–33) she is outraged. The dead child is no loss — it can be replaced — but a man who has lost his manhood is not even worth mentioning. The man must run for his life and does not get any help from the neighbor woman when the wife explains his "handicap" to her.[62]

One could assume that this man would be charged with and convicted of killing his own child and blamed for ruining the household, but this is not Frey's point. The man loses everything in life by his own doing, but is primarily blamed for having turned the world upside down, for having tried to be a woman for a day — for letting his wife do his duties, thus reversing the patriarchal order.[63] He has therefore made only one severe mistake: he has endangered and lost his masculinity, making him weak like a woman. With his penis gone, he even looks like a woman.[64] The wife shows no mercy with her husband when she realizes that he is no longer a true man:

> Er hatt ime unser füllyn im stall all sein hausgeschirr unden am bauch gar unnd gantz abbeissen lassen. Darumb mag ich sein kein gnad mehr haben; das ander wer alles gut zu verzeihen.[65]

The neighbor woman understands her anger and offers her a big, strong "knight" who will be able to satisfy her needs. She knows that he will serve her well — she has had an affair with him herself for six or seven years. Again female sexuality becomes the main topic of the story; Frey puts the blame on the women even though the idea was originally presented by the husband who wanted to learn about the everyday life of his wife. Both women in the text express what concerns them most — a man who can satisfy them sexually — or at least this is what the narrator makes the reader believe that they want. Hence, the story shows the danger not only of letting women rule but also of their immense sexual drive. The victim is the man who seems to be good for nothing. Neither man nor woman appears to mourn the dead child.[66] The father is too occupied with trying to correct his mistakes and worrying about the wife's reaction while she seems to feel nothing for the baby — as long as the husband has his "buppenhahn" there is no need to worry. The baby becomes an exchangeable object; the parents do not seem to have any personal ties to the child, which suppresses the discourse of family life and any feeling of empathy or compassion with the offspring. The man in this story might not signal any sexual desire for his wife or any other woman, but his nakedness and the castration that follows his failures in housekeeping clearly indicate what he is no longer capable of — satisfying his wife or himself.

The danger of female lust when combined with male weakness can also be found outside of marriage. In Schwank number 26, a goldsmith who has not yet found a husband good enough for his twenty-three-year-old sister finds out that she has had sex with an unidentified man of the Church at the time of the council of Constance. As a result of this she has become pregnant (15–16). By calling the pregnancy a "result of the holy council" and claiming it as an outcome of the meeting the woman is able to convince the brother of her innocence. He not only accepts her argument but also allows her continued freedom as long as the council meets — in fear of punishment by the Lord if he stops her. The reader is told that she obeys the wish of the brother to carry on what she has been doing for a long time without his knowledge. The brother thus encourages the prostitution of the sister. His stupidity makes him deserve her behavior. His misinterpretation of the situation and his unwillingness to save her from evil by letting her marry makes him a fool in the eyes of the reader. At the same time, the behavior of the woman is connected with pleasure; she is depicted as enjoying sexual intercourse with several men — monks and priests. The text suggests that she finds true pleasure in sex and thus makes her inability to control herself obvious to the reader. No man forces the young woman to have sex in the text. She is driven by instinct, as is the clergy. Monks and priests represent the hypocrisy of the Catholic Church and threaten the position of fathers, brothers, and husbands — the men who live according secular conventions and the norms of the reformed churches.

The Schwänke apparently show no mercy with men who cannot control themselves, and by pointing out the depravation of monks and priests and the improper behavior of most women, the threatened position of the norm — the married man — is accentuated. He has to focus on control in order not to be a victim of his own desire; male sexuality like female sexuality thus has to be suppressed if not used for procreation. The chapbooks do, however, stress that few men are able to subject themselves to this kind of self control or control over their wives. Frey tells one story of a man whose wife bears him a child every year — even when he is gone for three years to serve in a war.[67] Upon his return his wife welcomes him by explaining her incredible fertility; as soon as she dreams of "dem handtwerck" (the craft, 129) she becomes pregnant. She claims to have talked to the chaplain and the parish priest about the problem and they have told her to let God reign and to enjoy the blessing. The husband not only believes the tale, he accepts it fully and tells everyone who wants to listen to it, thereby making the adultery of his wife public and making a fool of himself. By calling the husband "der gut geck" (the good jester, 129), Frey makes his view of the husband apparent, but also relieves him of responsibility. A person of little understanding cannot be made liable for his deeds. Even though he has fought in a war the man is not a "real" man but rather a fool. He accepts the behavior of his wife and even brags about her fertility. This ignorance in a way makes him deserve the conduct of his wife, but his naivety can also grant him the status of the irresponsible fool.[68] His long absence from the house is not further commented upon, even though it could have been used as an excuse by the wife to find another spouse. She could have claimed that she thought that the husband had died in the war and that she needed a guardian. The author evidently seems less concerned with her actual behavior than with the reaction of the husband. Had he had complete control over his wife, had he been a true man, then nothing would have happened.

The same goes for a "good old shoemaker" who does not sleep in the same room as the wife and hence does not know of her nightly visitor, the young parish priest.[69] The cunning wife is able to make up a story about ghosts haunting the house so that the man does not get out of bed at night; she can consequently be sure that she will be alone with her lover. The husband is fooled but he never finds out about the affair, making punishment in the world of the chapbook less important. What is kept secret, what no one knows of, does not lead to legal consequences. This forgiving attitude among chapbook and other early modern authors might seem paradoxical, but can nevertheless be found in a great number of sixteenth-century texts, probably as a result of the search for stability and social order.

This is made evident in a story about a maid and the apprentice of a shoemaker.[70] They are caught in an intimate act on a Sunday morning when everyone is in church and the cleric assumes his maid to be there as well. The couple is found by their employers, but instead of punishing the young people they make fun of them and the story ends with the maid going to church, the apprentice leaving, and the shoemaker eating with the cleric at his house. Frey concludes: "Es hat auch niemands am leben kein schaden oder nachtheyl bracht; so ist auch ihr kein ripp zerbrochen" (It has brought no hurt or disadvantage to anybody alive; therefore no rib of hers has been broken either, 36). Neither maid nor apprentice suffer more than the shame of being caught while having intercourse, even though fornication could have justified harsh treatment — like the broken ribs mentioned in the last sentence of the story. The priest could be seen as unusually forgiving, but the point Frey wants to make is the secrecy surrounding the occurrence. It was hardly flattering for a man belonging to the clergy to have a fornicating maid in his house. The reputation of Catholic priests was poor in the sixteenth century and the picture given in most chapbooks usually make them the worst fornicators of all — women included. The story furthermore starts with the priest telling the maid that she is the lord of the house ("herr und meister im haus," 34). He has thus accepted that she rules the household, indicating that he has lost control, maybe without being aware of it himself. The image of the priest makes him a poor representative of the male sex. He is a man without the strength to control himself and others. He is unable and seemingly unwilling to bring order into a house that is evidently run by a maid, making it the perfect representation of the world turned upside down. The maid who cannot control her desire for sex and therefore calls for the apprentice at the time of the holy mass further emphasizes this. She shows no regret and goes to church as if nothing had happened. A comparison between the house of the priest with the town whorehouse is close. The text says nothing of a sexual relationship between the priest and his maid, but the reader gets a graphic description of the sexual act between the maid and the apprentice as a "wonderful fight" (35). It seems unlikely that this could have taken place without anyone being punished in any other place than the brothel with the priest as the pimp.[71] The maid is depicted as ruling the house, but this only emphasizes the poor management of the household. She does so because of the weakness of her master who does not live up to male norms. She never speaks for herself; the text only indirectly — through the voice of the narrator or one of the male characters — tells what she says and what she does. What remains at the end of the story is the picture of a man on top of a woman, the apprentice having sex with the maid. The image is thus stereotypical for male-female relationships while the priest represents a man who has lost his manliness.

The loss of dignity found among the clergy returns in stories on age difference. It is a hot topic for the chapbook authors as well as other guardians of good morals, as we saw in Wickram's *Rollwagenbüchlein*. The old man marrying a young woman and the old woman looking for a young man to marry were doomed to fall prey to the laughter of their neighbors and friends. In the chapbooks the loss of male virility required that the man marry an old woman who no longer desires sex, while young women need husbands who can satisfy their lust. One story depicts a rich old man who tries to hide his age in order to win the love of a young and beautiful woman.[72] When courting her he successfully hides his gray hair by always wearing a hat, but once married it is hard for him to fool his wife, who is very disappointed when she comments on his age. Arguments like his ability to provide for wealth, good food, clothing, and servants, do not impress the young woman, who angrily answers that he should know what is missing in the relationship.[73] The discussion is full of sexual allusions where man and woman make clear their positions. The husband compares himself with a gray stallion but the wife moves her hand downwards over her breasts and belly, referring to her body as full of dangerous ditches and holes, thereby calling for a red fox that would be more likely to pass the obstacles her body hides. She wants the wild and cunning fox while the man can only offer her a domesticated animal that properly and smoothly runs down even roads.[74] The dialogue expresses what a woman is presumed to want and thus claims to reveal her true nature while the metaphoric use of animals indicates her inherent sexual lust. The narrator comments at the end of the story, "es solt ein ungleich ziehens geben" (there would be an uneven pulling, 90), if one tried to make horse and fox pull together. The differences would make for a marriage where man and wife would fight and argue and not be able to pull evenly together as is done in a good marriage. The discourse of sexuality here once again interferes with the discourse of marriage, making human sexuality an obstacle for a happy marriage since it is impossible to channel into procreation only.

Another old man has even less success in seducing a young and pretty woman; her quick reply leaves him with no other option than to leave her alone.[75] When first encountering her he approaches her verbally and physically; the author-narrator tells how the "old fool friendly" touches her breasts, belly, and rear while insinuating intercourse. The woman does not hesitate in answering, using the image of a medieval tournament and the armored knight who fights for honor and love. The old man has no chance: if not a noble knight he will not be able to get the woman he wants. The answer leaves him speechless and he goes home with his "tail between his legs" like a dog (55). Unable to be in command of his desire for a woman the man makes a fool of himself and gives the woman the opportunity to take control. The beauty of women, their sexual appeal, and their tricks threaten the image of the perfect man as a person in complete power over himself, brave and God-fearing.[76]

Even when dealing with serious problems like infertility and unwanted childlessness Frey is more interested in telling an entertaining story about the joys of having sex than discussing the consequences (68). When regarded as enemies or as opposite poles on a scale, man and woman cannot unite in marriage to form a harmonious family; their natures do not allow for happy togetherness. The few stories involving children in Frey's work do nonetheless prove that family life was important for the construction of gender identities (if one disregards story number 20, discussed above). The rich woman in Schwank 68 is ready to do anything to become pregnant. Her maid tells an old priest that she and her mistress have had intercourse with many men without any success, and that out of desperation the woman has turned her beliefs to healing baths — to magic. The naive maid is very serious and does not see anything funny in what she states, even though the reader immediately realizes the point: the maid is a fornicator and her mistress most likely an adulteress. Their behavior has been made possible because of the lack of male control. The text does not mention a husband and leaves it up to the reader to imagine the social status of the women, but it is unlikely that the wealthy woman is single. If so she would have looked for a husband before trying to become pregnant. A homosexual relationship must be excluded since the maid has already told the priest that both women have had sex with men. What is a joke here is grim reality in other sixteenth-century texts, as can be seen in, for example, Wickram's *Goldtfaden*. The woman is willing to go through great trouble — even the danger of having sex with strangers — to become pregnant while still of fertile age.

Another story in *Gartengesellschaft* (number 37) shows the need of family ties from a male perspective. A man loses his children in an epidemic and shortly thereafter his wife, who mourns the children so deeply that she dies of her sorrows. Husband and wife are said to have lived "früntlich, fridlich und wol mit einander" (friendly, peaceful, and well together, 52) and the tone is serious from the first to the last line. The story ends with the man overcome by grief saying that the devil takes what one likes most (53). He has lost his family and is left alone. Despite the difference in phrasing, the two stories emphasize the importance of children and thus the importance of parenthood and the bonding between husband and wife. In the first story female sexuality overshadows the real problem, in the second the plot is focused on the man and his grief but both stories stress the need for family ties and kinship.

The reduction of the family to man and woman in most of Frey's Schwänke can be seen as a result of their emphasis on sexuality. Children are the outcome of sexual intercourse, not a part of it.[77] The discourse of marriage is hence so closely intertwined with the discourse of sexuality that it is often undermined by the latter. Human sexuality, especially but not exclusively female, threatens the concept of the good marriage, since human instinct is such a strong force that it causes men and women to break the ties of marriage and commit adultery. Marriage as a way for ordinary people to escape sinful living was nothing new to the sixteenth-century reader, but in the tides of the Reformation marriage becomes the only way for the common man and woman to live a God-fearing life and find grace before God.[78] The emphasis on marriage reduces the accepted options available to everyone looking for someone to share his or her life with and puts greater pressure on men and women to live according to secular and religious norms. The Schwank shows all negative aspects of marriage, turns matrimony into a straitjacket, and projects human weakness onto it. Marriage comprehended as a constraint leaves little room for a positive exchange of feelings and affection, or mutual understanding. Its perceived necessity for social and legal order in early modern texts makes it essential but also difficult.

Story number 64 (79–80) is the only text in *Gartengesellschaft* in which a man not only makes two Beguines[79] pregnant but in the end also marries one of them while finding a husband for the other. He thus makes sure that both women can live honorable lives and that his children are brought up well. The man who has taken advantage of the gullibility of two young women and forced himself onto them is also the one to save them from disgrace. By no means, however, does he do this voluntarily. The woman in charge of the Beguinage understands the innocence of the young women and talks to the young man's mother, who then confronts him. He tries to *play* stupid but does not get away with it. As opposed to the lovesick young man in story number 1, his foolishness is only apparent, and he must take responsibility for his immoral behavior. The father takes no part in this; it is a matter between the master Beguine, the mother, and the sinning son. The son keeps arguing with the mother, but in the end he reluctantly accepts his responsibility and marries one of the Beguines. The deviation from the common pattern of sexually obsessed women of the Church only seems possible because of the intercourse following the wedding. If this story is regarded as Protestant propaganda the man has actually saved the "sisters" from living in sin — behind the walls of the beguinage. His way of acting is therefore forgiven and since the Beguines are transformed into good housewives and mothers it is not possible to emphasize their sexual lust. The narrator instead focuses on their naivety, and the discourse of sexuality can move into the sphere of marriage and family life — the two weddings, childbirth, and the upbringing of the children.

The sinful act of sexual intercourse, to indulge in one's desires without the intention of procreation, still dominates the encounter between man and woman in Frey's texts. The threat to the well-ordered marriage is presented to the reader in the image of the parish priest, the monk, the soldier astray, or the wandering student, men who were not married or who were far away from their wives. The married woman rarely shows moral scruples when getting involved with these men, sometimes foreigners, sometimes friends of the husband. In the world of the Schwank there always seems to be empty rooms with thick walls for the lovers to hide in; the husbands are fooled — or fool themselves — since they do not see or hear anything until it is too late. The women in most of Frey's stories — young and old, married, unmarried, and widowed — are constantly searching for a man with whom they can dance "den Dannheuser" (91), and the most important characteristic of a man seems to be his "werckzeug" (100). The woman is reduced to the status of a sex machine with no other needs or desires than sexual intercourse. This combined with the lack of understanding of the society they are nevertheless part of makes them too caught up with their sexual liaisons to worry about their good reputation.

This is the state of affairs depicted by Frey in story number 95, in which a rich widow tries to defend her lover who is accused of murder (112–13). The woman is at first described as an honorable and God-fearing member of the community, but the irony is clearly expressed by the author-narrator. She soon makes public what no one has known — a long-lasting relationship with a clerk. The woman claims that the man has hardly slept a night outside her house in the past several years and that he has thus not had a chance to kill anyone. Her statement saves the man but makes her an "official whore" (111) when she is willing to claim his innocence under oath. Frey marvels over her "female stupidity" ("unsinnigkeit der frawen," 113); she would not have had to defend the man had he been innocent. He should have spoken for himself and her honor could have been saved. But what if her statement was correct? Then the affair would have become public as soon as the clerk made his statement. Frey seems to dislike the involvement of women in legal cases, questioning their reliability and ability to talk for themselves and others. An honorable man speaks up, and Frey's comment indicates that this kind of man would also try to save the honor of the woman he is involved with. The men are far from morally perfect, there are obviously enough men who are interested in having an affair, but the honor of the family and the social order is threatened only when the woman is sexually active outside of marriage.[80] Hence the importance of strong husbands who are capable of satisfying their wives themselves. If not, the wives will most likely look for a lover. Wickram mentions this danger, but Frey describes it vividly. As opposed to Wickram, Frey shows no fear of describing naked bodies or sexual intercourse. The somewhat surprising conclusion to be drawn from the discussion of Frey's Schwänke is that gender roles need to be carefully watched, not so much because of the evil inherent in woman but because of the weakness inherent in man, his tendency to act in opposition to the role ascribed to him "by nature," convention, and the Bible.

Frey is less interested in making relationships between men and women work than portraying stereotypical behavior at its worst. This makes him more conservative than Wickram but also more passive. He gives no solutions, no positive examples of good relationships, nothing more than an image of man and woman to fear. The texts express a desire to understand and to know the other sex from a male perspective. With few exceptions male sexuality is seen in opposition to female sexuality, while woman is opposed to man and is a part of the Schwänke only as his sexual (or spousal) counterpart. The effect is that the discourse of sexuality dominates in Frey's texts and is closely intertwined with the discourse of marriage, while at the same time undermining it by claiming that a happy marriage is a chimera.

With few exceptions Frey's stories represent an almost static view of what is typically male and female, of what is good and bad behavior. There seems to be little or no hope for a change. Women are not allowed the right to speak and act as respectable members of an imagined society as they are in Wickram's work. Did the audience accept discrepancies like this or should we rather understand the evil, stupid, or naive characters of Frey's texts as projections of fear that are meant to warn the reader, while Wickram's text is working from the perspective of the good example? There is no reason to believe that everyone regarded the figures of the chapbooks as living people of flesh and blood, but the repeated negative portrayals of male-female relationships must have had an impact on how men and women perceived themselves and others. The carnevalesque side of the Schwänke as an outlet for repressed fear and desires should not be neglected, but Mikhail Bakhtin's theories have been discussed and criticized thoroughly elsewhere and seem of less importance for the study of the construction of man and woman in these texts. Still, it would be wrong to deny that Frey in *Gartengesellschaft* expresses a great joy in narrating and an interest in human relationships.

It is striking that the women in Frey's texts — unlike the male protagonists — usually are characterized by their sexual or gendered status.

They are presented to the reader as (false) virgins, wives, or widows[81] and less often named by their profession — they are mostly maids[82] — or social standing. They are more likely to be defined by the profession of the husband or their father than by their own. They are daughters and wives of burghers and peasants, they are widowed and thus in need of a new man. This makes the position of women in the text extremely vulnerable and at the same time dangerous. The women appear as objects possessed by men — the subjects — but they still speak, nag, cuss, scream, and argue. They rarely take no for an answer and thus the man is not always able to control the woman he is in charge of in a way appropriate for a "real" man.

The men, on the other hand, are typically known by the profession they practice — they are introduced as peasants, monks, priests, soldiers, and so on. They might be weak, evil, or stupid but they are identified as independent subjects despite their stereotypical appearance. They might be obsessed with their own sexuality but they are for the most part more than simply sexed appendages of someone else. They have a life that does not necessarily have to be related to their sex, while the female characters are strapped in their roles as gendered stereotypes with no other function than tempting, trying, and aggravating the man and bearing children.

But is the construction of gender really fixed and without exception? If it were so, there would be no fear of reversal, anarchy, or female dominance. It seems to me that Frey's texts provide glimpses of a gendered discourse that is not as simple as it appears at first sight. About half of all stories told in *Gartengesellschaft* focus exclusively on men. They cover many aspects of human interaction, but women are absent in these texts. It is a man's world where men can make fools of themselves without jeopardizing their virility or fearing the loss of a patriarchal hierarchy. At the same time the men in these stories represent general human characteristics. These Schwänke cover topics such as gluttony, greed, foolishness, stupidity, violence, and blasphemy. The protagonists are in no way positive examples of the male sex but rather metaphors of human weakness. Their sex is not at stake but rather their position in society, the respect they enjoy among other people (men), and their lives as Christians. Soldiers, peasants, noblemen, monks, and priests — unpopular professions in the early modern towns — are the target of criticism as "bad men," but the man as such is never threatened in his position as man. This does not happen until Frey enters the discourse of marriage, family life, or sexuality.

The Battle of the Sexes

Two Chapbooks by Martin Montanus

Freündtlicher und lieber leser,
Deßgleichen auch du zuhorer,
Der du lust tragest zu kurtzweil,
Darneben frewd begerest vil,
Es sey in zechen eim und andern
Oder ob du über feld wilt wandern,
Kauff diß buchlin, zulesen lustig,
Ist darzu den jungen sehr nutzlich;
Dann vil historien drinn seind bschriben,
Welche dir ohn zweyffel werden lieben . . . .[83]

All die, so kurtzweil wollen haben,
Es seyen frawen oder knaben,
Inn gartten oder auff dem veldt
Oder auch inn krieges gezelt,
Die kauffen diss buchlin, welches schon
Und lustig ist, gantz wolgethon.[84]

Martin Montanus expresses the same interest in entertaining his audience and readership as Wickram and Frey do in their chapbooks. His two best known works, *Der Wegkürzer* (The Road Entertainer) and *Das ander theyl der Garten gesellschaft* (Part Two of the Garden Society), are written in the tradition of *Rollwagenbüchlein* and *Gartengesellschaft*. Montanus refers to both books at the beginning of *Wegkürzer*,[85] in the dedication to Jacob Herbroten, a man Montanus talks of in terms of high honors and dignity.[86] Like his predecessors, Montanus emphasizes the usefulness of his books and also welcomes women as readers,[87] but in *Wegkürzer* he concludes the introduction by mentioning a key topic of the book: "der frawen list" (the cunning of women, 9). The misogynist tone of many of the forty-four stories is thereby already set,[88] but it is possible that Montanus — like Frey — turns to a female audience in order to claim the harmfulness of the stories in front of the authorities and to stress the dictum *prodesse et delectare,* the usefulness of his stories for the reader. This continuously repeated Latin quotation in early modern literature, however, has little credibility in Montanus's works and only appears as a recurring and hackneyed phrase with little validity. Montanus first and foremost wants to entertain and does not shy away from depicting intimate and intimidating situations in explicit sexual language. When "teaching," Montanus delivers cliché-ridden phrases on celibacy and the danger of female rule. Despite the crudeness he nevertheless publishes his works under his own name — his family name, most likely a latinized version of a German name — and does not have to write anonymously. As in the case with Frey's work, censorship does not seem to have been a serious problem; most of Montanus's works were published by the well-known printers Knobloch and Paul Messerschmidt in Strasbourg.[89] In the preface of *Andreützo*, Montanus calls himself "Martin Montanus of Strasbourg," indicating his ties to the city where Wickram and Frey also published their texts.

With the exception of encyclopedic notes nothing has been written on Montanus since the nineteenth century when men like Wilhelm Scherer, Erich Schmidt, Karl Goedeke, and Johannes Bolte in their search for medieval and early modern manuscripts and prints came across his name. Montanus has since then been regarded as a poor follower of Wickram with less talent to work independently and with poor stylistic skills.[90] His texts are nevertheless valuable documents of their time. They give readers of later centuries an idea of what kind of texts were printed and read among the literate laity. Montanus moves within the sphere of the chapbook with few exceptions. His three adaptations of stories from Boccaccio's *Decamerone* — *Cymon und Iphigenia*, *Theobaldus und Ermilina*, and *Guiscardus und Sigismunda*[91] — were each published separately, probably due to their length, but they have much in common with the texts in *Wegkürzer* and *Das ander theyl der Garten gesellschaft* since they all rely heavily on Boccaccio. Three of his dramas — also based on texts by Boccaccio — have not been reprinted in modern times. Bolte did not include them in his volume of Montanus's *Schwankbücher*, probably because they did not fit the genre of the Schwank as well as the novellas by Boccaccio.

Montanus's interest in the female sex is exceptional in comparison to Wickram and Frey. He chooses the stories with the most problematic or sexually explicit relationships in *Decamerone* as well as in other texts that have inspired his narrative.[92] About half of all stories in Montanus's two main works depict adulterous, unreliable, cunning, and shrewish or stupid women, who with few exceptions make the lives of the male characters difficult. The men on the other hand are far from morally flawless, but they act and react differently and have functions in the text that women are not allowed. The novellas and dramas take the same approach; virtuous virgins occasionally appear in the texts but only as models of decorum, not as agents who influence the outcome of the plot. The relatively differentiated image of woman as presented by Wickram is replaced by an increasingly misogynist view, making for stereotypical representations with little room for positive characteristics of "woman." Thus, the most important questions are where "man" positions himself when constructing his image of the woman and what impact this has on the relationship between man and woman in the text.

Through the recurring descriptions of sexual intercourse between men and women — young and old, married and unmarried, rich and poor, nuns, monks, and priests — Montanus defines the nature of man and woman. Human sexuality seems to be a force so strong that very few people are able to stand up against it, making it the central point of reference when defining moral strength. Montanus writes in more than one story that women are primarily made for having sex, thereby not only emphasizing their role in procreation but their prime function as a creature driven by lust rather than reason. Herein lies the main difference between men and women. They all desire sex, but while women are exclusively made for it — which is proved by their ability to give birth — men have several functions and duties that make their life multifaceted. In *Das ander theyl der Garten gesellschaft* a newly wed young woman expresses her dissatisfaction with her rich but evil husband in a conversation with an older woman, who then explains the true nature of woman — and indirectly man:

> Unnd wann ich bedenck unnd mich sihe unnd find, als du wol sihest, unnd nicht finde, der mir ein fewr reiche, drumb gedenck, was pein mir das mag sein! Ein solchs sich bey den mannen nicht begibt; dann sie sein zu mancherley ander sachen beschaffen, darzu mir nit nütz sein, der frawen willen zu thun. Aber die frawen allein beschaffen seind das zuthun (du vernimbst mich wol) und kinder zutragen; darumb sein sie lieb gehalten. Und ob du es nie vernommen hast, so soltu es dabey mercken, das wir den mannen alzeit bereit seind, das begibt sich bey den mannen nicht.[93]

The major problem, so the reader is told, is that the man is disinterested in sex and therefore fails in his role as a husband; he simply is made for doing many things and does not need to focus on sex alone. Virginity, so closely connected with the unmarried woman, loses its meaning as soon as the woman marries. The marriage thus enables the woman to concentrate on what she is made for: procreation understood as sex and pregnancies. It is her duty to satisfy her husband and to bear his children. In Montanus's stories — as in most Schwänke — this results in an obsessive female sexuality that the man often is unable to control. The inability of the husband to fully satisfy his wife hence results in adultery and reverses the positions of the spouses. The woman can threaten the husband that she will take a lover, thereby making the husband obliged to serve his wife sexually. In this specific story the woman, who "would rather have married two or three men than one alone," is forced to live in chastity, which, as Montanus emphasizes, is against her nature (367) and dangerous to the marriage. The woman obviously cannot control her desire when the husband fails in fulfilling his duties. Out of despair she secretly sees the old woman who is known to be almost "holy," and who promises the young woman that she will help her find a secret lover, a man who can satisfy her so that she will not have to suffer from her desires. The old woman is not connected with magic or witchcraft in the narrative, but her position as mediator between the lusty woman and a secret lover makes her "holiness" dubious.[94] By helping a young woman find a lover when the man does not live up to his role as husband or when he is absent, the old woman is the central part of a conspiracy against the man. Having lost her sexual attraction because of age, she is still dangerous because of her experience. By portraying even the most faithful woman as a potential sex machine, Montanus presents women as unable to be in command of their desire and thus expresses strong doubts about giving women the right to a life of their own. They can reach salvation only through the man; they are strictly constrained to marriage.[95] The story thus ends with moralizing comments by the narrator and, so it seems, a woman regretting her adulterous behavior and a man in charge of his wife.

This need for a static social and gender order defined as male superiority over women is typical for Montanus. The result is that a man can be punished for not acting according to the norm, and that the woman is at fault for having caused his dysfunctional behavior. Montanus thus directs his critique exclusively towards women, unlike Frey, who put greater responsibility on the man. The first story in *Wegkürzer* portrays "wie ein junger gesell eines hirten tochter beschlafft" (how a young man has sex with the daughter of a shepherd, 9) after having promised to marry her. At first Montanus points out the wrongdoing of the man but immediately thereafter the immoral behavior among women is emphasized through the quick agreement of the woman to have sex before marriage. The text signals that the man has the right to test the virtue of a woman by asking her to sleep with him before marriage and that the woman has to decline the invitation regardless of promises. If she agrees to his suggestion, she is not worth marrying. The virtue of the man is not endangered, even though the narrator disapproves of the method as a test of female virtue. We are told that the man takes another woman to be his wife, a woman who has been suggested by his parents and who therefore seems trustworthy to him. This adds another problem to the plot since the behavior of the man makes him morally responsible for having broken the promise to the first woman. His sexual activities before marriage are irrelevant; his virginity is never an issue, but his way of approaching the woman under false pretenses is questionable and deserves punishment. Fortuna takes care of the problem: The young man ends up marrying a simple-minded and stupid woman. She turns out to be no better than the first woman in that she cannot keep quiet about her past and immediately tells him about her long-lasting relationship with one of the servants in her parents' house. Her affair with the servant can furthermore be regarded as worse than the behavior of the first woman, since it lasted for a long time and she probably had no intention of marrying the man. The first woman entered the relationship only because she believed the promise of the young man to be serious.

The man ends up paying for having damaged the reputation of the first woman and for having taken her virginity,[96] but the critique of the narrator is primarily aimed at the women. They cannot keep their mouths shut and always make public what should be kept secret. This view has already been seen in the texts by Wickram and Frey. The reputation of a woman can be saved if her sexual activities are kept secret, but her inability to control herself makes her a target of public ridicule. If she does not tell anyone about the loss of her virginity she can be saved from public disgrace, just like the women in Frey's stories. Silence and passivity are the virtues connected with femininity, with the ideal woman — especially with regard to sexuality and intercourse — but instead the women in Montanus's stories talk too much and engage in a sexual power play they cannot be allowed to win. The man in the first story thinks of himself as smart, but by making himself believe that he will be able to test a woman's fidelity by having sex with her and then marrying someone else, he transgresses legal norms and accepted behavior among men. The first woman has sex with him only because she thinks that they will marry — a common case in early modern German courts, especially when the promises were broken and the woman became pregnant.[97] She even talks to her mother, who seems to agree to the arrangement when she understands that a wedding is soon to be arranged. Had the woman felt hesitant, then she would hardly have discussed the relationship with her mother. Not even the most talkative women in the Schwänke want their parents to find out about their extramarital affairs. By marrying another woman the man thus damages the honor of a whole family. His new wife is the daughter of a family friend. She may be from a wealthy family with servants while the other woman is the daughter of a shepherd, but her virginity is long lost and she immediately tells her new husband about her previous affair. Instead of marrying out of love the young man marries a woman he hardly knows. Had he been able to control his desire for the woman he loved, she would still have been a virgin. Had she kept their relationship to herself or required that they marry before having intercourse, she could have saved her honor.

Even though one can find texts that call attention to the importance of marrying out of love, Montanus's stories show little or no interest in a spiritual relationship between man and woman. Gender equals sex, male-female relationships equal intercourse; a dialogue between the sexes is therefore unnecessary.[98] Schwank number 36 in *Das ander theyl der Garten gesellschaft* pictures a couple with serious marriage problems. Without going into details the narrator states that the husband sexually abuses his wife and hurts her so badly that the woman wishes that he were impotent.[99] However, when the husband in an argument claims to have lost his "buppenhan" (penis) the woman threatens to leave him. Does she prefer a life with the abusive husband to a sexually inactive life without him? Montanus seems to think so.[100] Her fear of living in chastity is greater than her fear of violence and abuse within marriage. Female lust thus appears insatiable. The women in Montanus's stories often need more than one man to keep them happy. Many Schwänke, including the longer ones, are reduced to pure action. As soon as the husband is out of the house the lover is in the woman. The women are assumed to enjoy sex more than anything else; any other thoughts or feelings they may have are suppressed and for the most part withheld from the reader. Although the women are not explicitly called witches, they are often given the features of the female witch as described in witch tracts like *Malleus Maleficarum* or *De Démonomanie*.[101] Due to their weak nature they are sexually obsessed, seem to have stronger ties to evil powers than to God, they like to gather in groups without their husbands or guardians, and are a constant threat to men because of their seductive nature.[102] Hence female weakness can be used as a powerful tool to challenge male strength and supremacy — a contradiction, it may seem, but nevertheless a frequent topic in the chapbooks.

In Schwank number 37 (another story adapted from Boccaccio's *Decamerone*) a young woman is mourning the man she had hoped to marry — a cherished clerk in the family trading company — but who was killed by her brothers when they found out about the relationship. The murder is well planned so that no one in the family can be linked to the crime. The honor of the brothers will consequently not be endangered even though they have murdered in cold blood. Secrecy may be used as an accepted way to hide improper or illegal behavior but these men transgress all boundaries. They even deny the sister the right to mourn the dead lover. The horrid story continues. The sister finds the body in the forest and cuts the head off to put it in a flowerpot. She wants to be close to the dead man at all times and therefore needs to be able to carry him — or rather his memory — with her. The woman grows fragrant herbs to hide the skull in the pot, well aware of the reaction of the brothers if they should learn what she is doing. The macabre pot is nonetheless discovered and taken away from her by the brothers; the woman dies from sorrow when unable to be close to her lover. Montanus does not comment on the behavior of the brothers with a single word but ends the story by warning young women about taking a man because of his money. The message transmitted to the reader is that a good woman should be willing to give up her life for the man she loves regardless of his wealth.

It is the awkward end to a story where the woman has all the money she needs and where money has not been an issue until the very last part. Towards the end, the narration switches from third to first person, abruptly involving the narrator, who comments on something that has been irrelevant to the plot so far. The woman is suddenly made responsible for the murder of her lover. Montanus has little in common with his predecessor Wickram, who even in his Schwänke looks for compromising endings. Montanus tricks his readership by leading the attention of the reader away from the tragic love story and instead focusing on female behavior. It always seems to correspond with his view of woman as evil.

A similarly twisted ending can also be found in the following story where a young man is sent away to a neighboring town because of his love for a woman of lower social standing. Upon his return he finds her married but he cannot forget her. One night he secretly enters her house and tries to talk to her after her husband has fallen asleep. She finally lets him lie down next to her; he does not touch her but dies from a broken heart when he realizes that she will never leave her husband. Fortunately the woman has a wise husband who believes his wife when he wakes up with a dead body in their bed and a wife who tries to account for the nightly drama. His wisdom saves the family honor, but when attending the funeral, the woman falls down dead over the man she used to love and who died next to her because she refused his invitations. The woman follows the man into death and Montanus again puts the blame on the woman. On the one hand the young woman is blamed for not having tried to save the young man's life by showing him her love. Having been his lover before marrying another man she had already sinned while assumed a virgin. On the other hand the narrator admires her faithful behavior towards the husband. The mother of the dead man is finally made responsible for the tragedy. She had not been able to resist her desire for her son to marry a rich woman. Had she not wished for a wife from a better family for her son and had she understood his desires, he could still have been alive (102). The single woman — here the widowed mother — proves to be the threat to the social order and nothing else is expected of her from the side of the male protagonists and the narrator. She acts exactly in accordance with the negative expectations of the men. The story thus closes with the narrator warning all women and telling them to watch themselves when falling in love. Even though the young woman in this story is passive and does nothing or little to encourage the relationship — especially not after having married another man — Montanus chooses to direct his warnings towards women instead of men.

Thus, not even the most innocent woman seems capable of resisting evil powers in Montanus's chapbooks. In these two stories in *Wegkürzer* he at first depicts the love between young, unmarried people and then ends up moralizing about female behavior.[103] When considering the fact that both stories involve virtuous and faithful behavior, the misogynist attack is far-fetched. A man's life does, however, seem to be indirectly determined by the women surrounding him and he can do little to change this. Hence her dangerous features in texts that otherwise claim her virtues.

More commonly found are stories depicting lascivious and voluptuous women. The second story in *Wegkürzer* tells of a woman who eats as soon as the man leaves the house, thereby reducing the food supplies and neglecting the household. When caught by the husband she is severely punished: "das sie mehr einem todten dann einem lebendigen menschen gleich sahe" (so that she looked more like a dead person than a person alive, 13). He shows no emotion when seeing the unconscious woman but leaves the house, and the wife soon seeks revenge. The quarrels are finally brought to court and the mayor — demanding peace and order — urges man and woman to be patient and quiet, but soon he reveals a different attitude. He smiles secretly when hearing the woman as if amused by her story (14).[104]

The mayor is able to reach reconciliation between the two at the first visit, but this does not stop the husband who soon wants to avenge himself on the wife. The quarrel escalates in a spiral of violence. The husband injures his wife badly a second time by pushing her down the stairs while dancing at a wedding. Once more she survives and takes her husband to court. Her reaction to the beatings in no way appears out of place in the text, and sixteenth-century courts records prove that it was at least not uncommon that women tried their cases in court in order to escape a violent husband.[105] Montanus's Schwank does, however, give women no hope to win a case. When told about the origin of the squabble the mayor laughs and immediately takes the side of the husband, meaning that the wife deserves the beating. He at first tries to hide his opinion — probably well aware of his position as a judge — but does not question the explanation given by the husband that the wife is so heavy that she fell out of his arms when he was holding her at the top of the stairs. The wife at first reacts strongly but then bows to her husband when she realizes "das sie dem mann nichts mochte abgewinnen, so hette sie auch wenig gunst mehr bey dem richter. Von des wegen alles das thete, so dem mann wol gefiele."[106] Order is reestablished; the woman has accepted her subordinate position, the man does not have to feel threatened in his position as head of the household.[107] He does not have to change his way of being or acting, as opposed to the woman whose life is threatened. He is willing to kill her if she does not obey his orders. There is no talk of the husband being punished after the mayor decides that the woman only has herself to blame. Gluttony is given the status of a deadly sin and the woman almost has to pay for it with her life. The husband makes use of his physical strength as well as his authority as a man in front of the mayor when seeking revenge. The "cunning woman" uses female friends and tricks to avenge herself on the husband before taking the case to higher authorities, but she has no chance of winning the case. A pattern of male and female behavior appears in the narrative: the man uses physical power to prove himself superior while the woman uses psychological tricks when trying to maintain her position, or when attempting to gain power over the man and thus to reverse the sex/gender roles. The difficult task of the husband is to prevent this from happening, and Montanus concludes one of his stories in *Wegkürzer* with the following remark: "Wann man aber die halßstarrigen weiber allsammen schlagen solt, wurden nicht gnug bengel da sein; man must auch etwan stein unnd andere instrumenta brauchen."[108] The notion of woman having seven lives as is presented in the frequently cited story of the woman with seven hides is conveyed to the reader also in Montanus's Schwänke.[109] Not even when beating an evil woman almost dead is it possible for man to tame her.

In yet another story taken from Boccaccio's *Decamerone*, Montanus in *Wegkürzer* goes as far as declaring male friendship much more valuable than the relationship between man and woman. His argument is that women in most cases are replaceable while good friends are not (113). He then goes on to tell the story of the successful and beautiful young

Roman Titi who falls in love with a woman, Sophrona. She is, however, given to his best friend, the Athenian Gisippus. After suffering through weeks of lovesickness, Titi opens his heart to the friend, who is immediately willing to give up his wife for his best friend. He obviously feels that he can find another wife for himself. At the night of the wedding Gisippus gets out of bed, leaves the room, and Titi takes his place. The woman does not notice any change and happily answers positively upon Titi's question if she wants to be his wife. He gives her a ring and the marriage is consummated through intercourse. When the woman finds out about the change in husbands she calls on her relatives. No matter how much she enjoys her nightly meetings with Titi, she and her relatives have been deceived and the "natural" order has been disrupted. She was originally given to Gisippus and he has insulted his friends, who offered him a wife. Which man Sophrona actually prefers is not of any interest to the author-narrator. Titi is able to convince everyone that he not only *is* but also *should* be her husband and he leaves for Rome with Sophrona. Her opinion in this matter is superfluous; like all "wise women" (121) she soon adapts to the situation, does what she is told to do, and loves the man to whom she is given. This act of self-effacement makes a harmonious marriage. The behavior of the woman is made to appear self-imposed in the text; her subordination is expected as soon as an agreement is reached with her relatives. As soon as they feel that their honor is reestablished, they do not seem to mind that the woman is given to another man. She is exchangeable and less important than the friendship between the two men.

This submissiveness before "man" is rare in Montanus's Schwänke. Stories proving the opposite dominate his oeuvre. The tensions between man and woman are so strong that they lead to constant battles. Because of their ability to attract men, women are able to seduce them into committing shameful acts. Hence the force of attraction of the women is stronger than the ability of the men to control themselves. If the woman is made responsible for arousing feelings in the man that he is able to control as long as she is not present, she can be blamed for causing the man to act in a way that harms or hurts her and also be punished for it. The Schwänke do, however, show that obsessive sexual behavior is inherent in certain men as well as in women. Monks and priests are the prime targets for Montanus's critique. Celibacy, voluntary or imposed, seems to evoke baser instincts in men and makes them act like women — that is, in constant need of sex. At the bottom of the sexual hierarchy one finds only one group that is even worse — the counterpart of the clergy, the nuns.

One story in *Decamerone* seems to have made a great impression on Montanus since he tells it twice, once in *Wegkürzer* (number 29) and once in *Das ander theyl der Garten gesellschaft* (number 96). It is the story of a convent where a young and strong gardener takes care of the gardens both literally and metaphorically, having sexual relationships with all of the nuns, sometimes with two at a time. The man in this Schwank goes through great trouble to get into the closed community of the convent — acting as if he were deaf and dumb. All of the nuns immediately get involved with the silent gardener, and the convent can best be compared to a brothel.[110] The silence of the gardener is symptomatic. There is no need for a conversation between the gardener and the nuns. The relationship is exclusively physical — sexual — and that is all that the nuns are interested in. The same goes for the young man as long as he is able to satisfy all the nuns, and he enjoys his position as the only man available to the women. At first the convent appeals to him as a paradisiacal island made for lovemaking, but after a while he changes his mind. His sexual appetite is replaced by exhaustion. He has had enough while the nuns cannot get enough of him. Just like the monks and priests the nuns are a threat to the male-dominated community outside of the convent. Using the nunnery as a brothel may seem appealing to the gardener, but he soon realizes that he cannot pay and leave after getting what he wants from the women. The paradox is that he is paid to work for them.

The nuns here appear as the worst example of human hypocrisy; they are women and hence sexually obsessed by definition, they are nuns and thus whores since the convent equals a brothel. They claim to be God-fearing and hardworking, but spend their days and nights having sex — all with the same man. This topic returns more than once in Montanus's work,[111] leading to the conclusion that the opening of the convents was of great importance for all those who believed them to be dens of promiscuity in the sixteenth-century society. Another problem then occurred: Enough single men must be found to marry the former nuns or they would challenge the social order by not subordinating themselves to male power, familiar or juridical.[112]

This interest in graphic descriptions of intercourse makes the discourse of sexuality stretch into the pornographic, especially when involving clergy.[113] Male and female genitalia are exposed and given a number of different names. The penis lives its own life when a man looks at a beautiful woman, making him unable to be in command of various parts of his body. When a young man watches a widow resting on her bed, "das seltzam thier" (the peculiar animal, *Wegkürzer* 103) keeps coming out of his pants since they only are tied together loosely. The penis acts as if independent of the mind of the young man but he does not seem to dislike it when recognizing the interest he receives from the woman, who notices the "seltzam thier" even before the man is aware of its "activity." The woman marvels over male virility, thinking that the man has two penises, and the man does nothing to correct her. They spend all night having sex and the woman is so fond of her lover that she does not let him go. After several days the man is completely worn out, because "dem jüngling solchs in die lenge so streng zutreyben nicht müglich sein wolt" (such long-lasting hard strain was not possible for the young man, 104) and he leaves the woman behind never to return. She does not seem to suffer from days of intercourse and lives up to the image of the woman as sexually insatiable. He in turn wants to leave for other things, thereby showing that sex is only one of many things that occupy man.

The same focus on the phallus can be found in a story in *Das ander theyl der Garten gesellschaft* where a man secretly lives in a women's convent. When the time comes for a body-search all nuns have to undress for inspection. The situation resembles the inspections of the city brothels in the late fifteenth- and early sixteenth-century Strasbourg, where male superintendents were to guarantee that law and order be upheld.[114] In Montanus's story the inspectors come to count, register, and examine the nuns. The young man consults the nuns who advise him to tie a string around his "entenschnabel" (416), pull it between his legs and tie the other end of the string around his neck. When the midwives and superintendents enter the room with the undressed nuns the man is no longer able to control his penis — watching the "schwartzen fledermeusslin zwischen den schneeweissen beinlin" (black little bats between the snow white little legs, 416) of the nuns is too much for this man. His erected penis is so strong that the string brakes; the man can no longer hide his true sex. The part following the graphic description of the naked women and the excited man makes clear who is to blame for this: "Da sahe man offentlich, was für frumme nünnlin im closter waren" (Then everyone could see, what virtuous little nuns were in the convent, 416). The irony in this sentence cannot be misunderstood. The cheerful tone and the explicit sexual language of the first half of the story are replaced by a long comment by the narrator about the low moral standards among the nuns in the convents. The man in this story is caught while living illegally among women, but his behavior is not questioned further. The narrator chooses to turn away from the protagonist and to instead focus on the behavior of the nuns. Their sheltered lives make it possible for them to live better than the common man, to hide men and illegitimate children, and to ignore the world outside the convent. The convent is depicted as a luxury brothel that provides everything a man wants while also allowing for the sinning nuns to live better than the more virtuous women outside of the nunnery.

Similar living conditions are expected of monks and priests. In one of many stories portraying the Catholic clergy, a priest fools a poor peasant couple into believing that he can make a mare out of the peasant wife.[115] The couple enjoys the thought of selling the mare at the market; husband and wife look forward to a better living and ask the priest to show them the trick. The priest undresses and then has sex with the woman in front of her husband until the husband cannot stand watching them any longer. No details are left out; the naked priest kneels down behind the woman, touches her all over with his hands while saying "Das werde ein schoner ross" (this will be a beautiful horse, 420), and giving examples of the various parts of the body. He finally closes the show by adding the "tail" to the horse after having chosen a place for it that pleases him. The act is completed and the woman does not seem to mind at all. Her snow-white breasts are stiff and hard, and she is angry with her husband who stops the priest. The image of the passive but excited woman, naked and down on her knees, presents one of the most humiliating representations of women in Montanus's work.[116] Sexuality and pornography are here used interchangeably, reducing the discourse of sexuality to a man's play with the female body. By being compared to a horse, the woman is given animalistic features and transformed into a commodity that can be bought, sold, or traded. This is further underlined by the fact that the wife encourages the husband to accept the suggestion made by the priest. Her naivety and stubbornness are used against her; while the priest and the husband both make fools of themselves because of immoral behavior and stupidity respectively, the woman is completely stripped of her clothes and her dignity.

The only time Montanus targets male sexuality for the same severe criticism as female is in Schwänke describing the lives of priests and monks. Their sexual drive is no less than the compulsive lust inherent in all women. Sexuality is here used pejoratively to characterize a whole person. Women and clerics are thus defined only through their sexuality, and this sexuality does not involve the senses. It is a mechanical act intended to satisfy a need. Neither women nor clerics are given a language that would enable them to express feelings. They are driven by sexual instinct and hence are hardly human.[117] The sexual drive controlling monks and priests is further a threat to other men in that it challenges their power over women, over their wives and daughters. The sexually active priest or monk not only disregards his vows but is suddenly a rival to the married man. He is no longer part of a social order that gives the married man the power to rule by nature but rather turns the world upside down — just like most women in the Schwänke.[118] He furthermore threatens the whole family structure by producing illegitimate children.

The discussion above has shown differences in the distribution of power between the sexes that are of importance for the construction of male and female characters in the texts. There is no simple common norm for the various Schwänke by Wickram, Frey, and Montanus; they deviate with regard to the amount of interest that the various authors attribute to male-female relationships and sexuality. This changes, however, when turning to the result of intercourse — pregnancies and children. The discourse of family life is not easy to trace in the chapbooks. Children are rare; despite all descriptions of sexual intercourse there are relatively few pregnancies.[119] Would this have been too much for the censor or the audience? The absence of pregnant women[120] and small children in the chapbooks could be a function of the genre: chapbooks primarily aim to entertain, and not to show the often difficult result of extramarital intercourse. It is nevertheless striking that authors, with very few exceptions, leave out pregnancies and childbirths.[121] It is therefore not surprising that the author who is most daring in his narrative is also the one who mentions small children more often than Frey and Wickram. Children occur in a number of Montanus's stories even if they do not have a prominent position in the text. They sometimes sleep in the room where the sex act takes place, they witness abusive fathers hitting their mothers, they are loved members of the family, or killed by desperate parents. They are simply a natural part of everyday life. The story about the young man working as a gardener in a convent is typical for Montanus; children are mentioned but are not part of the actual plot. Montanus tells us that many little "nünlein" are born,[122] but never says what happens to them after that.

Since marriages are generally unhappy and painful for those involved in Montanus's work there is hardly ever a happy family. The hierarchical pattern of the Schwänke involving husband and wife is extended to husband, wife, and children — with the children at the bottom of the hierarchy and no changes in the distribution of power. However, Montanus does not primarily portray children who do not obey their parents, but rather the problems involving parenthood. A peasant is called home by one of his sons because his wife is giving birth to another baby (274). The peasant, irritated by the message, asks when the wife will quit having babies since they already have enough children. His landlord (a count), not quite understanding the situation of the farmer, immediately emphasizes that it is a blessing to have children. Everyday life for the two men is clearly different: The peasant worries about another mouth to feed, the count has no such problems but gives him money when he realizes the hard living conditions of the poor. The story is unusual for Montanus with its happy ending and its way of describing a serious problem. The farmer — worried about supporting his family — tries to make his wife responsible for having too many children, but instead of joking about the sexual drive inherent in woman the count responds in a manner more often found in the works by Wickram.

One of very few times a marriage is mentioned in a positive way in Montanus's work is in a story depicting a husband who mourns his dead wife to the point where he leaves his home with a small son to live in solitude in the mountains. Without the wife he finds no pleasure in life. The son grows up isolated from other people, not unlike Wolfram von Eschenbach's Parzival, and his first encounter with life in the city opens up his eyes not only to a different lifestyle but also to the beauty of women. The story ends in moralizing comments about the danger of "civilization," but it is interesting with its highly unusual concept of a father living alone with his son after having had a good relationship to his wife. Maybe one should regard the fact that she is dead as symptomatic. The man can live with his memories without having to encounter the wife in everyday life. Considering that living women do not seem to offer their men much joy in the Schwänke, a good woman is likely to be a dead woman. Single parents in these texts, however, are usually women, widows who are made responsible for the well-being of their children and therefore closely scrutinized and criticized by the male narrator as long as they live without a male guardian.

Not only women but also children are the target of male violence. In *Wegkürzer* a father kills his two children out of desperation after having received a loan from a nobleman for his vineyard. He has wasted it on gambling, and then fallen sick so that he is unable to grow grapes he needs to support his family (89).[123] One day the man watches the youngest children at home while his wife and son are working in the vineyard. Worried to the point of insanity he at first thinks of committing suicide. He finds an axe and walks about the house looking for a place to hammer a nail into the wall so that he can attach a string and hang himself. The daughter — too young to understand what the father is thinking — then asks him to cut her a slice of bread and gives him a knife. As soon as the father feels the knife in his hand "stach er dem tochterlin die gurgel ab" (he cut his little daughter's throat, 89) and he then goes to do the same thing with the boy. Looking at the baby who laughs in his cradle when he sees the father, the man is at first unable to kill the child, but he soon returns and stabs the baby in its back several times so that it dies of the wounds. The father — probably in a state of shock — sits down at his front door watching people pass and telling them what he has done. At first no one believes him, but after checking the house some people keep him prisoner in his own home until the wife and son return from their work. The father then calls for his oldest son, telling him to be hardworking and God-fearing so that the devil cannot tempt him as he did with the father. The man here repeats what the reader was told at the beginning of the story — he committed his crimes while possessed by the devil. The reader is not told how the wife and oldest son react but that everyone should be able to figure out for himself if the mother was unhappy or not after having lost her beloved children.

Absolutely no blame is put on the woman who worked hard when her husband was ill, and who returns first to find two of her children murdered and then to see her husband sentenced to death. The man is clearly the only offender. The devil is said to have seduced him, probably at the time when his gambling addiction became uncontrollable. Only once does the man stop to think — when he sees his son smiling in the cradle. For a short moment his love for the child makes him aware of what he is doing, but then he falls back into the trance he seems to be caught in. Physical illness turns into mental illness, but is explained as the work of the devil. The woman is left alone with one child and nothing but debts and some vines. The man's desperation shows that he is aware of his position as head of the family. He reacts by trying to destroy it, to get rid of the ones he should support and take care of. Not until he has killed two of his children does he slowly wake up to understand what he is doing. By talking to the oldest son he passes on his authority to the boy. The message is apparent — the oldest son is supposed to take the place of the father so that order can be upheld. The readers are not told his age and the widow might be the one in actual charge of the broken family for years to come, but the son will guarantee that social order is not further disrupted. The man does not talk to the woman; her position obviously does not change even though her everyday life changes drastically.

A similar but less violent story is also found in *Wegkürzer*. Again the devil plays his evil games with a man, but this time he comes to him in person — "in gstalt eines menschen" (86) — and promises to give the man all the money he wants as long as he agrees to kill his wife and children. Greed makes him promise what the devil asks for in order to give him the money, but he has no intention of killing anyone, "villeicht auß gottes schickung oder sonderlichen affect, so er zu weyb und kinden gehabt" (perhaps thanks to the will of God or to a special affection, that he had for his wife and children, 86). Even after a second visit by the devil the man is unable to carry out what the devil demands. His love for his wife and children is stronger than his fear of the devil, but at the third visit the devil is tired of waiting. The man wants to pay back what he has received but the devil strikes the man with his tail, "darvon der mann als bald besessen ward" (by which the man was soon possessed, 87), abolishing his power of speech. The reader then is told that the man was saved by turning to God and that he no longer wished for money. By this point the family has lost its importance to the narration. Instead of describing the reaction among family members, Montanus chooses to moralize against greed and money, and the end of the story is somewhat surprising. He takes the side of the poor and expresses his understanding for people in need of money. No matter how hard they work, they can never make enough to meet their basic needs. Montanus therefore pleads for generosity among the rich and that they treat the poor well. He thus incorporates economic matters into the discourse of family life, moves away from the conventional, and becomes more reflective in his narration. Instead of focusing on stereotypical images of male-female relationships he moves on to the consequences of a certain kind of living in a way highly unusual for him.

Poverty, however, is no excuse for murder. The narrator does not show any mercy with a lazy man who accepts the help of some Jewish men in killing the unborn child of his pregnant wife. It is at first not explicitly stated, but the reason for his cruelty is made obvious to the reader — pure laziness. Tired of having to support a large family he simply decides to take the life of the unborn baby. The plan is simple. He makes his wife collect firewood in the forest without knowing of the dangers awaiting her there. She is attacked by the hired killers and tied to a tree, but she screams so loud that she gets the attention of a nobleman, even though the men quickly put cloth in her mouth to silence her. The nobleman arrives at the place just at the moment when the men are about to cut the woman open to take the baby. They quickly run off into the forest and the woman can be saved. The husband is nowhere to be found; he has fled in hopes of saving his own life. The image of the pregnant woman tied to a tree with no way to escape is gruesome. Although she is completely defenseless and very close to giving birth, her husband is willing to risk the life of his wife so that he will not have to feed another person. It is not quite clear if he intends to kill his wife too, but it is not likely that she will survive the assault. The decision to kill the unborn child nevertheless implies that the man still needs his wife to take care of the other children.

The narrator concludes that the man easily could have earned enough to feed his family, but that he is too lazy, he has a "schelmenbein im rucken" (387). He tries to get out of his responsibilities by committing the worst crime possible: killing his own child.[124] He is neither possessed by the devil nor mentally ill; there are no extenuating circumstances that could explain his behavior. He lives up to his duties as a father and a husband just as little as the adulterous or cunning women in Montanus's stories do, but there is one important difference — his personality is characterized by his laziness, not by biologically determined factors. Thus, he could have changed his way of being by his own choice, something impossible for most women in Montanus's work, who are slaves to their sexuality.

The stories discussed above express a concern with the head of the household, the father, when for some reason — it may be because of the devil or other powers — he becomes unbalanced. Montanus does not specifically discuss the position of husband, wife, and children, but the stories show the dangers of a system where only the man is made responsible for the family, with regard both to ethics and morals and to the income and physical well-being of the family members. As head of the household he has to be a good role model for his wife and children, but he also needs to make sure that they have food, clothes, and a place to live. Wife and children may be working too, but this is of no importance for the family structure. If the father/husband loses his mind, he opens up the possibility of a world turned upside down, of the reversal of social roles, and of his own downfall. The stories in Montanus's chapbooks show the vulnerability of the early modern family living on the margins. When the discourse of sexuality is suppressed for practical everyday matters as expressed in the discourse of family life, the readers are given an opportunity to recognize themselves in the images transmitted to them through the narrative to a greater extent than is the case with the salacious topic of deviant or illegal sexual practices.

Within the discourse of family life, the men seem to violate the social norms more often than the women, but there are exceptions. In one story in *Das ander theyl der Garten gesellschaft* a stepmother for reasons unknown to the reader hates her youngest stepchild and hatches a plot with the older sister.[125] The fairytale story takes the reader through schemes and evil plans that all aim at getting rid of or killing the youngest girl, yet without success. The father is not mentioned until the very last part of the story after the reader has been told that he remarries after the death of his first wife. He has no other function in the text than being the father of the children and bringing a new wife into the house. At the end of the story when the plans of the stepmother and the older daughter have been revealed, the father decides to allow the younger daughter to serve a wealthy man whose son's illness she had helped to cure. Again a family has been split up, first because of the death of a mother, then because of the evil stepmother. The stepmother is clearly at fault, even though the man is indirectly made responsible — he could have found a better mother for his children. The difference between the stepmother and her husband is that she is evil by definition while the man is simply ignorant. The male characters in Montanus's work normally commit crimes because they want something in exchange, while the woman in this story simply dislikes the stepdaughter. Her evil nature is stressed by her inexplicable hatred of the stepchild. As will be seen in the longer works of Wickram and Fischart, this is exceptional — women are for the most part portrayed as loving children because of their ability to become pregnant and give birth. There is no mention of poverty or anything else that could have caused the woman in this story to dislike her stepdaughter. It is not possible to explain her behavior because of their relationship — the child is not of her own flesh and blood — since she likes the older stepdaughter. The fairytale setting does, however, make for a different kind of story than most of the other texts in the chapbooks, whose plots, though often highly unlikely, always leave out supernatural elements. This story falls outside the standard Schwank setting as presented above.

It is well known that mothers are capable of killing or forced to kill their newborns for reasons such as rape, poverty, or fathers who refuse to take responsibility for their children or the woman they have had sex with, but Montanus avoids this topic.[126] Within the discourses of sexuality and marriage women prove themselves unreliable, cunning, and even evil,[127] but when moving to the discourse of family life the woman often seems to lose her sexual attraction in order to be, above all, a mother. The relationship to her husband, the father, is indirect and mediated through the children. This is completely different in the case of young women after they have reached puberty but before they marry. Their sexual attraction is at its peak and their desire is hard to please. One young girl complains to her mother about the man she recently married, stating that he cannot satisfy her sexually. She claims: "Du hast mir ein mann geben, der zu den wercken, darumb die ehe auffgesetzt ist, wenig oder auch gar nichts werdt ist; dann er hatt keinen."[128] The narrator asserts that he is unable to tell if the man or the woman is at fault, but the mother understands the seriousness of the situation and promises to help her daughter and ask her friends for advice. She says:

> Die [the friends, EWN] werden uns behilflich sein unnd verhelffen, damit du von dem lappen kummest und an ein ort gethon werdest, da du auch freud hast und deine junge tag nicht also vergebenlich verzerest.[129]

The mother-daughter relationship is close, but here it is hardly used to show the close family ties. It is used, rather, to prove that all women are the same, regardless of age. The mother invites her friends — male and female — to the daughter's house, and when the husband comes home he sees a group of worried people. When told about the problem he laughs and shows his "buppenhahn" to everyone. The women, impressed by his "haussrath," laugh and tell him that they are very happy with what they have seen — his penis is not missing, the marriage not endangered, and his masculinity not threatened. The reaction of the women show that they all desire the same thing, a man with a big "buppenhahn" who can satisfy their needs. There is little or no room for differences in character among those women, since their basic need is the same — a man.

The story is clearly written to entertain its readers, to give them something to laugh at, but it is more complex than one might think. It not only depicts the joys of an active sex life but also the seriousness of procreation. The female protagonist may be sexually obsessed like many other women in the Schwänke, but for the young couple it is not only a matter of satisfying sexual needs but also of having offspring. This could explain the interest among the neighbors and friends in helping the young woman; they not only want to see the husband, they want to make sure that he is able to fulfill his duties as a husband and father — as the head of the household. The distribution of power between men and women in Montanus's Schwänke is thus central for the roles they take. Gender roles are established in and by discourse, through the position "man" takes within marriage and the family, but also in the sex act. "Woman" is given her position by the man — the male author, the male narrator, and on the fictive level by the male protagonists. While convinced of the unreliability of women, the narrator is also aware of the weak sides of his own sex with regard to women — yet without questioning conventional stereotypes of male superiority over women. The (heterosexual) man therefore has to watch what he does and says at all times, but unless he belongs to the clergy he does not have to really fear his position at the top of the gender hierarchy.

Notes

[1] Johannes Pauli, *Schimpf und Ernst,* ed. Johannes Bolte (Berlin: H. Stubenrauch, 1924).

[2] Elfriede Moser-Rath, *"Lustige Gesellschaft." Schwank und Witz des 17. und 18. Jahrhunderts in kultur- und sozialgeschichtlichem Kontext* (Stuttgart: J. B. Metzler, 1984). See especially 116–17 and 251. On the origins of the "Schwank," see Erich Strassner, *Schwank,* 2nd ed. (Stuttgart: Metzler, 1978) and Wilfred Deufert, *Narr, Moral und Gesellschaft: Grundtendenzen im Prosawerk des 16. Jahrhunderts* (Frankfurt am Main: Peter Lang, 1975), 5–21.

[3] This was probably the case with a text such as Schwank 55 in Wickram's *Rollwagenbüchlein.* See further discussion below.

[4] Peter C. M. Dieckow, "Um Jetzt der 'Katzenborischen Art Rollwagenbücher' zu Gedenken — Zur Erforschung deutschsprachiger Prosaerzählsammlungen aus der zweiten Hälfte des 16. Jahrhunderts," *Euphorion* 90, no. 1 (1996): 85. Dieckow notes, however, that also this term causes certain problems, for instance when pieces of verse poetry are incorporated into the prose.

[5] During the second half of the sixteenth century Wickram's and Frey's texts were published together with Montanus's *Wegkürtzer* but I will only discuss the first editions here.

[6] For comments upon the selection of texts in these collections and on generalizations, see, for instance, Moser-Rath, *"Lustige Gesellschaft,"* 280–82. It is well known that *Decamerone* was very important for the depiction of lovers and marital problems among early modern authors, and it does not need to be further discussed here. The loathing of women and adultery, and of monks and nuns obsessed with their sexuality, have furthermore been frequently recurring themes in both fictional and scientific texts ever since Aristotle. Only the context varies, and there are both deviations from and changes made in the opinions that colored previous centuries. As Peter Dinzelbacher says, "conceptions of marriage, sexuality and love have changed over time": "Mittelalterliche Sexualität — Die Quellen," in *Privatisierung der Triebe? Sexualität in der Frühen Neuzeit,* ed. Daniela Erlach, Markus Reisenleitner and Karl Vocelka (Frankfurt am Main: Peter Lang, 1994), 279. See also: "Epochenwandel sei dann weniger in einem bestimmten Moment oder einem einzelnen Text zu konstatieren als vielmehr immer nur in einer 'Differentialanalyse' verschiedener Texte und ihrer Verschiebungen im System der Fragen und Antworten" (The transition between eras is less likely to be determined in a certain moment or in one single text than through a "Differential analysis" of different texts and their displacement in the system of questions and answers), Hans-Jürgen Bachorski, "Diskursfeld Ehe: Schreibweisen und thematische Setzungen," in *Ordnung und Lust: Bilder von Liebe, Ehe und Sexualität in Spätmittelalter und Früher Neuzeit,* ed. Hans-Jürgen Bachorski (Trier: Wissenschaftlicher Verlag, 1991), 520. See also page 525 about the signs indicating that the discourse field of "marriage and family" is reshaped during the early modern era.

On generalizations, see Deufert, *Narr, Moral und Gesellschaft,* 35.

[7] On taboo limits, Ernst Englisch, "Die Ambivalenz in der Beurteilung sexueller Verhaltensweisen im Mittelalter," in *Privatisierung der Triebe? Sexualität in der Frühen Neuzeit,* ed. Daniela Erlach, Markus Reisenleitner, and Karl Vocelka (Frankfurt am Main: Peter Lang, 1994), 175.

[8] Monika Jonas has, however, discussed the importance of including chapbooks in the study of gender in early modern Germany: "Hinter der — vor allem durch vordergründige Komik vermittelten — 'Harmlosigkeit' der Texte verbergen sich potentiell Reaktionen auf außerliterarische Bedingungszusammenhänge. Der Schwank kann als Einfache Form . . . oberflächlich (sprich: trivial) erscheinen; auf einer tieferliegenden Ebene lassen sich zuweilen aber durchaus auch innovative Züge aufspüren" (Behind the 'Harmlessness' of the texts — conveyed through above all ostensible humor — lie potential reactions to conditions outside of literature. The Schwank may appear superficial [read: trivial] as simple or primary Form . . . ; at a deeper level, however, there are sometimes definitely also innovative traits to be found throughout the texts): "Idealisierung und Dämonisierung als Mittel der Repression: Eine Untersuchung zur Weiblichkeitsdarstellung im spätmittelalterlichen Schwank," in *Der Widerspänstigen Zähmung: Studien zur bezwungenen Weiblichkeit in der Literatur vom Mittelalter bis zur Gegenwart,* ed. Sylvia Wallinger and Monika Jonas (Innsbruck: Universität Innsbruck, 1986), 68. See also Joy Wiltenburg, *Disorderly Women and Female Power in the Street Literature of Early Modern England and Germany* (Charlottesville, VA: UP of Virginia, 1992) on gender in street literature, and Moser-Rath, *"Lustige Gesellschaft,"* 282. On sexual pessimism, see Englisch, "Ambivalenz in der Beurteilung," 168.

[9] Elfriede Moser-Rath, among others, has pointed out that chapbooks preserve traditional and conservative viewpoints: "Jegliche Form des Aufbegehrens gegen bestehende Regeln ist personalisiert und als Einzelfall behandelt; kollektiver Protest kommt nicht zum Ausdruck" (Every form of protest against remaining rules is personalized and treated as an isolated case; collective protest is not expressed, Moser-Rath, *"Lustige Gesellschaft,"* 274).

[10] The definition of mass literature for the early modern era has been a topic of discussion to scholars in the field. The fact that the printed word spread faster and faster and to more and more people during the first half of the sixteenth century has not, however, been questioned. Mass production became possible, and the channels of distribution were expanded and improved, although it would take a long time before literacy was spread to all levels of society. See the works of Rolf Engelsing, *Der Bürger als Leser. Lesergeschichte in Deutschland 1500–1800* (Stuttgart: Metzler, 1974); Elizabeth L. Eisenstein, *The Printing Press as an Agent of Change: Communications and Cultural Transformations in Early Modern Europe* (Cambridge: Cambridge UP, 1985); Elizabeth L. Eisenstein, *The Printing Revolution in Early Modern Europe* (Cambridge: Cambridge UP, 1993).

[11] Keith Moxey, *Peasants, Warriors, and Wives: Popular Imagery in the Reformation* (Chicago: U of Chicago P, 1989), 4.

[12] Moxey, *Peasants, Warriors, and Wives,* 6.

[13] Moxey, *Peasants, Warriors, and Wives,* 7.

¹⁴ The number of scholarly publications on "popular culture" is immense, but Peter Burke's book on popular culture in early modern Europe and the work of Bob Scribner on the German empire are important starting points for further research within this field: Peter Burke, *Popular Culture in Early Modern Europe* (Aldershot: Wildwood House Ltd, [1978] 1988); Robert W. Scribner, *For the Sake of Simple Folk: Popular Propaganda for the German Reformation* (Cambridge: Cambridge UP, 1981); Robert W. Scribner, *Popular Culture and Popular Movements in Reformation Germany* (London: Hambledon, 1987).

¹⁵ Moxey, *Peasants, Warriors, and Wives*, 9. See also Dinzelbacher, "Mittelalterliche Sexualität," 48; and Moser-Rath, *"Lustige Gesellschaft,"* 279. I would here like to emphasize the importance of the reader as an active and constantly changing part of the reading process and hence of the analysis.

¹⁶ See Moxey's discussion of Althusser in *Peasants, Warriors, and Wives*, 8. Moxey here refers to Louis Althusser and his definition of ideology, where "ideology is to be equated with systems of social signification," which creates a definition of ideology as cultural semiotics.

¹⁷ "Vermittler von Werten und Meinungen, in diesem Fall der massiven Bestätigung der Herrschaftsansprüche des Mannes" (mediator of values and opinions, in this case the confirmation of the male claim to power and despotism, Moser-Rath, *"Lustige Gesellschaft,"* 117). Although I find that in her study Moser-Rath seems to overrate woman's opportunities for influencing her situation in the early modern society, she has conducted a very thorough examination of the theme of marriage and family life in the sixteenth- and seventeenth-century texts that can be defined as "Schwänke." See for instance her comment on "Weibspott," or the insulting of women (101–5). Hans-Jürgen Bachorski discusses the thematic field of "marriage and family" and its importance to early modern society in "Diskursfeld Ehe." Bachorski underlines the ever changing nature of terms like love, marriage, and family, and warns about interpretations where these terms are seen as constants. This cannot be sufficiently emphasized. None of the terms are constant givens.

¹⁸ Moxey, *Peasants, Warriors, and Wives*, 121. See also Deufert, *Narr, Moral und Gesellschaft*, on the danger of generalizing when discussing texts as heterogeneous as chapbook stories. This is in line with Schnell's discussion of the expected readership: the authors tried to bring their work in line with the readers they were turning to, thus changing the focus when switching between men and women; Rüdiger Schnell, "Geschlechterbeziehungen und Textfunktionen. Probleme und Perspektiven eines Forschungsansatzes," in *Geschlechterbeziehungen und Textfunktionen. Studien zu Eheschriften der Frühen Neuzeit*, ed. Rüdiger Schnell (Tübingen: Niemeyer, 1998), 32–39, and Rüdiger Schnell, "Geschlechtergeschichte, Diskursgeschichte und Literaturgeschichte. Eine Studie zu konkurrierenden Männerbildern in Mittelalter und Früher Neuzeit," *Frühmittelalterliche Studien* 32 (1998): 309. Also see Lyndal Roper, "Sexualutopien in der deutschen Revolution," in *Ordnung und Lust: Bilder von Liebe, Ehe und Sexualität in Spätmittelalter und Früher Neuzeit*, ed. Hans-Jürgen Bachorski (Trier: Wissenschaftlicher Verlag, 1991), 327. Ernst Englisch discusses the sexual pessimism that colored the opinions of the Catholic Church, in "Ambivalenz in der Beurteilung," 168. Cf. Moser-Rath, *"Lustige Gesellschaft,"* 86.

[19] See Bärbel Schwitzgebel, *Noch nicht genug der Vorrede. Zur Vorrede volkssprachiger Sammlungen von Exemplen, Fabeln, Sprichwörtern und Schwänken des 16. Jahrhunderts* (Tübingen: Niemeyer, 1996). On how these familiar texts are told in a new fashion see especially chapter 5.2.3. As has already been said, Fischart, Frey, Montanus, and Wickram used well-known stories and plots for their writing and this was most likely not only accepted but also expected among the readers.

[20] The societal status of the clergy and the celibacy imposed on monks and priests had indeed been questioned by many people already before the Reformation, but the split of the Catholic church during the sixteenth century had far-reaching consequences not only in the reformed parts of Europe. People were not only critical towards priests, monks, and nuns who did not live up to their vows, but their position in society in general was questioned. In texts like the Schwänke, whose main purpose was to entertain, the frustration that many people felt towards the long-criticized double standards of the Church could be expressed without anybody coming to direct harm.

[21] Cf. "The content of sexuality is ultimately provided by human relations, human productive activities, and human consciousness. The history of sexuality is therefore the history of a subject whose meaning and contents are in a continual process of change. It is the history of social relations": Robert A. Padgug, "Sexual Matters: On Conceptualizing Sexuality in History," *Radical History Review* 1 (1979): 11; for further readings on sexuality, see the theoretical discussion by Frank X. Eder, "'Sexualunterdrückung' oder 'Sexualisierung?' Zu den theoretischen Ansätzen der 'Sexualitätsgeschichte,'" in *Privatisierung der Triebe? Sexualität in der Frühen Neuzeit*, ed. Daniela Erlach, Markus Reisenleitner and Karl Vocelka (Frankfurt am Main: Peter Lang, 1994), 7–29, and a presentation of the sources to the discussion of human sexuality in the Middle Ages in Dinzelbacher, "Mittelalterliche Sexualität." Even though brief, Dinzelbacher's study gives a very good overview over the discourse of sexuality in the Middle Ages.

[22] A widow at first does not want to remarry since she would then have to give up her independence; she is later punished when she marries a younger man who abuses her (44). One woman is having a relationship with the parish priest, another is eating too much (gluttony), yet other women are naive, "einfältig" or simply annoying, but few if any are described as stupid, sexually obsessed, or otherwise dangerous for their male counterparts.

[23] Georg Wickram, *Sämtliche Werke*, ed. Hans-Gert Roloff, vol. 7, *Das Rollwagenbüchlein* (Berlin: Walter de Gruyter, 1973), 7. The Roloff edition will be used for all quotations from *Rollwagenbüchlein*. The page numbers refer to this edition. In the longer quotes the translation appears in the notes.

[24] Dann diß mein büchlein allein von guter kurtzweil wegen an tag geben / niemants zu underweysung noch leer / auch gar niemandts zu schmach / hon oder spott / . . . (that this little book of mine is only to make the day shorter, not to lecture or teach anyone, and not to offend, scorn or insult anyone [. . .]," 5).

[25] Wickram's first prose novel *Galmy* is written anonymously but scholars have agreed that Wickram is the author of the book. By signing his texts Wickram makes clear that they are his, that they belong to him. This does not mean that Wickram *is* the

narrator or that he invents an author who communicates with his characters but rather that he is not yet able to distance himself from the text and explicitly make use of a narrator to tell the story. The same can be said for Frey and Montanus. See also chapter 2, on Wickram's novels.

[26] "Der Münch kam zu der tochter unnd begriff ir den fuß mit dem dorn / darvon sich die tochter ein wenig übel gehube / aber die Muter meindt / der Münch arbeyt sich also an dem dorn / unnd schreye der dochter zu / 'Leid dich mein liebs kind / so wirt dir geholffen'" (The monk came to the daughter and grabbed the foot with the thorn, which made the daughter scream a little, but the mother thought that the monk was working on the thorn and shouted to the daughter "Let him help you, my child," 41).

[27] "And as the mother came to the daughter, she found that he had done other things to her than what concerned the thorn," 41.

[28] Michel Foucault's definition of power as a creative and productive as well as destructive force forming the discourses of knowledge can be used as a starting point for an analysis of gender roles. See *The History of Sexuality I* (New York: Vintage Books/Random House, 1990), 81–102 for his analyses and definition of power in relation to sexuality. Power to Foucault is polymorphous, multifarious, and multiform; it is polyvalent and consists of force relations produced in and by all social settings. Power in Foucault's terms becomes a moving force characterized by transgression, transformation, and transference; "It is the name that one attributes to a complex strategic situation in a particular society" (93) and it is closely intertwined with resistance(s). This power structure deviates from what Foucault regards as the common Western European concept of power, which can be "formulated in terms of law" (87). Foucault finds its roots in the juridico-discursive conception of power in the Middle Ages with its emphasis on obedience, interdiction, and a strictly hierarchical juridical and political system, and sees a development towards new power systems in the eighteenth and nineteenth centuries (83–88).

[29] He "ließ hinfürbaß seinen eyfer faren / und ward ein rechtgeschafner Hawßman" (from now on let go of his anger, and became a righteous head of the household, 162).

[30] He never mentions female jealousy — this could never affect the family in the same way.

[31] Schwank 87 makes even more evident that jealousy does not lead to anything but trouble. The very short story depicts a wedding where the husband-to-be hits the bride with his fist so that she falls over. The reason for his anger is that she has smiled at the priest when entering the church. All the blame is put on the groom. The bride is described as a pious and honest woman ("die doch ein fromme ehrliche Tochter was," 166), and the young man appears as uncontrolled, violent, and stupid. The punishment is immediate; the guests are sent home and he is forced to spend some time in jail — "das dann auch sein verdienter lohn was" (which was indeed what he deserved, 166). In this story there are no sexual allusions. The discourse of sexuality is reduced to imaginative thinking: what if the woman had done more than just smile? What if the priest had tried to initiate a relationship (just as is the case in so many other Schwänke)?

[32] The old woman and young husband and lover as well as the young wife and her old husband appear as motifs on a number of sixteenth-century paintings, prints, and wood cuts. Difference was regarded as one of the reasons for disagreement within marriage that could result in a "battle of the sexes." See Keith Moxey's study of Nuremberg broadsheets, *Peasants, Warriors, and Wives*, especially chapter 5, and also Joy Wiltenburg's book on "disorderly women," chapters 5, 6, and 7, in *Disorderly Women and Female Power*, and "Family Murders: Gender, Reproduction, and the Discourse of Crime in Early Modern Germany," *Colloquia Germanica* 3–4 (1995): 357–74. Tilmann Walter states that the old man marrying the young woman was regarded as the worst combination, since this disrupted the power structures. The woman had the advantage over the man, since he no longer was able to sexually satisfy her: *Unkeuschheit und Werk der Liebe. Diskurse über Sexualität am Beginn der Neuzeit in Deutschland* (Berlin: De Gruyter, 1998), 222–24. See 263–66, where Walter discusses the problem surrounding sexuality and age and points out that aging couples often are the target of ridicule if they have sex. This must be seen in the light of procreation. A woman who no longer can bear children should not feel desire.

[33] See Miriam Usher Chrisman, "Women and the Reformation in Strasbourg 1490–1530," *Archiv für Reformationsgeschichte: Internationale Zeitschrift zur Erforschung der Reformation und ihrer Weltwirkungen* 63 (1972): 143–67: "The exception to this was the widow who, on the death of her husband, took over the responsibility for the business. Sometimes she would remain until her son achieved his majority, more frequently she married a journeyman in the same trade and the continuity of the business was secured," 143. See also Merry E. Wiesner, "The Religious Dimensions of Guild Notions of Honor in Reformation Germany," in *Ehrkonzepte in der Frühen Neuzeit: Identitäten und Abgrenzungen*, ed. Sibylle Backmann, et al. (Berlin: Akademie Verlag, 1998), 223–33, on women, honor, and the guilds.

[34] See Joy Wiltenburg, *Disorderly Women and Female Power*, 7: "The cultural perception of women's power as disorder, and of their disorderliness as power, reflects male anxieties about the success of patriarchal rule." She proves that this anxiety was commonly expressed in her study of cheap prints, but it is important not to mix the representations of women as expressed in discourse with the lived reality of sixteenth-century women. Many of the cheap prints belong to genres that exaggerate the negative aspects of male and female behavior.

[35] Schwank number 16 (33–34).

[36] "Also was er ir darnach befalch zu kauffen / richt sy fleissig auß / und ward nümmen irr in den nammen" (and what he thereafter told her to do she did correctly and never erred again, 34).

[37] "Was wolt ich mich aber zeihen / das ich ein alten mann nemmen wolt / übernacht so legen wir beidsammen da unnd wißt keins dem andren zu helffen / weren beidsammen kranck und schwach" (what would make me take an old man, In the night we would lie together and do not know what to do with each other, if we were both sick and weak, 83). It is not clear if this should be understood as a sexual allusion as well. The comment that the spouses would not know what to do with each other at night is definitely ambiguous.

[38] "As she now finally gave up her folly, and thus did not annoy the man anymore, he also gave up some of his anger," 84.

[39] See Marga Stede, "Ein grausame unnd erschrockenliche History. Bemerkungen zum Ursprung und zur Erzählweise von Georg Wickrmas Rollwagenbüchlein-Geschichte über einen Mord im Elsass," *Daphnis* 15 (1986): 124–34. Stede gives the background to the story.

[40] "Das Thema Sexualität jedoch — und das verweist bereits auf seine grundsätzliche Problematik — wird in den Sammlungen sehr unterschiedlich behandelt. Vor allem bezüglich der Darstellung sexueller Details sind die Unterschiede signifikant: In einem Falle können sie völlig fehlen, im anderen einen Großteil der Texte maßgeblich bestimmen. Die Grenze, die markiert, wann eine Darstellung als verletzend oder provozierend empfunden wurde, scheint unmittelbar mit der Hervorhebung des 'Details' verbunden zu sein" (The theme of sexuality, however — and this is already a sign of the basic problem connected to it — is treated very differently in the various collections. Above all regarding the description of sexual details are the differences significant: In one case there might not be any, in another color a large part of the text. The limits that decide when a description could be seen as insulting or provoking seems to be closely connected to the attention paid to the "Details"): Kyra Heidemann, "'Grob und teutsch mit nammen beschryben': Überlegungen zum anstössigen in der Schwankliteratur des 16. Jahrhunderts," in *Ordnung und Lust: Bilder von Liebe, Ehe und Sexualität in Spätmittelalter und Früher Neuzeit*, ed. Hans-Jürgen Bachorski (Trier: Wissenschaftlicher Verlag, 1991), 416. Heidemann writes further: "In den 'groben' Texten steht das Detail im Mittelpunkt, es ist keine entbehrliche Zutat zum Erzählten, sondern ein die Handlung wesentlich mitkonstituierendes Element" (In the "crude" texts the detail is at the center of the story. It is not a dispensable addition to the narrative but an element important to the creation of the plot, 417–18).

[41] Schwank number 40 (71–73).

[42] In the text it is said that the soldier might become the owner of the house and the land. Wickram, *Das Rollwagenbüchlein*, 72.

[43] The stories are numbers: 4, 16, 17, 20, 40, 44, 45, 49, 55, 62, 66, 75, 79, 84, 87, 91, and 107. A number of stories were added to *Rollwagenbüchlein* in editions published after Wickram's death. See also Hans-Gert Roloff on the different editions of the text (315–16).

[44] Jakob Frey, *Jakob Freys Gartengesellschaft (1556)*, ed. Johannes Bolte (Tübingen: Literarischer Verein, 1896), 6. The Bolte edition will be used for all quotations from *Gartengesellschaft*. The page numbers refer to this edition.

[45] The fear of the woman controlling the man was great if looking at popular prints and learned texts of the sixteenth century. The image of "the woman on top" was common in literature and art, as was mentioned above. See Natalie Zemon Davis, "Women on Top," in *Feminism and Renaissance Studies*, ed. Lorna Hutson (Oxford: Oxford UP, 1999), 156–85, Moxey, *Peasants, Warriors, and Wives*, chap. 5, and Wiltenburg, *Disorderly Women*, 131–39. Wiltenburg stresses that it may not be forgotten that the majority of cases involving dominance and violence in German literature depict a hierarchic world with the man as evident ruler and the wife as his

submissive companion (137). As for the lived reality, it is evident that the women more often were the victims than the perpetrators and that their legal rights were few. Merry Wiesner in her research has shown that the actual rights of women were shrinking in the sixteenth century, even though it needs to be emphasized that not all women were treated in the same way. According to Wiesner the legal status of a woman was determined by her relationship to a man (maiden, wife, widow) and to her physiological status (virgin, pregnant, nursing mother, mother), which was a direct result of her relationship to the man: *Gender, Church and State in Early Modern Germany* (Harlow: Longman, 1998), 84–93. See esp. 85.

[46] See Werner Röcke, "Liebe und Melancholie. Formen sozialer Kommunikation in der *Historie von Florio und Biancefora* (1587)," in *Variationen der Liebe. Historische Psychologie der Geschlechterbeziehung*, ed. Thomas Kornbichler and Wolfgang Maaz (Tübingen: Diskord, 1995), 129–48. The changing notion of melancholy found in sixteenth- and seventeenth-century learned texts leads to a new belief of this mental state as creative. It cannot, however, yet be found in popular literature of the time. From antiquity until the Renaissance melancholy was regarded as an imbalance of the four humors (black bile, yellow bile, blood, and phlegm) that caused illness.

[47] Frey, *Jakob Freys Gartengesellschaft (1556)*. See the introductory remarks, xxv–xxviii.

[48] Frey, *Jakob Freys Gartengesellschaft (1556)*. See Bolte's remarks, xxvi.

[49] Frey, *Jakob Freys Gartengesellschaft (1556)*, 6.

[50] "Jacob Frey, stattschreiber zu Maurmünster" (JF, town clerk of M, 5–7).

[51] On the readership in early modern Europe, see Rolf Engelsing, *Analphabetentum und Lektüre: Zur Sozialgeschichte des Lesens in Deutschland zwischen feudaler und industrieller Gesellschaft* (Stuttgart: Metzler, 1973), and Engelsing, *Der Bürger als Leser*. See also Elizabeth L. Eisenstein's work on the printing press, *The Printing Press as an Agent of Change: Communications and Cultural Transformations in Early Modern Europe* (Cambridge: Cambridge UP, 1985) and Eisenstein, *The Printing Revolution in Early Modern Europe*, and Tessa Watt's study of the medium of print as modifying traditional culture, *Cheap Print and Popular Piety 1550–1560* (Cambridge: Cambridge UP, 1991). A very good introduction to the early modern book industry is a text that was originally published in 1958, Lucien Febvre and Henri-Jean Martin, *The Coming of the Book: The Impact of Printing 1450–1800* (London: Verso, 1990).

[52] Number 54: "Ein fraw begert, das die orgel zu Straßburg im münster zu ir in ir haus komen solt" (A woman demands that the organ in the cathedral of Strasbourg be moved into her house, 69).

[53] See Alfred Götze, *Frühneuhochdeutsches Glossar* (Berlin: De Gruyter, 1967), 94. "Gaffelstirn" is explained as "vorwitziges Mädchen," "Fratz," a crazy person of female sex.

[54] Number 123: "nam sie ein groß glaß, bruntzt es fol, ließ kalt werden und brachts im" (she took a large glass, pissed it full, let it cool off and brought it to him, 140).

[55] Walter, *Unkeuschheit und Werk der Liebe*, 210. See also 63–64.

[56] "Du bist ein solche miserere hur, du hast mehr ertzknappen, blotzbrüder, kämetfeger und buppaper gehabt, dann die pfaffen zwüschen ostern und pfingsten alleluja

singen" (You are such a miserable whore, you have had more sexual partners than the priests sing alleluia between Easter and Pentecost, 41).

[57] Ralf Georg Bogner has written an interesting book on oral communication and the repression of speech in the early modern society, *Die Bezähmung der Zunge. Literatur und Disziplinierung der Alltagskommunikation in der Frühen Neuzeit* (Tübingen: Niemeyer, 1997); see also Wiltenburg, *Disorderly Women*, 97–98.

[58] "Also was und blib eine eben als gut als die ander" (each was and remained just as good as the other, 41).

[59] On woman's reluctance to subject themselves to and obey man, see Bachorski, "Diskursfeld Ehe," 516.

[60] His clothes have been stolen at an earlier point and he tries to cover himself up with the grass intended for the hungry horse.

[61] The reader does not get to follow the woman who is doing "male" work. Frey does not even mention her experiences while carrying out her husband's duties away from home. It is irrelevant for the plot, but nevertheless interesting, considering that she must be equally inexperienced in performing typically "male" duties.

[62] "Als bald die nachbeurin das erhort, das er seines scharwechters beraubt war, da wurde sie ime auch feindt" (as soon as the neighbor woman heard that he had been robbed of his penis she also became angry, 33).

[63] The household must be seen as one of many parts in the societal structure colored by religion (in both Catholic and Protestant countries). God's power over the human being is reflected in the worldly hierarchy based upon a long chain of dependent links. The married man is supposed to rule his family as God rules human beings. At the same time he is subordinate to other worldly rulers. The family is therefore the smallest entity with a power hierarchy of its own. See for example Lyndal Roper in her study of life in Augsburg: "the distinct offices of master, mistress, children, and servants were structured in a hierarchy of benign authority of age over youth, master over servant, and man over woman. It was a patriarchal ideal which sanctified the existing exclusion of women from independent household-workshop enterprise, and from political power": *The Holy Household: Women and Morals in Reformation Europe* (Oxford: Clarendon, 1989), 252, and see also 266–67; see also Moxey on the two-country theory of Luther and its importance to the hierarchy in society and in the family: "Luther saw in the hierarchical structures of the family a model for the organization of the state" (*Peasants, Warriors, and Wives*, 122).

[64] See Moser-Rath (*"Lustige Gesellschaft,"* 19) on reversed roles. She talks of the "Potenzangst des Mannes," of the fear of man of not being able to fully satisfy the woman at intercourse.

[65] "He has let our foal in the stable completely bite off all his tools down by his belly. Therefore, I will have no more mercy on him; the other things would have been easy to forgive," 33.

[66] On the importance of children, see Eva Labouvie, *Andere Umstände. Eine Kulturgeschichte der Geburt* (Cologne: Böhlau, 1998), especially the chapter entitled "Gewünschte Schwangerschaften," 35–44, and Heide Wunder, *He Is the Sun, She Is the Moon: Women in Early Modern Germany* (Cambridge: Harvard UP, 1998), 12 and

119. The reaction of the wife in the Schwank runs counter to all reactions documented in historical records.

[67] Frey, *Jakob Freys Gartengesellschaft (1556)*. Schwank number 112 (128–29).

[68] The idea of man and woman deserving each other when one part — usually the man — acts against the norm is common in Schwänke. Frey lets a wife talk back to her husband with the argument that they are both imperfect, number 50 (66) and in a later edition (from 1618; see number 131, 151 in Bolte's edition) the text tells of an old knight marrying a woman who is no longer a virgin. Because of his previous lifestyle the moral of the story is that the knight has no right to demand a virgin.

[69] Frey, *Jakob Freys Gartengesellschaft (1556)*. Schwank number 94 (110–11).

[70] Frey, *Jakob Freys Gartengesellschaft (1556)*. Schwank number 21 (34–369).

[71] The poor behavior of the Catholic clergy as described in the Schwänke cannot be discussed in detail in this study. At times they are successful in seducing the wives of their parishioners but at other times the women refuse their invitations, thus adding to the image of the cleric as sexually obsessed and at the bottom of the sex/gender hierarchy. In Schwank 97 a monk tries to impress a group of women by referring to himself as a stallion (114–15) but one of the women quickly answers that he should then get a saddle and let the devil ride, an answer that makes the monk disappear quickly and hide in the monastery. A majority of the stories do, however, portray women who show great interest in having an affair with the clergy, such as numbers 25, 87, 94, and 112. The message seems to be that the relationship woman-monk is unavoidable and therefore not to worry too much about as long as it is kept secret. Even if the husband finds his wife with a priest or a monk he should take advantage of the close relationship to the clergy and make sure that it does not become public. Schwank 87 emphasizes the similarity of all monks by letting the brothers help a lovesick monk who has been caught during the love act. Their way of acting — they arrange a procession with the pants that the monk has left in the house of the woman when he had to leave quickly — not only makes them appear foolish but also makes Catholic traditions seem ridiculous. The story ends with the husband kissing the pants in the belief that he is holding a holy object, thus indicating stronger critique of the Catholic Church and faith than of the adulterous wife. The Catholic man is no man but rather a fool.

[72] Frey, *Jakob Freys Gartengesellschaft (1556)*. Schwank number 75 (89–90).

[73] "'Das solten ir wol gedencken,' sagt die fraw, 'was mir mangelt'" (You should think about what I lack, said the woman, 89).

[74] "Die fraw streich die hand uff ir brust bitz für den bauch hinab und sprach: 'Ja, aber auf der strassen nit. Dann da sind gräben und geforliche löcher, das man eins satten, steiffen zugs wol von nöten ist. Das selbig kan ein roter junger fuchs vil baß dann ein alter grawer schimel ausrichten'" (The woman moved her hand over her breasts and belly and said: 'Yes, but not in the streets. There are dangerous holes there where one needs a strong and stiff tool. Here a red young fox is much more likely to make it than an old gray roan, 90).

[75] Schwank number 40 (54–55).

[76] The type of Schwänke involving the "aller närriste mensch" (the most foolish people, 8) make little difference between men and women. If a person is character-

ized as someone of "groben unnd dollen verständtnus" (serious and crazy understanding, 8) who in his or her way of acting transgresses all social boundaries, the themes of the jokes may change according to the sex/gender of the person, but the image conveyed to the reader is that of the fool, of a social outcast not fitting into any social class, sex/gender-model, or other hierarchy. Uncontrollable and unpredictable, he or she personifies the world turned upside down, as in the first story of the volume where the not so bright adult son of a wealthy widow falls in love with a "beautiful, well-shaped and bright young virgin" (8). The mother is torn between her feelings for her son and the knowledge that he is dangerous for himself and others. She tries to help him, probably hoping for her son to come to his senses — but in vain. The young woman understands what is going on and plays jokes on the poor fool who is incapable of interpreting speech in any other way but quite literally. No blame is put on the mother who does what is expected of her — she tries to find a wife for her son and thus bring order into his life. The woman he loves can trick him without reversing any power structures; the fool is not part of a gendered discourse here. Mental illness seems to function as castration — neither other men nor women nor their positions in society are threatened. The use of the fool does not reverse hierarchical structures, but rather points to their weaknesses.

[77] Schwank number 58 depicts the christening of a baby and how the priest in an annoyed manner claims to know the sex of the baby; since it has a slit it must be a girl. This is the only story involving a child where the narrator alludes to sexual organs: "ich sihe an dem schlitz selber wol, das ein meydtlin ist" (Of course I can tell from the slit that it is a girl, 72).

[78] The literature on marriage was immense in the sixteenth century. Especially the so-called "Ehespiegel" (mirrors of marriage or manuals for marriage) were very popular and the reformers wrote extensively on the topic, as did the humanists. The research in the field is vast and constantly growing. The concern of especially Martin Bucer but also other Strasbourg reformers for marriage has resulted in a number of interesting scholarly works that stress the special position of the city as situated between the Lutheran and Swiss reformation. See H. J. Selderhuis, *Marriage and Divorce in the Thought of Martin Bucer*, trans. John Vriend and Lyle D. Bierma (Kirksville, MO: Thomas Jefferson UP, 1999); Thomas A. Brady, *Ruling Class, Regime, and Reformation at Strasbourg 1520–1555* (Leiden: Brill, 1978); Thomas A. Brady, *Communities, Politics and Reformation in Early Modern Europe* (Leiden: Brill, 1998); Miriam Usher Chrisman, *Strasbourg and the Reform: A Study in the Process of Change* (New Haven: Yale UP, 1967); Miriam Usher Chrisman, *Lay Culture, Learned Culture: Books and Social Change in Strasbourg 1480–1599* (New Haven: Yale UP, 1982).

[79] Beguines was the name for women who joined in associations similar to convents but who never took any vows and who were not subject to the rules of any convent. Devoted to religious and charitable work, the associations were first established in Belgium and the Netherlands in the high Middle Ages and moved from there to Germany and France. After originally having been in favor of the protection of the Catholic Church, the Beguines in the late Middle Ages often were the target of accusations of heresy. These associations of women living without male supervision were an easy target for secular and church authorities in their search for immoral behavior and by the middle of the sixteenth century they were scattered refuges for

poor women. See further, Ernest W. McDonnell, *The Beguines and Beghards in Medieval Culture with Special Emphasis on the Belgian Scene* (New Brunswick, NJ: Rutgers UP, 1954).

[80] This is made clear in the first story where a young man of very poor understanding and conduct tries to win the love of a rich young woman. Cf. Bachorski, "Diskursfeld Ehe," 517.

[81] Just to mention a few: Schwank number 1 speaks of a rich widow, number 6 of a "sister," numbers 20, 37, and 45 of a wife, number 40 of a young woman, number 50 of a wife and a virgin.

[82] See for example numbers 21, 60, 89.

[83] Martin Montanus, *Martin Montanus Schwankbücher (1557–1566)*, ed. Johannes Bolte (Tübingen: Der literarische Verein in Stuttgart, 1899), 5–6. All quotes from or about Montanus's works are taken from this edition.

[84] Montanus, *Schwankbücher*, 255.

[85] "Unnd wiewol diser schöner buchlin hievor vil geschriben sind, als nemblich *Schimpff und ernst, die Gartengesellschafft, der Rollwagen* unnd andere vil kurtzweylige historien mehr, denen diß mein buchlin vil zu gering ist" (And even though many nice texts like this already have been written, like *Schimpf und Ernst, Die Gartengesellschaft, Das Rollwagenbuch* and many more, to which my booklet cannot be compared, 4).

[86] The dedication says: "Dem wolgebornen edlen gestrengen herren, herrn Jacob Herbroten, römischer kayserlicher mayestet rath unnd churfürstlicher pfaltzgrävischer gnaden statthalter zu Laugingen, meinem gnedigen herrn" (To the honourable noble strict gentleman, Mr. Jacob Herbroten, . . ., my gracious lord, 3).

[87] In *Wegkürzer* Montanus claims: "habe ich dises buchlein, wiewol als ein unverstendiger unnd unwürdiger sollicher lieblichen stücklin zuschreyben, inn truck geben lassen, darinn sich die jungen gesellen zuersehen haben, unnd nicht allein die jungen gesellen, sonder auch den mannen unnd allen weybspersonen zu gutem fürgeschriben ist" (I have let this little book be printed — although I may be of no knowledge and unworthy of writing such lovely little pieces — in which the youngsters can recognize themselves, and which is not only meant for the good of the youngsters, but also for that of the men and all female persons, 3). See also *Das ander theyl der Gartengesellschaft*, 255.

[88] Bolte in a footnote points out that the last two Schwänke (numbers 43 and 44) were added to the 1565 edition printed in Frankfurt. He does not comment on the authorship of these stories (Montanus, *Schwankbücher*, 126).

[89] The undated editions of *Wegkürzer* and *Andreützo* were not printed in Strasbourg like Montanus's other works, according to Bolte, who believes these texts to first have been published in Augsburg (Montanus, *Schwankbücher*, xix–xxii).

[90] See also the introduction. Montanus's own texts give no clues to his life besides his ability to read and write. The quality of his writing however, does not indicate a very long education, and he probably did not know much Latin — despite his last name.

[91] Bolte dates these texts to the period between 1558 and 1560 (Montanus, *Schwankbücher*, x).

[92] For a discussion of the sources Montanus has used for his work, see Bolte: Montanus, *Schwankbücher*, xiii–xvi. Bolte has found many other sources for Montanus's texts besides Boccaccio: the Latin *facetiae* by Poggio and Bebel, broadsheets, folk tales, and other texts with a long oral tradition.

[93] "And when I think about it and see and find myself, like you see yourself, and do not find, that he will give me a fire, imagine what pain that would be to me! Something like that never happens to the men; for they are made for various other things than to serve the women. But the women are made for intercourse (I think you understand what I mean) and bearing children; because of this they are cherished. And if you have never felt it, you will know it through the fact that we are always ready for the man, which is not the case with the men," 369. Further comments on female sexuality can be found in stories 7, 58, 62, 84.

[94] She is not explicitly given the features that Sigrid Brauner has referred to in her discussion of the "modern witch," but the old woman has supernatural powers in matters regarding sexuality, a major theme in early modern literature about witchcraft. Sigrid Brauner, *Fearless Wives and Frightened Shrews: The Construction of the Witch in Early Modern Germany*, ed. Robert H. Brown (Amherst: U of Massachusetts P, 1995), 7–13. On young and old women accused of witchcraft, see Gerhild S. Williams, *Defining Dominion: The Discourses of Magic and Witchcraft in Early Modern France and Germany* (Ann Arbor: U of Michigan P, 1995), 79–80.

[95] "While the ends of a wife might be different from that of a witch, their means are surprisingly, indeed, uncannily alike," Allison P. Coudert, "The Myth of the Impovered Status of Protestant Women: The Case of the Witchcraze," in *The Politics of Gender in Early Modern Europe,* ed. Jean R. Brink, Allison P. Coudert, and Maryanne C. Horowitz (Kirksville, MO: Sixteenth-Century Essays & Studies, 1987), 79.

[96] Montanus writes that the man "deß hirten tochter für ihr junckfrawschafft ein abtrag thun solte" (should repay the shepherd's daughter for her virginity, 11).

[97] See Labouvie, *Andere Umstände*, 50–64.

[98] This is vividly described in story number 59 where two men have sex, each with the other man's wife. It can also be found in story 86: A man, his wife, and daughter let two young men who are pretending that they are looking for shelter spend the night in their house. The house is small and everyone sleeps in the same room, husband and wife in one bed, the daughter alone in one bed and the visitors in the third bed. By "accident" (it is dark, no one talks) the two men end up in bed with the wife and the daughter and have sex with them all through the night. In the morning one of them says: "seither ich von dir uffgestanden bin, sechs mal mit ir über feldt geritten bin" (since I left you I have been riding with her over the fields six times, 348–49). The horse or stallion as a metaphor for the virile man is once again used in a Schwank and the bed is the substitute for bucolic fields, making the act appear smooth and pleasant rather than wild and dangerous. The husband/father has slept through the night and has not heard a sound. The cunning women are able to make up a plausible story and an excuse for the shift in sleeping arrangements. Since no one knows of what has happened in the dark the family honor has not been damaged and the head of the family is spared from public disgrace. The story is unusual for Montanus because the discourse of sexuality is here closely intertwined with the discourse of

family life. By doubling the women and letting both mother and daughter have sex with the strangers Montanus doubles the weakness of the husband/father. He is in control of neither his wife nor his daughter. Only complete silence can save him from becoming a public joke. See also Roper, "Sexualutopien," 329.

[99] On violence and abuse, see Wiltenburg, "Family Murders," especially 367.

[100] See Moxey on the usage of violence to reestablish order, *Peasants, Warriors, and Wives*, 114–20. See Wiltenburg on male violence, "Family Murders," 367, also Moser-Rath, *"Lustige Gesellschaft,"* 116–17, 280. The courts definitely had several cases where the judges had to face the question of how far the man was allowed to go in his abuse of the wife before he was to be punished. He did after all have the right to chasten his wife as well as his children and servants.

[101] The most famous one — *The Hammer of Witches* or *Malleus maleficarum* by Heinrich Institoris — was published already in 1486 and followed by a great number of texts like *De praestigiis daemonum* by Johann Weyer (1563), *De démnomanie* by Jean Bodin (1580; translated into German by Johann Fischart 1581).

[102] I have found only one exception. Schwank number 80 in *Das ander theyl der Gartengesellschaft* is the only story that portrays a good woman. Moser-Rath claims that the women lose their individuality because they are given certain — negative — qualities. Although the male characters of the Schwänke are also often described in a stereotype manner, it is the female characters that are portrayed in the most uniform way (*"Lustige Gesellschaft,"* 108).

[103] Montanus, *Schwankbücher*. Schwank numbers 37 and 38 (90–102).

[104] Here parallels to sixteenth-century jurisdiction can be drawn: early modern society allowed the head of the family to punish wife, children, and servants, but downright beating was illegal. See Elisabeth Koch, *Maior dignitas est in sexu virili: Das weibliche Geschlecht im Normensystem de 16. Jahrhunderts* (Frankfurt am Main: Vittorio Klostermann, 1991), passim.

[105] See Wiltenburg, *Disorderly Women;* Wiltenburg, "Family Murders"; Heide Wunder, "'Weibliche Kriminalität' in der Frühen Neuzeit. Überlegungen aus der Sicht der Geschlechtergeschichte," in *Von Huren und Rabenmüttern. Weibliche Kriminalität in der Frühen Neuzeit,* ed. Otto Ulbricht (Cologne: Böhlau, 1995), 39–62; Ulinka Rublack, *The Crimes of Women in Early Modern Germany* (Oxford: Clarendon Press, 1999).

[106] "That she would not win anything from the husband, and that she was also in little favor with the judge. Therefore, she did everything that the husband liked," 15–16.

[107] There are a number of studies on the perception of social order in the Middle Ages and the early modern era. See for instance *Infinite Boundaries: Order, Disorder, and Reorder in Early Modern German Culture,* ed. Max Reinhart (Kirksville, MO: 16th Century Journal Publishers, 1998), and Gerhild S. Williams, "Der Teufel und die Frau: Textformen und Aussagen," in *Text und Geschlecht. Mann und Frau in Eheschriften der Frühen Neuzeit,* ed. Rüdiger Schnell (Frankfurt am Main: Suhrkamp, 1997), 280–302.

[108] "But if one should beat all stubborn women at the same time, there would not be enough cudgels there; one would also need stones and other instruments," number 23, 48–49.

[109] Cf. Wiltenburg, *Disorderly Women*, 111–12.

[110] In a paper at the Sixteenth Century Studies Conference in Cleveland, Ohio, October 2–5, 2000, Amy Leonard gave an account of her research on the convents in Strasbourg. Leonard has found that the arguments for closing the convents were similar to those that were used in the debate about the city brothels.

[111] Cf. *Das ander theyl der Garten gesellschaft,* in Montanus, *Schwankbücher.*

[112] See also Bachorski: "Der Mikrokosmos des Hauses und der Makrokosmos des Gemeinwesens entsprechen einander, ebenso wie sie sich gegenseitig ergänzen und stabilisieren. . . . Dieser neuen gesellschaftlichen Funktion der Familie entspricht eine Ausweitung des diskursiven Feldes 'Ehe und Familie,' und so könnte die Integration des Themas 'Obrigkeit' in den Ehediskurs einer 'Differentialanalyse' verschiedener Texte Zeichen für eine überschrittene Eposchenschwelle sein" (The microcosmos of the home and the macrocosmos of society correspond to each other at the same time that they complete and stabilize each other. . . . This new societal function of the family corresponds to an expansion of the discourse field of "Marriage and Family" and therefore the theme of "Authority" in the discourse of marriage found in a "Differential analysis" could be an indication that a new era has begun, "Diskursfeld Ehe," 527–28).

[113] See *Wegkürzer* numbers 30, 31, 32, 33, and *Das ander theyl der Garten gesellschaft,* numbers 87, 98–103, 105–7, 109, 111.

[114] See chapter 5 on moral ordinances.

[115] Montanus, *Schwankbücher.* Schwank number 111 (418–20).

[116] In one story in *Wegkürzer* a priest kills a pregnant woman because she does not want to give him a sack with money that belongs to a knight (number 33, 83–85). There are no sexual insinuations, just plain violence aimed at a woman in no position to protect herself or her unborn child. The story is similar to Schwank 55 in Wickram's *Rollwagenbüchlein,* not so much because both stories portray pregnant women who are killed, but because of its brutality and complete lack of humor.

[117] See Moser-Rath, *"Lustige Gesellschaft,"* 101, on the discussion as to whether woman is human/a human being.

[118] Schwank 106 in *Das ander theyl der Garten gesellschaft* can thus be regarded as the perfect revenge of married men, had it not been the cruel joke of a young man. A married woman has an affair with the parish priest and one of the young men in the village knows of their secret meetings. He goes to the husband asking if he can have the farm if he makes sure that the woman loses her ability to speak. The husband is stunned but likes the idea of a quiet wife and promises the young man what he asks for. The youngster then dresses up like the wife and at a meeting with the priest cuts off his penis — his buppenhahn. The priest runs off and thinks of revenge. The following day the woman, who is unaware of the meeting between the priest and the young man, decides to visit her lover and bring him food. The joker then puts the cut-off penis in the basket without her noticing. When the priest sees his missing body part he asks the woman to put her tongue in his mouth, claiming that it will cure him. The woman, already shocked, agrees and the priest bites her tongue off. She loses her ability to speak and her husband has to give the farm to the young man. The priest is castrated and the woman quiet. It could have been the ideal situation

for the male protagonist, but instead he has to leave his home and live a life in misery. By wishing for things to happen that are against "nature" — celibate clergy and silent women — the farmer changes the social order. Montanus sends out a message in this story that makes any change impossible, even if one at first thinks of it as good.

[119] Moser-Rath, *"Lustige Gesellschaft,"* 119.

[120] Exceptions are Schwank 55 in *Rollwagenbüchlein*, Schwank number 29 in the *Wegkürzer*, and number 96 in *Das ander theyl der Garten gesellschaft*.

[121] There is a clear difference in class when looking at children in the sixteenth century. Few children were allowed to be children for very long. Most had to contribute to the survival of the family at an early age. Furthermore, the mortality rate of children was so high that crude jokes about children might have been regarded as improper. Handbooks on childrearing were on the other hand very popular among the wealthy, and the interest in the body, especially the female body, grew with scientific and medical advancement. The chapbook authors have definitely made a conscious choice when leaving out children. On the position of the child in the Schwänke, see for instance Moser-Rath, *"Lustige Gesellschaft,"* 122; for a wider summary, see Philippe Ariès's famous and controversial study on childhood, *Centuries of Childhood* (London: Pimlico, 1996), and Carmen Luke, *Pedagogy, Printing, and Protestantism: The Discourse on Childhood* (Albany: State U of New York P, 1989). On the relationship between parents and children, see Steven Ozment, *When Fathers Ruled: Family Life in Reformation Europe* (Cambridge, MA: Harvard UP, 1983); Steven Ozment, *Flesh and Spirit: Private Life in Early Modern Germany* (New York: Viking, 1999). Ozment's very positive view of affectionate parents and spouses at the time of the Reformation can be questioned since the lack of sources make a study of the lower classes in society almost impossible. There is on the other hand little or no proof for the argument that parents did not love their children. Poverty and diseases put a strain on everyone regardless of age.

[122] Montanus, *Schwankbücher*, 387; similarly one story mentions that a mother is carrying a child in her arms when she goes into the bedroom to have sex ("der liebe mit einander spylten") with a friend of the family, a man who has entered a convent: "Und er mit seiner lieben gefatterin, die das kindt am armb het, in die kammer gieng" (And he entered the room with his beloved who had the child upon her arm, 75).

[123] This is one of few Schwänke by Montanus where a character has a full name. Mostly the characters are not characterized by anything else than the function they take in the story.

[124] The anti-Semitism of this story is clear but cannot be further discussed here. The Jews are portrayed as cunning, cruel, and evil.

[125] Montanus, *Schwankbücher*. Schwank number 5 (260).

[126] Also this is discussed by Labouvie out of the perspective of court records in *Andere Umstände*.

[127] The author/narrator claims: "Dann kein boserer teufel ist dann ein weib" (For there is no devil more evil than woman, 267); "Es ist ein teufelisch thier umb ein weib: wan man in ein ding verbeut, so thund sies erst. Aber ich kan gedencken, das

es ein angeerbt bose, gifftige natur ist" (There is something devilish about woman; if you forbid them to do something they will immediately do it. But I can imagine that it is due to their inborn evil and poisonous nature, 269).

[128] "You have given me a man who is of little or no use when it comes to the work upon which marriage is built," 316.

[129] "They will be of help to us and help you get away from the poor bastard and come to a place, where you will be happy and not waste the days of your youth," 316.

Illustration from Georg Wickram, *Vom guten und bösen Nachbarn*.

2: The Novels of Georg Wickram

"And they lived honestly and well with their women and children"[1]

GEORG WICKRAM'S INTEREST IN well-functioning relationships between man and woman, young and old, master and servant is well documented; scholars of early modern German literature have shown his prose novels an increasing interest over the past two decades because of their exemplary images of perfect marriages and harmonic family life.[2] Especially in his later works where he writes more independently of his sources, Wickram makes up his ideal version of an early modern society — almost as an antithesis to the world turned upside down in the chapbooks or in texts written in the tradition of Sebastian Brant's *Narrenschiff* (1494) — yet without having an explicit political intention. He generally avoids everything that could appear provocative in the eyes of the reader, but his idealistic visions of urban life are nevertheless regarded as interesting, especially because of the scarcity of similar texts in German.[3]

Because of the greater originality of his works from the 1550s, I have chosen to focus on *Der jungen Knaben Spiegel* (Manual for Young Boys, 1554) and *Von guten und bösen Nachbarn* (Of Good and Bad Neighbors, 1556). Wickram's early works are adaptations of older texts and they focus almost entirely on courtly love, although in a version far removed from middle high German poetry and epic in time and space and heavily influenced by sixteenth-century Alsatian town life.[4] Since Wickram frequently uses plots, themes, and characters from a wide array of sources, it is difficult to prove what is exclusively original and what is borrowed, what is new and what belongs to convention. Building his stories on traditional themes, he mixes well-known literary figures and *topoi* with matters of topical interest to his contemporaries. He thus moves freely from the courtly setting in *Galmy* and *Gabriotto und Reinhardt* to the urban life in *Nachbarn* while giving the nobility of a distant past the traits often ascribed to early modern burgher and at the same time letting sixteenth-century merchants or craftspeople practice courtship in a manner typically found in courtly literature. Despite his fear of controversy, Wickram is thus one of the first German authors to give characters from the lower and middle social classes a status long reserved for the nobility in literature.

Family Feud: *Der jungen Knaben Spiegel*

The prose novel *Der jungen Knaben Spiegel* is based on the biblical parable of the prodigal son. Wickram makes use of the topic frequently in his writings, but adapts it freely for his own purposes.[5] The novel is set at the court of the "Hochmeister" of Prussia,[6] but Wickram is more concerned with questions regarding marriage, child-rearing, and education than with chivalry and courtship. The story sets off:

> Es ist gewesen vor langen jaren ein frummer alter Ritter an dem hoff zu Preüssen / welcher seine tag in mannlichen und Ritterlichen thaten hinbracht biß auff fünfftzig jar / so das er keinem Ehlichen weib vermehlet ward / . . . .[7]

The first lines appear familiar to readers educated in the tradition of medieval literature: Wickram presents an old knight who has fought successfully for his lord for many years but adds that he has had no time for marriage. Over three pages the reader then is told that the knight — Gottlieb — is given a wife, that the wedding is held, and that the couple prays to God for a child. Gottlieb is thus quickly brought into a sphere probably much better known to Wickram's readership than was the world of professional warriors in armor — that of the family. The first words, "once upon a time," suggest a story of past times, while the armored knight represents a topic that can be regarded as a leitmotif in medieval European literature and that was thus known to many readers. The sentences following do, however, make the story seem a bit odd; knights of the kind described by Wickram may originate in medieval epics and poetry, but medieval literature hardly deals with knights thinking of "retirement" at the end of their careers, or their worries about not being married. "Love" might be of major importance in medieval — as in other — literature, but the lonesome bachelor longing for a spouse is rarely a middle-aged, retired knight, and the problems surrounding childlessness were not often a topic of discussion in that kind of literature. It is impossible to draw any conclusions about the lives of medieval soldiers and knights from the highly stylized images found in medieval literature, and the same goes for the protagonists in Wickram's texts. The lack of sources regarding what often is called "real life" makes for speculations and theories that are hard to prove, and we can only assume that a knight had needs and desires similar to those of other people of his time, but that this is of little interest to an author trying to express certain values. At stake here is rather what Rüdiger Schnell has regarded as a merger between the discourse of love and the discourse of marriage caused by the growing interest in marriage as an instrument of control by the authorities not just of the individual but of the whole social structure.[8]

The themes in Wickram's text are thus not new in themselves, but they are put into new contexts. Wickram puts great effort into describing all the problems that surround marriage and family life, making the story particularly interesting for studying gender-related questions. Here I will focus on the representation of women and men in the text by looking at how Wickram makes use of his characters: how he uses them as carriers of a gendered discourse. At first glance it seems easy to discuss the construction of woman and men in texts that focus so intensively on marriage, family life, and the bringing up of children as Wickram's works — topics generally establishing stereotypical gender identities and regarded as the center of heterosexual relationships — but it is not.[9] His production is so large that any topic of investigation is by necessity contradictory.

The phrase "once upon a time" might explain the free use of the parable; the author makes a point of being removed from his topic in time and space. He can reconstruct his image of "the past," its spatial and temporal settings as well as its personages without any obligations to his contemporary reader. He does so by telling his own story, by writing "Ein schön Kurtzwyligs Büchlein" (a nice, entertaining little book). By no means revolutionary, the *Knaben Spiegel* makes the (post-) modern reader aware of the problems surrounding the study of early modern literature: how are we to read what seems familiar and yet different? By reading the opening lines of Wickram's text closely, the multitude of problems immanent in seemingly simple texts — linguistic, historical, cultural — emerge and force us to ask questions of the text.

Knaben Spiegel starts where many other stories end: with a marriage. Wickram does not want to tell about the glorious victories of a knight but rather of his life as husband and father. Gottlieb is given a wife as a reward for his loyalty to the Hochmeister, a reward that the Hochmeister makes use of in different situations throughout the book.[10] Every time a male character needs to be awarded for his outstanding success in life, he is given a wife by the Hochmeister, who cannot think of a better "gift" for a bachelor. The woman thus becomes a trophy, the prize for serving well. A born matchmaker, the Hochmeister not only finds spouses for his protégés, he is successful in finding the "right" person for his men, maybe a sign of his interest in and good knowledge of his subjects. Like a *deus ex machina,* he enters the scene every time a character has accomplished something that deserves rewarding, while at all other times he is absent. An almighty God of marriage, the Hochmeister rules his lands and people like a Protestant preacher believing in happy marriages as the key to peace and order. But it would be underestimating Wickram's skills as an author to see only the repetitive pattern of matchmaking for the sake of Reformation propaganda. The Hochmeister might find spouses for everyone, but the men and women involved react differently upon the suggested marriage, showing that they are less stereotypically portrayed than a first reading might suggest. This allows for Wickram to examine the concept of marriage from different perspectives and to point out not only what he regards as the positive sides of marriage but also its possible negative effects, a concept also used in *Rollwagenbüchlein*.

The first proposal does not meet any resistance. Gottlieb responds with gratefulness when the Hochmeister suggests that he marry the wife of a dead servant and also take on his job. The woman is "pretty, young, and pious" (8), making her an ideal wife. The narrator does not seem to have a problem with a young woman marrying a man who is fifty years old, even though marriage tracts and chapbooks alike never stop short of expressing the danger of age difference. At a later point he also moralizes about old women who marry young men with the intention of being taken care of instead of having to provide for their aging husbands (111). It is possible that Wickram distinguishes between men and women, making a relationship between an old woman and a young man appear less appealing to the reader than if the woman is younger than the man — a view still held by many men and women in the twenty-first century. Although most sixteenth-century texts disapprove of all kinds of differences between spouses (age, class, race, religion), it is still more likely that Wickram downplays the problem because he needs a younger wife for Gottlieb in order to continue the story. She has to be of childbearing age. Gottlieb is fifty years old and a woman of his age has gone through menopause. It is further possible that it is a simple slip of the pen, the word "young" being part of the phrase expressing the perfection of the woman. This woman, Concordia, has furthermore been married once before but no children were born before her husband died. It can thus be assumed that "young" is relative to Gottlieb's age.

The Hochmeister might be pushing marriages, but he follows the advice found in most marriage tracts and in the writings of the reformers. At no time in the text does he consider a wedding ceremony before talking to the parties involved and he does not force a man or woman to marry against their will. In accordance with the teachings of Martin Luther and other reformers the Hochmeister calls for Concordia to discuss the marriage with her after having talked to Gottlieb.[11] She does not bring a male guardian but talks for herself; as a widow she is allowed a certain freedom and independence, something seen again when the other marriages in the text are being negotiated. When finding wives for Gottlieb's and Concordia's stepson Friedbert and his teacher Felix, the Hochmeister sends for the widow of his previous chancellor, and when looking for a wife for their son Wilbald he lets Friedbert and Felix talk to the widow of a wealthy merchant. These women are also consulted without further male involvement. In the first case he talks to the widow in her position as mother, since he wants her daughters to marry Friedbert and Felix. The text does, however, make clear that the Hochmeister himself is the legal guardian of the woman and her daughters, since her husband had asked for this favor on his deathbed. This reduces her freedom to act on her own, but on the other hand the Hochmeister does not make the important decision without her knowledge. Expressing her gratitude she confirms what the husband has wished for by saying: "So ergib ich mich mit meinen Tochtern / in deren schutz und schirm" (so I give myself together with my daughters / to their protection and safeguard, 65). The two young women are left out of the discussion with the explanation that they are so well behaved that they would never question a decision made by the mother (65). The statement can be read as a passive approval and a strong belief in the judgment of the mother, although Wickram does not repeat this sort of indirect courtship in his last novel, *Nachbarn*. When focusing on early modern urban life and leaving the courtly sphere, he leaves much of the literary tradition behind and seems more influenced by contemporary ideas.

Hence in *Knaben Spiegel* — just as in Wickram's earlier novels — some sort of imagined ancient time and place make the marriage negotiations seem unintentional caricatures of medieval epics. Having no firsthand experience Wickram can only consult older texts he has read or heard of and use them as references. For the most part he is in the firm grip of Reformation propaganda. The need for women and men to marry remains as strong throughout the book as it does in all of his prose novels regardless of the setting — courtly or urban. This can be seen in the emotional reaction of the widow when approached by the Hochmeister and asked if she would like to see her daughters married. She cannot think of any better message than that he is trying to find a spouse for her daughters:

> . . . was mocht mir glückseligers auff diser erden zuston / dann so ich meine lieben Tochtern also glückselig in ehlichen staht kämen sehe / mir armen Wittfrawen aber ist semlichs zu vollbringen nit moglich.[12]

Her gratefulness is explained by the last part of the sentence. The widow does not have the right to initiate a marriage, but depends on male agency for this important decision that involves not only emotional but also financial aspects and the future of the family. She has to wait for a man to propose to her daughters; anything else is obviously a violation against convention, and she does not for a moment think of overthrowing it. Her only right is to turn down a proposal if found inappropriate and a dishonor for herself and her daughters. This leaves her with few choices but to passively wait and try to present the most well-behaved and beautiful daughters in town.

Knaben Spiegel does not yet explicitly claim the need to discuss the marriage with man and woman as is found in *Nachbarn* and often stressed by reformers like Luther and Martin Bucer, but the message transmitted to the reader is clear: a wedding should not take place unless both spouses are in agreement. Since all women asked in the *Knaben Spiegel* happily submit to the Hochmeister, putting themselves under his protection, no problems arise. They may not immediately agree to his suggestions but have complete trust in his choice of partner for them, as does the hesitant widow who is asked to marry Wilbald at the end of the book. Having at first lost her beloved husband and then had a miscarriage because of the depression following her husband's death, her initial hesitation does not in any way seem out of place. After four years of widowhood she is nevertheless ready to reconsider her previous desire to remain a widow for the rest of her life. The text does not explain why but several reasons appear probable: she may be thinking of her age and the possibility of having a child, but also of the restrictions surrounding a single woman living on her own. Her openness towards the proposal further show her willingness to oblige her visitors. This complete trust in male judgment of course make the women in Wickram's prose works better wives; they do not question male authority but rather show their submissiveness and willingness to obey. It should not be overlooked, however, that Wickram here as in *Rollwagenbüchlein* allows women the right to express their opinion, even though he is clear about a strict gender hierarchy. No virtuous woman should have to put up with a violent gambler or drunkard, but in the best of worlds the men are as virtuous as are the women and all arguments unnecessary.

The men have the same right to object to a marriage proposal as the women, but they are also given the advantage of always having the right to actively engage in the process, while the women have the right only to agree to or turn down a proposal. The men are allowed to initiate a marriage themselves while women have to wait for a proposal. The difference can be seen in the phrase "und noch wol eines ehrlichen mans wert was" (and was still an honest man, 111). A man has to prove himself worthy of starting a family; he has to prove himself skilled and knowledgeable. A woman on the other hand has a certain value attached to her, depending on her birth and her virtue — including such aspects as age, social status (or class), and beauty. Her most desired characteristics are submissiveness and passivity. She can thus hardly shape her life actively unless submissiveness is regarded as a skill one actively acquires and passivity is seen as an activity. In sum, if found virtuous enough, the woman "deserves" a husband and she will be married to someone who has proven himself worthy marrying her through honorable deeds.

Not everyone shows the same compliance with the marriage proposals suggested by the Hochmeister. When he approaches Friedbert and Felix to express his appreciation for their skills they at first do not react according to his expectations. Friedbert has been chancellor at the court for two years and shows no intention to marry. This seems to bother the Hochmeister and Wickram comments: "Fridbert was jetzund bey zweien jaren Kantzler am hoff zu Preüssen gewesen / hat aber kein weib" (Fridbert had now been chancellor at the Preussian court for two years / but had no woman, 61). Felix, who is even older than Friedbert, is also still a bachelor. As a sign from above the Hochmeister comes to think of the two daughters of the previous chancellor but he is at first met with suspicion. The young adults Friedbert and Felix are content living with Gottlieb, Friedbert's mother Patrix (who is working as a maid in the house after the death of her husband), and Gottlieb's wife (43). When asked about marriage Friedbert answers that he is unwilling to give up his freedom unless given a wife with whom he can live in peace and happiness ("friden und freüden," 61). When in doubt he would rather remain a bachelor and he prefers to live without a "good and virtuous" wife in order to avoid risking continuous fights with a shrewish wife.[13] The Hochmeister is amused by this answer, maybe ascribing it to Friedbert's young age, but he then receives a similarly quirky answer from Felix, who claims to know that every human being is born to suffer and that he patiently has accepted this. Hence, the Hochmeister should not hesitate to find him a wife. If the marriage is happy, he says, he has to thank God kindly.[14]

This seems to satisfy his master who immediately acts on behalf of his two young and successful disciples, while they hurry to report the good news to Gottlieb; their hesitancy is suddenly gone. Wickram has been able to use two of his main characters to express the dark sides of marriage and the dangers of marrying the wrong woman and can now return to the story itself. The two bachelors look forward to their new social status as married men and do not for a moment question if their soon-to-be wives have any objections. This would simply have implied uncertainty about the power of the Hochmeister.

The doubts of Friedbert and Felix about female virtue do, however, reappear when the Hochmeister wants their assistance in finding a wife for the returned son, Wilbald, as a sign that he has done penance and needs to be reintegrated into the world he was born into. Instead of dubbing Wilbald to knighthood — as would have been the obvious reward for a nobleman whose father had belonged to the Teutonic knights, and which also was Wilbald's desire when a child — the Hochmeister appoints him his successor and gives him a wife. Knighthood might be a part of this gift but Wickram does not find it worth mentioning explicitly.

This deep belief in marriage as the one and only way of living that seems to characterize the *Knaben Spiegel* does not quite correspond with the image of women expressed by two of the main characters. Or does it? When Friedbert discusses a potential wife with Felix they fear that the person considered — a widow — will reject their proposal because of her love for her dead husband (106). Friedbert — who despite his name and its allusions to peace sees conflict inherent in every woman — believes he has found the solution. If Wilbald first is appointed successor of the Hochmeister, the woman will be so flattered to be considered his wife that she will not be able to resist a marriage proposal. Friedbert points out that women forget easily: "so gewiß das ist das die weiber lang hor und lang kleider gern haben / so gwiß tragen sie auch ein kurtzen sinn" (just like women surely like to have long hair and long clothes / they also have a short memory, 106). He shows the mourning widow little respect, talking about women in general terms as if they were all the same. However, since the narrator already has told the reader that time has healed the wounds and that the woman is reconsidering her refusal to enter a second marriage no further discussion of one particular woman and her position among "women" is needed. Freidbert is saved from making another misogynist statement, but is allowed to make his point. He can state what he considers typical female mentality while the reputation or good intentions of the widow need not be examined in detail.

The vigilant behavior of the widow shows that she is aware of her dangerous position as a single woman and knows that any movement from her side can be used against her. She cannot simply admit feelings for other men and has to cautiously watch her reputation. The distribution and circulation of power between men and women becomes very clear in this passage. The widow is allowed certain independence as long as she does not express any interest in another man; this includes thinking and talking with others about a possible remarriage. Correct female behavior thus excludes all notions of sexuality. As soon as her desire becomes public, she has to abandon her independence and submit herself to male dominance. This leaves her with the choice pointed out by the narrator — complete chastity until remarriage. Friedbert on the other hand sees only the weakness in woman by claiming that all women — just like Eve when taking the forbidden fruit — want more than they have. The thought of marrying into the nobility will hence make many, if not most women forget all previous principles. His comment not only shows disrespect for a woman's feelings for her dead husband, but also makes her way of thinking compulsory, leaving a woman with no option to make her own choice.

In this specific case the woman is yet another example of female virtue. When approached by Felix and Friedbert — who in no way reveal their previous thoughts — she invites them to enter her house. The woman is thoughtful, flushes at the right points, answers all questions modestly, and does everything Friedbert and Felix expect from a virtuous woman. When hearing about Wilbald's wild youth, she only makes the comment that it is irrelevant since he has turned away from that life. She is thus willing to be his wife and to live under his protection.[15] The men do not have to deal with a rejection. They are themselves such examples of morality that they are able to convince even the most difficult widow about the positive effects of a second marriage despite their own initial doubts. Since asked first, she in turn does not have to be forced into something against her will. The text makes the decision of the woman appear completely voluntary and unforced, but did she really have a choice? What would have happened if she had turned down the offer? The text is fictitious and can thus not provide the reader with any answers, but by discussing the marriage with the woman and by giving her the opportunity to answer for herself, she is given the same freedom as when Concordia was asked to marry Gottlieb. This freedom is, however, a chimera; the women make a decision because they have complete trust in the men, not because they trust their own judgment.

After all parties have agreed on the premises — the Hochmeister as usual promising a valuable gift — the wedding is quickly arranged and the ceremony celebrated. Even though Friedbert's and Felix's weddings are described more vividly than the other two weddings in the book,[16] the festive occasion in itself is of little interest to Wickram, who is focused on the result of the wedding, the married couple and their future children.[17] Marriage may be regarded as a reward for the protagonists in *Knaben Spiegel,* and the women "given" to them examples of unusual virtue, but the use of characters such as Gottlieb and Concordia shows that not even the best qualifications among spouses guarantee a happy marriage. In *Knaben Spiegel* Wickram points out two issues of importance for a successful marriage: children and the relationship between the spouses. The birth of healthy children as well as their appropriate upbringing are a necessity for the marriage, thus making the marriage between Gottlieb and Concordia doomed to fail. Wickram is evidently more interested in the complications surrounding this marriage than in the later marriages in the book that are instant successes, with many children brought up to fear and love God and their parents (74, 116–19).

In *Knaben Spiegel* as well as in *Nachbarn,* children can in many ways be regarded as the center of the stories, while Wickram always avoids discussing sexuality — whether it is expressed as desire towards another person or the sexual act itself.[18] If the women, but also often the men, in the chapbooks seem obsessed by sex, they appear almost asexual in Wickram's novels. Like most authors influenced by the Reformation, Wickram emphasizes the importance of married life, but he seems to find no contradiction in being unmarried and capable of virtuous conduct, or in being married and living in chastity. In his novels virtuous women appear to remain some odd sorts of virgin after marrying and even after giving birth — just like the Virgin Mary.[19] Virginity becomes the metaphor for a life lived according to existing social and religious norms, and sexuality loses its importance for the plot while making room for a presentation of life after childbirth.[20] This is made clear in the comparison between Friedbert and Felix and Wilbald and his so-called friend Lothar. While Friedbert and Felix live harmonious family lives, the two misfits spend their time in taverns with prostitutes or "beautiful women," as Wickram prefers to call them in this text.[21] Lothar goes as far as promising a woman marriage if she has sex with him — a common chapbook tactic, but in *Knaben Spiegel* leading to no happy ending. The woman becomes pregnant but keeps it a secret until the baby is born. Chased out of the house by her parents the young woman turns into a beggar and the infant dies. In a way this creates a continuation of the chapbooks that focus on intercourse per se but not so much on the result — pregnancies and babies. Only when dealing with childlessness do the novels and chapbooks seem to agree — it is generally regarded as a serious problem for the parents.

Gottlieb and Concordia pray to God for a child but Concordia does not get pregnant until after they have assumed responsibility for the upbringing of Friedbert, a peasant's son. The reader is told that their prayers focus too much on the birth of a child and that little attention is given the personality of the baby that is completely dependent on godly grace. It is as if Gottlieb and Concordia think too much of the child and too little of the responsibilities of parenthood.[22] Since it is a gift from God, it is presumptuous to regard pregnancy as a right, something every married couple has the right to experience. It is a blessing and has to be accepted as such rather than something unfairly distributed among humankind. Concordia's frustration is obvious when she expresses her longing for a child to God. She compares her earthly wealth with the poverty of the peasant woman Patrix who is blessed with many children (11), but she soon realizes the difference in "wealth." The poor woman is given "Sun und Tochteren / in deren angesicht sie sich mit grossen freüden ersehen mag" (sons and daughters / in whose faces she may see herself reflected with great joy, 11) while Concordia has more money than she can spend and no children to share it with. Concordia's solution to this problem is to ask the peasant couple to let her and Gottlieb bring up the child they are about to have. It is a suggestion that seems to satisfy everyone despite the demanding tone of the question: "diewyl mich Gott nit erhoren wil von meiner sünd wegen / so soll mir dise Frauw einen trost geberen / damit ich mein zeitlich freüd haben mag" (whereas God will not hear me because of my sins / this woman will bear me comfort / so that I will be happy, 11). Concordia and Gottlieb both suffer from not having a child, but no blame is put on the woman for not getting pregnant, even though she refers to herself as a sinning person. It is a problem belonging to both spouses and seemingly nothing uncommon to the expected readers, judging by the way it is presented in the text. The topic is treated with great sincerity by Wickram, making it the focus of the first pages of the book. By showing childlessness a problem man and woman have in common, a great burden is taken off the woman. One should, however, keep in mind that sixteenth-century medical discourse did recognize that childlessness could be referred to either man or woman, so that this acknowledgment is not limited to Wickram's work.[23]

When Concordia and Gottlieb are allowed to take care of Friedbert as their own son their joy is unmistakable, but they never end their prayers for a biological son. Concordia gives birth to Wilbald about a year after Friedbert was born. The happiness of the parents has no limits, and they have no intention of returning Friedbert to his biological parents. The two boys are raised together, but while Friedbert grows up to be a well-behaved young man, Wilbald ends up a criminal before regretting his evil deeds and returning home. The parents are at all points regarded as equally responsible for the children but have distinct roles as "mother" and "father" that correspond with their roles as "woman" and "man." It is hence possible to put the blame for Wilbald's behavior on the mother, who always tries to protect the son from being corrected or punished by his teacher or his father, by stressing that her son is too young and sensitive for harsh treatment.

This lenient attitude among mothers towards their children is commonly described in early modern didactic texts and often explained by their weak disposition due to a combination of wet and cold humors, and this also characterizes Concordia.[24] She makes the mistake that she and Gottlieb had both promised Friedbert's parents not to make (11) — that of treating the two boys differently — and it has a deadly outcome. Friedbert may not need to be controlled by their teacher Felix like his brother, but the love Concordia feels for the biological son — protecting him when stealing, gambling, and lying — is as obvious as it is dangerous. The wife acts without consulting her husband and is finally made responsible for the destruction of the family. As soon as Wilbald is caught by Felix or Gottlieb he runs to the mother, complaining that he should not have to study. As the son of a knight he sees himself as living off a family fortune and entertaining himself in tournaments with other knights (16, 28). Believing in what he thinks of as traditional male values he ends up being what he fears: a nobody without a home, a family, or wealth. The mother speeds up the decay of the son while wanting the opposite, exposing her inability to control herself or her son. She immediately calls for the teacher when Wilbald complains and goes as far as to tell him that her husband by no means needs to know everything: "hey es muß mein Herr und gemahel nit gleich alle ding so gar eigentlich wissen / mein Felix du must zu zeiten ein aug zu thun" (My master and husband does not really have to know of everything. Felix, you will at times need to keep your eyes shut, 29). Felix, tired of her schemes, does not agree with her but tells himself: "wolan der Son ist dein" (well, the son is yours, 29). Despite calling Gottlieb her master, Concordia refrains from discussing the problems with him and refuses to see the severity of Wilbald's evil deeds. Finally Wilbald has to leave town after hurting his teacher with a knife, but Concordia keeps sending him money and spends a great part of the family fortune before dying of the depression that torments her after the prodigal son leaves the parents (43).[25] Her behavior is addressed by the narrator, who takes every opportunity to castigate the feeble mother. He at first carefully points out that one at times finds fathers as well as mothers who try to keep school teachers from upholding order among their pupils by claiming that they know their children better and know when and how to punish them (16–17). Then it becomes evident that the mother is regarded as the greater problem due to her unstable mentality. Concordia is unable to treat her son with anything but leniency,[26] and this passivity is the downfall for them both. Concordia is made to personify the weak mother, a person who is in need of strict male guidance in order to function in her role as wife and mother — in her role as woman.

    The category "woman" as mediated through *Knaben Spiegel* is complex and contradictory. The text can be described as at once misogynist and pro-women, at once claiming male superiority and showing male weakness. It oscillates between the desire to stick to stereotypical portrayals of men and women as presented in literature since antiquity and a need to differentiate by means of everyday experience. Concordia and Gottlieb at first appear as the perfect match, but Concordia's desperate attempts to please her son do not seem to correspond with the initial description of her as virtue personified. On the one hand, it seems possible that her previous marriage had been childless for more than one reason. Though not explicit, the text leaves the reader feeling that a woman like Concordia never should have had children. Her only pregnancy indirectly results in her own death because of the uncontrollable behavior of her son. Also contradictory is that the main characters of the book are told to live in relationships where the spouses discuss family matters with each other,[27] whereas Concordia still so ruthlessly acts behind her husband's back. Gottlieb in turn is not able to control his wife. He does not even seem to understand the extent of the problem. When she dies he promises never to remarry, but not out of bad experience; he never shows any anger with his wife, only compassion. On the other hand, Concordia cannot be blamed for loving her son. Even though Wilbald does not prove himself worthy of this love until after her death, his mother only does what she thinks is right. No matter what Wilbald does, he is still the son that she longed for. The narrative makes very clear that the strong ties between mother and child need to be controlled, that the mother is incapable of being in charge of her own feelings, but that Concordia in all other aspects remains a virtuous woman.

    The rights given to the women in *Knaben Spiegel* as wives and mothers do not hide the fact that this text expresses greater doubts about women than do other novels by Wickram. Friedbert and Felix may be portrayed as perfect examples of male virtue, but their misogynous comments on women would seem out of place unless regarded as a response to women like Concordia. Her punishment is immediate; just like some of Montanus's women, Concordia has to die for acting independently without consulting her husband. She has access to money but only wastes it on her son; she has influence over the teacher but she misuses her position and makes a problematic situation worse; she has two sons but neglects the adopted and well-behaved son because of her worries over Wilbald; she is married to a husband who loves her but she lies to him and does not obey him. Hence Concordia breaks all rules possible and does not accept her subordinate role as a wife. This can only end in the ruin of the family, but the text also stresses that Gottlieb's compassionate attitude towards his wife is partly to blame. Had he taken full responsibility and punished wife and child, the family order would not have been disrupted. His punishment is a lost family. It would, however, be wrong to say that there is no difference in the punishment of man and woman in Wickram's text. Gottlieb is only punished indirectly when his beloved wife dies and his son turns into a criminal. He lives to see the prodigal son come home, and he is allowed to die happy. He is given a second chance while the woman loses her life. The main difference then between Montanus's and Wickram's portrayals of weak father figures is that Wickram in *Der jungen Knaben Spiegel* never questions the family as an institution, while Montanus in his texts expresses strong doubts about it.[28]

A further aspect adding to the complexity of the gender roles in *Knaben Spiegel* is the difference in class. The category woman is not exclusively reduced to the image of the middle-class woman as mother and wife. The rights and obligations of "woman" is thus not always the same. The noblewoman Concordia holds an important position when married to Gottlieb. This can be seen in her relationship to Patrix, who is depicted as very grateful when her newborn is promised a secure home, even though this means that she has to give him away while still an infant (11). The wealth of Concordia and Gottlieb is further emphasized by the description of the cottage where Patrix lives with her husband Rudolf and their children. When Patrix later serves as a maid in the household of Gotfried, her relationship with her son is not even mentioned as we might expect; Wickram focuses rather on the distribution of power between men and women. Patrix is said to be in charge of maids and household-related tasks, but Friedbert who is coming of age and given an increased authority is made responsible for the male servants — obviously a task more appropriate for a man. This indirectly points out Patrix's position in the household and especially her position in regard to Friedbert. She is his biological mother but considered a servant without the right to represent her son, and much less Gottlieb, if they are away from home.

Concordia on the other hand does not hesitate to talk to Felix about Wilbald. He respects her will and does not question her authority, even though he disagrees with her and finds her behavior irresponsible and incorrect. He even admits to Gottlieb having feared her wrath: "auch der frawen zorn geforcht" (34). Concordia thus takes active part in her two sons' lives while Patrix only gratefully adapts to her role as head of the maids. Concordia is superior to Patrix and other women of lower birth, but also to men like Felix who serve her husband.

There is a difference in class that at times overshadows the category gender, even though the wealthy Concordia, like most other women in the text, first and foremost appears as wife and mother. Training for the future starts in early childhood when learning the household chores, while the boys are trained for a profession outside of the family — just as God decided:

> [S]under must ein jedes nach dem und es von Gott begnadet was / arbeiten leren / die tochteren leret ir Muter erstlichen spinnen / demnach nehen / wircken / sticken / und weben / dann sie wol kondt ermessen das mußiggang nichs guts geben thut. . . .[29]

The women are thus primarily defined by their relationship to a man — a dead man, in the case of the widows — and they have to submit to male authority. It is nevertheless important that "class" is brought into the text as a factor that divides women into different subgroups, thereby allowing a more productive construction of woman than the common dichotomy Mary-Eve or wife-witch.

Paradise Equals Family Life:
Von guten und bösen Nachbarn

Von guten und bösen Nachbarn can be read as the answer to *Knaben Spiegel*; it is the positive example of family life at its best. The last novel of Wickram to be published, *Nachbarn* is also his first work written more or less completely independently of older sources. It is furthermore the first long prose text in German with characters exclusively taken from the growing urban middle class. Wickram in this text leaves the sphere of the court and instead turns to the portrayal of merchants and craftsmen with their families. The text has been blamed for its stereotypical images of the urban middle class, but considering its uniqueness in German literature of that time one should rather stress Wickram's originality in his choice of plot and characters. The book depicts everyday life in the early modern town and city — its problems and its joys. In no way a "realistic" text,[30] it nevertheless gives the reader an idea of how Wickram would have liked his fellow citizens to live and how he perceived some of them. Focusing on friendship, Wickram repeatedly and vividly describes the dichotomy expressed in the title of the book: of good and bad neighbors.[31]

The story begins with Robertus and Sophia who leave Antwerp for Lisbon after having inherited a relative's business. The death of nine of their ten children to disease, along with quarrelsome and cunning neighbors, make their decision to leave easy. In Lisbon the family creates a private sphere, including only good and trustworthy friends and neighbors and excluding anyone who does not live a pious and quiet life. The daughter Cassandra marries Richard, a young friend of the father, and another family soon moves in next door after the men have become friends on a business trip. The friendship is extended to the wives and children, making "Frid" (peace) the head of the family at the end of the book.

If the wedding was the reward for obedience and hard work "given" to the men in *Knaben Spiegel,* it loses its status and is replaced by life after marriage — family life — in *Nachbarn.* The men are not given wives as a reward for their service but rather marry out of love.[32] Richard expresses his interest in Cassandra to her father, who in turn talks to her and her mother before the marriage is arranged. Later on their daughter Amelia falls in love with the neighbor boy, Lasarus Jr., at such a young age that courtship is never an issue. Their love grows as they grow up, and the question of marriage is mostly just a matter of waiting until they have come of age.

The marriages may be very convenient for all persons involved, but they are not initiated from "above." Richard falls in love with Cassandra upon his arrival in Robertus's house. Her beauty makes him get over his illness quicker, and he decides to speak to her father, feeling that his love for the young woman is reciprocal and also that the parents will accept the proposal. This at first excludes Cassandra and her mother from participating in the discussion, but Robertus's answer is a pledge for consent:

> Mir aber wil dannocht geburen / die muter und die dochter darunder anzusuchen / damit harnach kein verwiss daraus ervolgen thue / so wolt ich auch (sie die dochter) nit gern zwingen / das sie wider iren willen einem jüngling oder witwer solt vermehelt werden / zu welchem sie keinen willen het.[33]

Richard answers with a question:

> Von gantzem grund meins hertzen solt mirs leid sein / Es wer gleich ewer tochter oder ein andere / solt ich deren wider iren willen vermahelt werden / Was lieber stund würden wir doch bey einander haben?[34]

In *Von guten und bösen Nachbarn* it is assumed that the men consult with their wives and children before making decisions of importance for the family as a whole. The women are not given to men without first being asked for their opinion. Robertus even says that he would deeply regret forcing his daughter into marriage (36). Regarding marriage as the beginning of a life of togetherness, of parenthood and partnership, this attitude seems the only one possible, but it is not fully developed by Wickram until *Nachbarn*. It makes the involvement of the women more important than in *Knaben Spiegel* where marriage was a reward in itself. Robertus's conversation with Sophia shows that husband and wife can disagree without starting a fight. Sophia does not want her daughter to leave the house, fearing the loss of her only living child. When told that Cassandra would stay in the house and marry Richard (who wants to move his business to Lisbon) and also that Robertus has no intention of making Cassandra marry against her will,[35] Sophia is willing to agree to the arrangements with certain hesitancy. Cassandra, on the other hand, does not have to think twice. Trusting her father she says: "An herr Richarten dem jüngling / habe ich gantz keinen mangel" (I have nothing against young mister Richart, 39).[36] It can hardly be denied that the men are in charge of the process and that the women listen to them as authorities, but the women are heard and their reactions respected.

There are, however, clear limits for female agency. Wickram advocates mutual respect and understanding between man and wife, and "it seems as though the wives' opinions have equal status with those of their husbands. Yet that equality exists only in theory."[37] When Amelia later falls in love with Lasarus Jr., the two at first keep their love secret, but when caught — Amelia is heard talking to herself by the father — they set off a process involving all of their parents (88–90). The reaction of the parents explains why Amelia and Lasarus had tried to keep the affair secret. The parents hope for a later marriage between them but fear a clandestine marriage, not only because Amelia and Lasarus are too young to support themselves and to keep house on their own but also because children should not act behind the backs of their parents. The topic is well known from sixteenth-century didactic and educational texts and probably well familiar to the early modern urban reader.

There is of course no need to worry; Amelia and Lasarus would never marry without parental consent, but their parents take full responsibility together — men and women. The fathers first discuss the future of the children (91) but agree that the wives need to be consulted for a "geschwinden rhat" (quick advice, 94). The experience and the advice of the women as spouses and mothers of the two children are important.

They are an integral part of the family and important for the upbringing of the children. They talk to their children but with the difference that Amelia primarily talks to her mother (99–101) while Lasarus listens to his mother but then waits for his father and his advice (103). The family ties are close and openness within the family is required. The men clearly take their roles as head of the household seriously, despite many journeys and other obligations. It is, however, puzzling that the wives are given such importance in family matters while at the same time being restricted to a very limited sphere — their houses. There is no difference between men and women in their basic functions, but when we turn to the texts and look at what men and women are expected to do within the family, clear differences are found that make for gender roles that do not allow for any transgressions. It therefore seems appropriate to look for the construction of woman — and man — within the discourse of family life.

The image of the father leaving the house for work while the woman stays home and takes care of the household is often used as *the* image of the capitalist society, and sometimes its roots date back to the sixteenth century with its growing cities.[38] Equal with man before God, the woman has to submit to her husband or guardian in all secular matters. She is allotted her own sphere at home, where she is assigned household duties and child-care while he is gone.[39] The *oikos* is presented as its opposite, a household or community based on communal values and characterized by the reciprocal dependence of man and woman for the survival of the household.[40] The gender roles in the medieval society are thus regarded as subsidiary and as opposed to the complimentary character of the early modern relationship between men and women with its stricter division of labor. An immediate problem arises, however, since the man of the early modern society is given the right — and is obliged — to rule over his family at home while at the same time representing the outside by working "in public," away from home. This makes him the bridge between public and private — reducing the gap between them,[41] — but it also means that he is the person in charge of both spheres and that the woman is allowed to substitute for him only while he is away. If the woman is supposed to be truly the representative of "the private," she must also have the rights associated with the man. The other problem is that this model hardly can be applied to those men who worked in or from their own home, craftsmen but also men of other occupations who combined living quarters with their businesses and who often worked closely with their wives. Even if characterized as subsidiary, such reciprocity of the medieval household should in no way be confused with more recent concepts of equal rights between men and women.[42]

In *Nachbarn*, the image of public and private as discussed in many scholarly works does have certain relevance.[43] The female characters rarely have any contact with the world outside their homes. The women seem totally cut off from the rest of the community. They seem neither to participate in everyday life, like shopping at the market or going to the communal well, nor to work in the family business.[44] Active within the family, they do not spend any time away from home.[45] They make sure that food is on the table, they take care of the children, supervise the maids, and support their husbands in decisions and discussions regarding the household, but they do not leave the familiar area unless necessary. The two children Amelia and Lasarus are brought up to fit into this enclosed world of family life. Surrounded by strict but loving parents and friends they live a life that is characterized by the same dichotomy of voluntary restraint as the lives of the adult women. Wickram devotes one full chapter (85–87) and several passages to the discussion of proper child-care and education. At first a matter primarily under the tutelage of the mothers, the upbringing of the children is nevertheless of parental concern, "dann wo vatter und mutter mit der straaff zu waich sind / nemend die kinder gar bald einen halsstarck darvon ab" (for where father and mother are too weak with punishment the children soon become defiant, 85). In "good" families the use of physical punishment does not seem necessary, but the children are taught to obey their parents by their exemplary wisdom and behavior. As is shown by the "bad neighbors" at the beginning of the book, poor parental — especially male — behavior results in poor behavior among the children. They grow up to be loud, rude, and quarrelsome.[46] This includes the shaping of "man" and "woman" respectively.

The young Lasarus is sent off to school at the young age of five and the teacher is informed by both parents to be strict with the son (85–86). Lucia, the perfect mother and wife, does not make the mistake Concordia did with Wilbald in *Knaben Spiegel*, and the result is striking. Lasarus Jr. grows up to be a model student and a good son who respects his parents. Only once does he complain: when the parents want him to spend some time in foreign countries to learn his future profession — working as a goldsmith — and to learn languages (93, 104). He then expresses fear of being far away from home and distrust in his parents' love for him (105). The arguments of the father leave him with no option, but he agrees to the trip "mit grossem unwillen" (with great reluctance, 106) and claims: "Mein lieber vatter / wiewol mir die raiß gar zu wider ist / noch dannocht lernet mich kintliche trew und liebe / dieweil dir die sach also gefallen will / das ich mirs auch gefallen lassen sol" (My dear father, as little as I like the trip my childish loyalty and love tells me that I must comply with what you want, 106). Young, worried, and in love with Amelia, Lasarus has no interest in traveling or training for adult life. He, the young man, is sent away to prove himself worthy of marrying, starting a family, and running the family business while Amelia is taught reading, writing, and some math ("sampt dem rechnen," 86) before being taught to make silk embroideries (86–87). He is given no choice if he wants to be a successful craftsman, husband, and father.

Nor is Amelia really able to influence her own situation, since she will never go far away unless together with her father or husband. Her theoretical education is brief, judging by the text.[47] Lasarus is taken out of school to work in the business at age twelve and Amelia at that time has already finished her education. It is said that she enjoys the fact that Lasarus will be "home" to work and that she often sits with her embroidery-frame next to him in his father's business (87).[48] Still young and not yet sure of their feelings for each other, they seem more like siblings than lovers, but as soon as their love is made public, they find it harder to communicate and even start writing each other letters — overwhelmed by their emotions.[49] Amelia, however, does not hesitate to contact Lasarus personally or in writing, a skill she must have acquired during her formal education.[50] She actively works for their relationship without transgressing the restricted sphere of female agency as depicted in the image of the closed off house.[51]

When the men are gone on business, the women are left alone with the servants, but they seem to be in charge of the private — "female" — part of the household exclusively. The women only say that they need to keep an eye on the maids, the female servants. They do not mention male servants or apprentices even though the wealth of the families indicate that there must have been a number of people living in the house.[52] Someone else must be taking care of them and the business; business and household matters have been distinctively separated.[53] The result is that the wives feel responsible for the household when their husbands are gone but that anything related to their businesses is put on hold. It is simply not mentioned until the men return. This division is like the distinct areas of responsibility as depicted in *Knaben Spiegel*, where Friedbert is in charge of male servants while Patrix supervises the maids. In Wickram's texts the discourse of marriage thus seems to advocate an even stricter division of labor and responsibility than historians like Merry Wiesner-Hanks and Heide Wunder have found in their research on sixteenth-century German men and women in urban areas. Ideal and reality do not correspond; limiting the female sphere to the home was not really possible in the material reality of sixteenth-century women. It would have been disastrous to the family economy, unless the family belonged to the very small rich upper class that did not have to work for a living.

Despite the closeness in space and the close relationship between the families, Cassandra — as a sign of her virtue — is very reluctant to visit her best friend Lucia and to leave the servants on their own when the men are gone. In a discussion with her daughter she says:

> O mein tochter/ wie übel es staht einem weib / in abwesen ires mans gastung zu halten / so wenig ziert ein weib in irs mans abwesen / zu gast aus dem haus zu gon [. . .] darumb will mir / O liebe tochter / bass gezimmen dahaim / zu bleiben / und meines haus zu warten.[54]

Amelia is able to convince her mother by calling Lucia spiritual kin and reminding her of a door that minimizes the contact with the outside world.[55] The women in *Nachbarn* do not have to be seen in public in order to visit each other. The men build a door between the houses to ensure that evil gossip can be repressed before it starts and the honor of the women will hence not be endangered.[56] The number of doors leading to the outside is thus reduced to one, preparing for the merger of the households at the end of the book. There is, however, no discussion of the men's needing a door to keep them from being the target of neighborhood rumors. They already belong to the world outside the two houses and can move about freely.[57]

In order to avoid all risks, Cassandra brings the female servants so that they can be observed, but also so that they can observe her. They should not be able to gossip about her and her daughter, as is evidently expected of the maids when not closely watched, and it implies distrust in them. If a female character has doubts about the women's ability to keep their mouths shut, the decision to bring the servants appears logical and makes Cassandra stand out as a perfect exception from the rule. Able to control herself — her mouth included — she can allow herself to visit her neighbor. She would not dream of wasting the time on useless nonsense.

The women spend the evening discussing female conduct, emphasizing the importance of chastity before marriage, honesty and moral discipline, humbleness and submissiveness to the husband and to God. They are exemplary representatives of the ideal woman and wife as depicted in the religious and moral tracts of the fifteenth and sixteenth centuries.[58] They would not dream of acting on their own, without the permission of the husband or against his will, but rather discuss how they can be of help to their men while they are gone (138–39). They also try to prepare Amelia for married life by presenting examples of extraordinary women, thereby stressing Lucretia as the most admirable.[59] Even though innocent, she was willing to take her life in order to save the reputation of her husband. Her innocence made her death tragic, but suicide seems to be the correct reaction of a good wife; Lucretia finds her own life less important than the life of her husband.[60]

When Amelia in youthful naivety expresses interest in entering a nunnery because of a disagreement with her beloved Lasarus, Cassandra and Lucia immediately convince her of the terrible state of morals in the cloisters. They quote marriage tracts and other texts written by men when trying to give the young woman the "correct" view of marriage and help her to self-control.[61] Married life is regarded as the natural norm and the basis for a well-functioning society. Referring to Erasmus of Rotterdam's two texts "Virgo misogamos" and "Virgo poenitens" from his *Colloquia Familiaria* (Friendly Conversations, 1522) Lucia points to the importance of married life as opposed to the life of a nun, echoing the reformers.[62] It is, however, noteworthy that Wickram chooses texts by the well-known humanist Erasmus instead of Martin Luther or Martin Bucer. Wickram on several occasions expresses great admiration for Erasmus and seems more hesitant towards Luther in his texts.[63]

It is neither new nor original to claim that the man is the undisputed head of the household, but the obligations assigned to the men in *Nachbarn* are manifold. Wickram in his dedication and in his foreword to the reader points to the importance of modesty, friendship, wisdom, generosity, and self-control, but also the need for strict control of other members of the family, especially the children. A man who cannot control himself is unable to be in command of his family and servants; hence the image of the bad neighbors at the beginning of the book. Robertus's wife Sophia has "ein gut lob vonn wegen ihres tugentlichen unnd holdtsaligen wandels / sie was ein weib der ehren ein liebhaberin" (been praised due to her virtuous and lovable appearance; / she was a woman who praised virtue, 12). The neighbor on the other hand has a wife who is "ein schaum von einer bosen befftzin" (a scum of a mean woman, 14) and who "barks like a hunter's dog." The women are mere reflections of their husbands, determined to live in their shadows. The difference is, however, that a good man listens to his wife, that he respects her opinion, and that he loves her at least as much as she is expected to love him. Good husbands and wives fear the loss of each other while men and women in bad marriages slowly wear each other out, unconsciously causing the destruction of the marriage and the family and in the end the destruction of society. Unlike the chapbooks, the *Nachbarn* expresses a belief in the ability among women to control themselves. They are not born evil but rather made evil by negative forces inherent in all people. This gives the men a great responsibility to carry. Regarded as the stronger sex, they have to live up to the expectations as expressed in the text. They have to act "manly" in order not to be regarded as a "weibisch jüngling," which Lasarus Jr. fears that Amelia will blame him for after his departure for Antwerp when he is unable to talk to her (125). His reaction makes an awareness of gender categories clear, but this is the only passage I have found in the two texts by Wickram discussed here where a man is considered female because he is unable to control his emotions.

The reader no doubt hears a man talk through all women in the text; there is a male voice and a male perspective constructing gender relations. Male domination is taken for granted, even though Wickram emphasizes a dialogue between man and woman. He regards married life as a necessity for adult women, but less as a way to reach salvation after death than to reach perfection in life. Amelia, the young virgin, is a virtuous and innocent young woman with little resemblance to the sexually obsessed women in the chapbooks, and this innocence does not end with marriage. Amelia nevertheless shows that there are ways for women to act — in her conversations with Lasarus and when convincing her mother to visit her neighbor and best friend. However, she never transgresses the threshold of female agency — the family house. Even though the families in *Nachbarn* expand the area within which they feel safe, they prefer to move within a closed-off sphere, isolated from fellow citizens.

At the same time the outer world gets perilously close. The men, who are forced to travel because of their businesses, are the target of violence, intrigues, and illness. They have to fight evil people and powers like the medieval knights in order to prove themselves as good men while the women wait patiently at home — with few and extraordinary exceptions just like women have done in literature since antiquity. Wickram stresses the dangers of a world inhabited by people who do not live in accordance with the Ten Commandments and secular legislation, but there is still hope for a better world. In that world men and women live in harmony with each other, each knowing his or her rights and obligations. As opposed to the world of the Schwank, people in Wickram's utopia never question what is presented to them as a God-given world order. They struggle and adapt, content with the world as long as nothing changes and no social or other roles are reversed. This makes for a world where people can be divided into "good" and "bad," where some people live in accordance with given norms and some people do not. The result is characters that are less complex than a figure like Wilbald who has bad as well as good sides and whose personality is marked by social norms and ethics rather than biological or "natural" causes.[64]

Wickram in *Nachbarn* defines "man" and "woman" just as little as he does in *Knaben Speigel*. They are made to belong to two categories that do not seem to need any further explanation. Men and women simply exist — they appear as biological givens in the text, and their primary role is to raise a well-functioning family. The wives — Sophia, Cassandra, and Lucia — are shown great respect by their men, they are always consulted in family matters, and their opinions are thought important before a decision is made, but they almost always agree with their husbands. It is easy to give them the right to talk knowing that they will exhibit self-control and complete submissiveness to male authority. "Woman" thus appears to be exactly what "man" makes her — the ideal wife. This leaves little room for conflict.

Sexual difference or gender difference at first glance seems to be of less significance for the right to speak up, to act, and to take responsibility in Wickrams's novels than in some other sixteenth-century texts, but a distinction between men and women is nevertheless clearly upheld. Women are by definition regarded as subordinate — they are considered mentally as well as physically weaker than their counterpart, the men. This is often expressed by the female characters themselves, making the argument strong; a person admitting weakness can hardly be questioned. The weakness inherent in woman makes her an easy target for evil powers. This in turn makes women potentially dangerous; it is thus necessary that they obey their guardian, a father, brother, or husband. Whereas Montanus, Frey, and other chapbook authors make fun of men who have rebellious wives but never let them lose complete control, Wickram, especially in his later works, is more interested in a well-functioning family, bringing forward suggestions and solutions for problematic situations. The women are not to be tamed and controlled for the sake of it but because they are needed within the family. They should not be repressed, but strictly controlled by their husbands or masters, unless the control turns into self-control, the voluntary restriction of freedom to act and speak found among the women in *Nachbarn*. If the man fails in his role as head of the family he is punished, albeit indirectly like Gottlieb.

This still does not answer the question of what makes a woman a woman and a man a man in Wickram's novels. Wickram himself does not go into details, but judging by his emphasis on marriage one could claim that a woman is a person a man marries in order to procreate. She is defined as the opposite to man, a person who can bear children. This gives her a central role in the family, the microcosmos of the world as depicted in the texts. Female sexuality is not, however, a topic of discussion. The need for the human being to procreate might be the reason given by Montanus and Wickram for marriage, but Wickram suppresses the sexual aspect in favor of order. Children are born but descriptions of sexual contact between men and women, husbands and wives never appear in Wickram's works. As long as sexual intercourse is restricted to an act between husband and wife, there is no need to discuss it. It is made evident by the context. A well-ordered family life guarantees a well-ordered community where everyone lives in harmony with his neighbors and disruptive tendencies can be avoided. "Woman" can be pregnant and give birth but is otherwise much like the Virgin Mary, a mother and virgin alike.[65] A woman is thus primarily seen in comparison to man as a wife, mother, or widow.

What conclusion is then to be drawn from people of female sex who are not married? A few characters in the texts are referred to as "she" or "woman" without enjoying the respect of a married woman. They are not married and hence need to support themselves, but the number of possible professions seems very limited. In Wickram's novels the only occupations mentioned are maids/servants or prostitutes (hübsche Frauen, 6), occupations with few rights and little or no recognition. Unmarried and disrespected, these women turn into non-women of female sex. (Social) gender and (biological) sex thus only partially overlap. The man, on the other hand, has problems in finding himself in his role as "Hausvater" (father of the house). In Wickram's novels he is allowed feelings, he is thoughtful, and he cares for his wife and children. He listens to everyone and allows for the wife and children to express their own ideas, but he continues to function as a predefined norm — as expressed in the Bible and "by nature" — that has all that woman has not.

Notes

[1] The quote is taken from Wickram's *Der jungen Knaben Spiegel* and slightly altered: "Friedbert und Felix lebten gar ehrlich unnd wol mit iren weibern und kindern." Georg Wickram, *Georg Wickram: Sämtliche Werke,* ed. Hans-Gert Roloff, vol. 3, *Knaben Spiegel — Dialog vom ungeratnen Sohn* (Berlin: De Gruyter, 1968), 119. All page numbers referring to the *Knaben Spiegel* in the text are from this edition. The translation of long quotes can be found in the notes.

[2] I will not further digress into the genre debate regarding early modern German prose literature here. Wickram's prose works and a number of other fifteenth- and sixteenth-century texts commonly referred to as "Volksbücher" are more often

labeled "prose novels" (Prosaromane) in accordance with Jan-Dirk Müller's definition of the term as discussed in his excellent research report from 1985. Jan-Dirk Müller, "Volksbuch/Prosaroman im 15., 16. Jahrhundert: Perspektiven der Forschung," *Internationales Archiv für Sozial- und Literaturwissenschaft* Sonderheft 1 (1985): 1–128. The theoretical discussion of the prose novel has mainly been a "German" matter. See Alois Brandstetter, *Prosaauflösung. Studien zur Rezeption der höfischen Epik im frühneuhochdeutschen Prosaroman* (Frankfurt am Main: Athenäum, 1971), Hans Joachim Kreutzer, *Der Mythos vom Volksbuch. Studien zur Wirkungsgeschichte des frühen deutschen Romans seit der Romantik* (Stuttgart: Metzler, 1977), and Norbert Thomas, *Handlungsstruktur und dominante Motivik im deutschen Prosaroman des 15. und frühen 16. Jahrhunderts* (Nuremberg: Hans Carl, 1971).

[3] Since finishing my dissertation on Wickram's prose texts, I have come to reevaluate some of my conclusions, particularly in regard to the female characters. I now believe that the dissertation expresses a view of the female characters that is too positive. See Elisabeth Wåghäll, *Dargestellte Welt — Reale Welt: Freundschaft: Liebe und Familie in den Prosawerken Georg Wickrams* (Bern: Peter Lang, 1996).

[4] See Wåghäll, *Dargestellte Welt — Reale Welt,* especially pages 13–54, and Jane Emberson, "Of Good and Bad Neighbors: Middle-Class Life in the Work of Jörg Wickram," *The Sixteenth Century Journal* 26, no. 3 (1995): 533–45. See also Irene S. Cannon-Geary, *The Bourgeoisie Looks at Itself: The 16th Century in German Literary Histories of the 19th Century* (Göppingen: Kümmerle, 1990), 134–52.

[5] He published the play *Ein schönes und evangeslisches Spil von dem verlornen Sun* (A Beautiful and Evangelical Play about the Prodigal Son) in 1540 and a drama based on *Der jungen Knaben Spiegel* — the plot presupposes familiarity with the prose text — probably in 1554.

[6] "Hochmeister" was the name of the leader of the Teutonic Order of Knights according to *Wahrig. Deutsches Wörterbuch* (Gütersloh: Bertelsmann, 1986), 660.

[7] "There was many years ago a virtuous old knight at the Preussian court who for fifty years had spent his days performing manly and knightly deeds so that he had not been married to any woman," 7.

[8] Rüdiger Schnell, "Liebesdisdurs und Ehediskurs im 15. und 16. Jahrhundert," in *The Graph of Sex and the German Text: Gendered Culture in Early Modern Germany 1500–1700,* ed. Lynne Tatlock (Amsterdam: Rodopi, 1994), 77–120.

[9] The female characters in Wickram's work are often mentioned in scholarly texts, but Anna Hirschberg's dissertation from 1919 is to my knowledge still the only long publication on the topic: "Darstellung der Frau in den Romanen Jörg Wickrams und Untersuchung des Kulturgeschichtlichen Wertes der Schilderungen" (Ph.D. diss., Greifswald, 1919).

[10] The repetitive pattern stresses the importance of the married state. By limiting the number to three weddings the text resembles the fairytale while at the same time alluding to the Christian doctrine of Trinity. About marriage and control, see Lyndal Roper, *The Holy Household: Women and Morals in Reformation Europe* (Oxford: Clarendon, 1989), 133–64.

[11] Hans-Jürgen Bachorski calls Luther's work on marriage a "programmatic topic or theme" (programmatisches Thema), in "Diskursfeld Ehe: Schreibweisen und thema-

tische Setzungen," in *Ordnung und Lust: Bilder von Liebe, Ehe und Sexualität in Spätmittelalter und Früher Neuzeit,* ed. Hans-Jürgen Bachorski (Trier: Wissenschaftlicher Verlag, 1991), 520–21. Marriage according to Luther is initially regarded as the way for the common man to avoid a life lived in sin if he or she is unable to live in chastity, but towards the end of his life Luther increasingly stresses marriage as the only way for man and woman to live: Martin Luther, *Vom ehelichen Leben und andere Schriften über die Ehe,* ed. Dagmar Lorenz (Stuttgart: RUB, 1978). See also Steven Ozment, *When Fathers Ruled: Family Life in Reformation Europe* (Cambridge, MA: Harvard UP, 1983); Michael Dallapiazza, *Minne, Husere und das Ehelich Leben: Zur Konstitution bürgerlicher Lebensmuster in spätmittelalterlichen und frühhumanistischen Didaktiken* (Frankfurt am Main: Lang, 1981); Maria E. Müller, *Eheglück und Liebesjoch: Bilder von Liebe, Ehe und Familie in der Deutschen Literatur des 15. und 16. Jahrhunderts,* ed. Maria E. Müller (Weinheim: Beltz, 1988); and Joel F. Harrington, *Reordering Marriage and Society in Reformation Germany* (Cambridge: Cambridge UP, 1995).

[12] ". . . what in the world would make me happier than seeing my dear daughters come happily into matrimony, but some things are impossible for me, poor widow, to carry out," 64–65.

[13] Freidbert says: "wo er wußt eine / bey welchern er in friden und freüden laben mocht / wolt er sich darin begeben / wo er aber des in sorgen ston solt / wolt er eh von der freyheit in welchern er jetzunder wer nit abtretten / und vil lieber einer guten und tugentsammen frawen manglen / dann mit einer wunderlichen zenkischen hauß halten" (if he knew of one with whom he might live in peace and happiness, then he would agree to marriage but he would rather not give up his present freedom and would rather live without a good and virtuous wife than to have a household with a strange shrew, 61).

[14] "Darzu wußt er wol / das alles menschlich geschlecht zu leiden erboren / dieweil es dann je gelitten mußt sein / wolt er sich mit gedult darin begeben / geriet es im dann nach dem besten / so het er Gott des mehr zu dancken" (He is also aware that all human beings were born to suffer and since there will always have to be suffering, he will endure it patiently. If things would then turn out for the best he would have to be the more grateful to God, 61).

[15] Armin Schulz in his study of Wickram's *Goldtfaden* refers to "love" as the medium that makes it possible for people to rise in society. This advancement is, however, available only to men. Women of noble birth marry non-noble but virtuous men in Wickram's texts but noble men do not marry women of lesser birth: Armin Schulz, "Texte und Textilien. Zur Entstehung der Liebe in Georg Wickrams *Goldtfaden* (1557)," *Daphnis* 30, no. 1–2 (2001): 53. Cf. Stephan Pastenaci, "Tragischer Liebestod versus sozialer Aufstieg in Georg Wickrams Prosaromanen *Gabriotto und Reinhard* und *Der Goldfaden* — Zwei Verlaufsvarianten einer Novelle von Boccaccio," *Wolfenbüttler Renaissance-Mitteilungen* 19, no. 2 (1995): 49–58.

[16] Their weddings must be seen in sharp contrast to Wilbald's life at the same time. They reach the first peak of their careers, while Wilbald can be found at the very bottom of society.

[17] In *Knaben Spiegel* the glamorous weddings of Felix and Friedbert only further stress the destructive life of Wilbald (70–74). Wilbald's own wedding is less glamor-

ous (113–16). The weddings are in themselves never given much attention in Wickram's work, maybe a result of the increasing restrictions surrounding wedding festivities in German towns and cities in the sixteenth century. Modesty is often stressed in Wickram's work; in *Galmy* the wedding between Galmy and the duchess is only mentioned briefly towards the end of the book as a reward for Galmy's virtue: *Wickram: Sämtliche Werke*, vol. 1, *Ritter Galmy* (Berlin: De Gruyter, 1967), 226. The weddings in *Nachbarn* are quiet celebrations that give emphasis to the modest and virtuous lives of the protagonists — maybe as a response to the excessive lifestyle often ascribed to the nobility and the patricians (40–45 and 174–78): *Wickram: Sämtliche Werke*, vol. 4, *Von guten und bösen Nachbarn* (Berlin: Walter de Gruyter, 1969).

[18] This corresponds with Volker Mertens's discussion of Wickram's *Goldtfaden*. Mertens finds it conspicuous that sexuality is completely suppressed in Wickram's work; it is mentioned neither as a positive nor as a negative factor as is the case in other early modern texts like *Melusine* or *Magelona:* "Aspekte der Liebe: Ihre Semantik in den Prosaromanen Tristrant, Melusine, Magelone und Goldfaden," in *Personenbeziehungen in der Mittelalterlichen Literatur*, ed. Helmut Brall, Barbara Haupt and Urban Küsters (Düsseldorf: Droste, 1994), 132.

[19] Cf. Dyan Elliott, *Fallen Bodies: Pollution, Sexuality, and Demonology in the Middle Ages* (Philadelphia: U of Pennsylvania P, 1999). "Perhaps the most compelling measure of the persistence of the pollution beliefs associated with women's physiology was the continued effort to separate the Virgin Mary from all such sources of contamination. The Virgin was widely believed to have been spared not only the pain of parturition but also the polluting effects of childbirth." Elliott uses a psychoanalytic concept in his study of men's and women's bodies, sexuality and demonology in the Middle Ages.

[20] Schulz ("Texte und Textilien") comes to the same conclusion in regard to sexuality in many sixteenth-century prose texts. Schulz sees the lack of explicit sexuality in those texts — as opposed to medieval love epics — as a result of a stronger emphasis on discipline and moral in the sixteenth-century society, thus referring to external forces that make for a change in literature. This conclusion, however, makes it hard to explain the very graphic depictions of human sexuality found in the chapbooks and other texts from the same time. The problem needs to be explained by means of tradition and genre and is more complex than Schulz suggests in his otherwise very interesting article on the "love" as a semiotic process in the *Goldtfaden*.

[21] Wickram writes: "musten alzeit schone Frawen und Seytenspeyl bey ihn sein" (he had to have beautiful women and music around him at all times, 39); "ja ich meyn in Wirtzheüsern / mit würffel / karten / wein und beir / auch mit schonen Frauwen . . ." (yes, I mean in taverns, with dice, cards, wine, and beer and also with beautiful women, 61). Cf. 49.

[22] On parenthood in the fourteenth and fifteenth centuries, see Claudia Opitz, "Mutterschaft und Vaterschaft in 14. und 15. Jahrhundert," in *Frauengeschichte — Geschlechtergeschichte*, ed. Karin Hausen and Heide Wunder (Frankfurt/New York: Campus, 1992), 137–53. Opitz discusses the role of the mother in Germany before the Reformation. Her duties were much the same as in later centuries and often left little time for the children, since many wives and mothers worked in the family shops

or otherwise were preoccupied with the household. Childrearing was thus far from the only obligation assigned to the woman.

[23] Eva Labouvie's research on pregnancy in the early modern period shows the importance of childbearing and the rituals surrounding the pregnant woman. Labouvie focuses on the rural areas of Germany, but it is evident that much of women's lives was centered around pregnancy and birth and that married women who did not give birth were excluded from many rituals and were thus outsiders in the community just as the unmarried women who had illegitimate children were: *Andere Umstände. Eine Kulturgeschichte der Geburt* (Cologne: Böhlau, 1998). The great effort put on helping the pregnant (married) woman, on having a network of women surround her, left the childless woman alone. At a time when children were needed for work and often regarded as securing the lives of aging parents, the childless couple was left with nothing. Heide Wunder states: "Women of early modern society did not share modern women's interest in contraception. Their concern, rather, was barrenness, which was seen as divine punishment or, at the very least, as a severe test. Women left nothing untried to escape the blemish of childlessness: they underwent treatment prescribed by physicians, went on lengthy journeys to baths, undertook pilgrimages to miracle-working pictures of saints, and did not even shrink from magic": *He Is the Sun, She Is the Moon: Women in Early Modern Germany* (Cambridge: Harvard UP, 1998), 119.

[24] The belief that the human being was composed of wet, dry, cold, and warm humors goes back to antiquity and was the object of study among many scholars of the sixteenth century. Cf. "In keeping with the theory of the humors, physicians of this era recommended a different diet for men and women. Man was seen as warm and dry, woman as moist and cold" (Wunder, *He Is the Sun, She Is the Moon*, 39–40).

[25] For different types of marriage, see Merry Wiesner, *Gender, Church and State in Early Modern Germany* (Harlow: Longman, 1998), 86–87. Wiesner there discusses the growing restrictions for women in financial matters.

[26] See, for instance, 16, 21, 29, and 33.

[27] Gottlieb discusses the education of Friedbert and Wilbald with his wife (13) and he immediately tells her about his feelings when asked (25). She may protect her son but she is nevertheless concerned when seeing her husband sad. This is not to be followed as easily in the later marriages where perfection is reached at the moment of the wedding and everyone lives together happily ever after (74, 118–19).

[28] In another story by Wickram, *Gabriotto und Reinhart*, a similar situation is described as in Montanus's text, but Wickram's story focuses more on family life in general, and the men and women who die are the most virtuous young people. In Wickram's work the king obviously is at fault, whereas in Montanus's story the father has to kill the lover in order to control the daughter.

[29] "Everyone had to learn to work in accordance with what was given to them by God. The daughter was first taught to spin by her mother, then to sew, to knit, and to weave so that she would know well that idleness leads to no good," 119.

[30] The tendency to regard Wickram's work as a mirror of sixteenth-century society is mainly found in scholarly work from the former GDR. See for instance Hans Jürgen Geerdts, "Das Erwachen des bürgerlichen Klassenbewusstseins in den Romanen Jörg

Wickrams," *Wissenschaftliche Zeitschrift der Friedrich-Schiller-Universität Jena* 2 (1952–53): 117–24; Wolfgang Friedrich, "Bemerkungen zu den Romanen Georg Wickrams," *Wissenschaftliche Zeitschrift der Martin-Luther-Universität Halle-Wittenberg. Gesellschafts- und Sprachwissenschaftliche Reihe* 10, no. 4 (1961): 1037–42; Ingeborg Spriewald, "Jörg Wickram und die Anfänge der realistischen Prosaerzählung in Deutschland" (Ph.D. diss., Potsdam, 1971); Ingeborg Spriewald, *Vom Eulenspiegel zum Simplicissimus. Zur Genesis des Realismus in den Anfängen der deutschen Prosaerzählung* (Berlin: Akademie-Verlag, 1974); and Hannelore Christ, *Literarischer Text und historische Realität. Versuch einer historisch-materialistischen Analyse von Jörg Wickrams Knabenspiegel- und Nachbarn-Roman* (Düsseldorf: Bertelsmann, 1974).

[31] There are a number of publications on the cultural setting of early modern Germany, most of them in German; see among others the three volumes by Richard van Dülmen on everyday life: *Kultur und Alltag in der Frühen Neuzeit: Erster Band — das Haus und seine Menschen 16.–18. Jahrhundert* (Munich: C. H. Beck, 1999); *Kultur und Alltag in der Frühen Neuzeit: Zweiter Band — Dorf und Stadt 16.–18. Jahrhundert* (Munich: C. H. Beck, 1999); and *Kultur und Alltag in der Frühen Neuzeit: Dritter Band — Religion, Magie, Aufklärung 16.–18. Jahrhundert* (Munich: C. H. Beck, 1999). Also see Robert W. Scribner's work on early modern popular culture, *Popular Culture and Popular Movements in Reformation Germany* (London: Hambledon, 1987). On the Swiss territories, see E. William Monter, *Enforcing Morality in Early Modern Europe* (London: Variorum, 1987). On the role of women in society see Sherrin Marshall, ed., *Women in Reformation and Counter-Reformation Europe: Public and Private Worlds* (Bloomington: Indiana UP, 1989); Merry Wiesner, *Working Women in Renaissance Germany* (New Brunswick, NJ: Rutgers UP, 1986); Roper, *The Holy Household;*, and Wunder, *He Is the Sun, She Is the Moon*.

[32] It can be argued that their feelings seem very rational and correct and that the decisions are characterized by reason rather than by love. The men always fall in love with women who will contribute to increased wealth and extended family ties. There is no tension between emotions and rational thinking but the text nevertheless stresses love between spouses as most important.

[33] "I would, however, like to ask the mother and the daughter, so that there will be no mistake, and I also do not want to force her (the daughter) to marry a young man or a widower, whom she does not want against her will," 36.

[34] "I would be sorry of all my heart if I would marry your daughter or another against her will. What good times would we have together?" 36.

[35] Robertus emphasizes the importance of love by expressing the danger of marrying in order to gain wealth and power: "Ich bin einmal des vorhabens / ir keinen man zu geben / sie habe dann ein lust zu im / und wann er gleich eines Fürsten gut hette / und vermocht" (I have decided not to give her to any man unless she wants him, not even if he had land and wealth like a prince, 38).

[36] Schulz ("Texte und Textilien," 66) concludes that the knowledge of being loved is enough for love to arise in the other person. A couple thus does not have to meet. One person just has to make sure that his or her object of desire finds out about the feelings in order to encounter the love as expressed in words.

[37] Emberson, "Of Good and Bad Neighbors," 544.

[38] For the following discussion, see also Maria E. Müller, "Naturwesen Mann," in *Wandel der Geschlechterbeziehungen zu Beginn der Neuzeit,* ed. Heide Wunder and Christina Vanja (Frankfurt am Main: Suhrkamp, 1991). See pages 44 and 50. Cf. Sigrid Brauner, "Gender and its Subversion: Reflections on Literary Ideals of Marriage," in *The Graph of Sex and the German Text: Gendered Culture in Early Modern Germany 1500–1700,* ed. Lynne Tatlock (Amsterdam: Rodopi, 1994), 179–200. Brauner sees a clear connection between the stress on complementary gender roles and the need among the urban male elite to define a new identity, because of changing living conditions.

[39] There are growing numbers of scholars researching the dichotomy public-private and the position of women in the early modern society. Here I can only recommend a few studies: Barbara Becker-Cantarino, "Vom 'Ganzen Haus' zur Familieidylle. Haushalt als Mikrokosmos in der Literatur der Frühen Neuzeit und seine spätere Sentimentalisierung," *Daphnis* 15 (1986): 509–33; Karin Hausen, "Öffentlichkeit und Privatheit: Gesellschaftspolitische Konstruktionen und die Geschichte der Geschlechterbeziehungen," in *Frauengeschichte — Geschlechtergeschichte,* ed. Karin Hausen and Heide Wunder (Frankfurt/New York: Campus, 1992), 81–88; Labouvie, *Andere Umstände;* Dagmar Lorenz, "Vom Kloster zur Kirche: Die Frau vor und nach der Reformation Dr Martin Luthers," in *Die Frau von der Reformation zur Romantik,* ed. Barbara Becker-Cantarino (Bonn: Bouvier Verlag Herbert Grundmann, 1980), 7–35; Ozment, *When Fathers Ruled;* Steven Ozment, *Flesh and Spirit: Private Life in Early Modern Germany* (New York: Viking, 1999); Roper, *The Holy Household;* Wiesner, *Working Women;* Merry Wiesner, *Women and Gender in Early Modern Europe* (Cambridge: Cambridge UP, 1993); Wiesner, *Gender, Church and State;* Joy Wiltenburg, *Disorderly Women and Female Power in the Street Literature of Early Modern England and Germany* (Charlottesville, VA: UP of Virginia, 1992); Wunder, *He Is the Sun, She Is the Moon.* For an interesting study of early modern England, see Susan D. Amussen, *An Ordered Society: Gender and Class in Early Modern England* (New York: Columbia UP, 1988).

[40] Cf. Becker-Cantarino, "Vom 'Ganzen Haus' zur Familieidylle."

[41] "Niemand käme auf die Idee, die Privatschaft nicht der Öffentlichkeit zuzurechnen, doch ebenso selbstverständlich denken wir bei Privathaushalt nur an Privatheit" (Nobody would think of not regarding the private sphere as part of the public one. Still we associate a private household only with the private): Gisela Bock, "Frauenräume und Frauenehre. Frühneuzeitliche Armenfürsorge in Italien," in *Frauengeschichte — Geschlechtergeschichte,* ed. Karin Hausen and Heide Wunder (Frankfurt am Main, New York: Campus, 1992), 23. See also: Hausen, "Öffentlichkeit und Privatheit," 82.

[42] See Müller, "Naturwesen Mann," and Brauner, "Gender and its Subversion."

[43] See Wiesner, *Gender, Church and State,* 78. Wiesner here discusses the importance of social standing in connection with gender.

[44] Jane Emberson has commented on the isolated situation of the wives in *Von guten und bösen Nachbarn* ("Of Good and Bad Neighbors, esp. 543). Even though I elsewhere have disagreed with her on Wickram's confessional status, her comments

on the women in *Von guten und bösen Nachbarn* are noteworthy. See also Roper, *The Holy Household,* 46, and the introduction to Karin Hausen and Heide Wunder, "Frauengeschichte — Geschlechtergeschichte: Einleitung," in *Frauengeschichte — Geschlechtergeschichte,* ed. Karin Hausen and Heide Wunder (Frankfurt/New York: Campus, 1992), 15: "Denn auch Frauen verließen schon immer täglich den durch die Schwelle des Hauses markierten Innenraum der Privatheit, um in der Öffentlichkeit des kirchlichen Gemeindelebens, der wohltätigkeit oder der kulturellen Veranstaltungen mitzuwirken" (For women also left the inner room of privacy — marked by a threshold — every day in order to partake in the public activities of religious community life, charity, or cultural events).

[45] The only exception I have found is when Lasarus sets off for Antwerp and everyone sees him off at the harbor (118).

[46] The first chapter of *Nachbarn* gives a graphic description of the neighbors, 11–16.

[47] Merry Wiesner-Hanks has published extensively on women and work in the early modern period. See for example *Working Women* and *Women and Gender;* see also Roper, *The Holy Household.* Heide Wunder has written a very interesting and brief comment on gender specific work and the values attached to various occupations in an article entitled "'Jede Arbeit ist ihres Lohnes Wert.' Zur geschlechtsspezifischen Teilung und Bewertung von Arbeit in der Frühen Neuzeit," republished in Heide Wunder, *Der andere Blick auf die Frühe Neuzeit: Forschungen 1974–1995,* ed. Barbara Hoffmann, et al. (Königstein/Taunus: Ulrike Helmer Verlag, 1999), 170–86.

[48] This is to be compared with Schulz's statement that Lewfrid and Angliana in *Goldtfaden* never make anything out of their relationship until it is legitimized through marriage. They only assure each other eternal love; they only use language to express desire. Rarely do lovers touch each other (Schulz, "Texte und Textilien," 67. Cf. 69, 70).

[49] See Irmela von der Lühe's article on the letters in *Nachbarn,* "Wolan, Hin ist Hin: Brief und Exemplum in Wickrams 'Nachbarn-Roman,'" in *Erzählungen in Erzählungen: Phänomene der Narration in Mittelalter und Früher Neuzeit,* ed. Harald Haferland and Michael Mecklenburg (Munich: Wilhelm Fink, 1996), 411–23. Lühe comments on the letter Lasarus writes to Amelia before his departure to foreign countries and claims that it is central to the didactic concept of the book — the preservation of order and harmony. This point is important, since the letter, first, is the reason for Amelia's anger with Lasarus when he leaves without talking to her, then it works for consclidation, and in the end it strengthens the ties between the lovers and points toward their future as a married couple.

[50] Far fewer women than men were able to write in the sixteenth century, but Charlotte Woodford has pointed out that the number of writing women was growing and that they consciously used letter writing to communicate matters of importance to them: "'Es werd nu wol zeit, das si wartet. Was einem frumen ee Weib zu Stund.' Women's Letters from the Reformation," *Daphnis* 30, no. 1–2 (2001): 37–52. See also Barbara Becker-Cantarino on the literacy of women at the time of the Reformation, "Renaissance oder Reformation? Epochenschwellen für schreibende Frauen und die Mittlere Deutsche Literatur," in *Das Berliner Modell der Mittleren Deutschen Literatur: Beiträge zur Tagung Kloster Zinna 29.9.–01.10.1997,* ed. Christiane Caemmerer, et al. (Amsterdam: Rodopi, 2000), 69–87, and Miriam Usher Chrisman

on print culture in Strasbourg, *Lay Culture, Learned Culture: Books and Social Change in Strasbourg 1480–1599* (New Haven: Yale UP, 1982).

[51] Peter Frei has found an interesting correspondence between character and room or space in Wickram's *Goldtfaden* that indicates a growing need of privacy and causes tensions between the general and individual: "Das Zufallen der Türen, der Zufall: Raumdarstellung in Jörg Wickrmas Goldfaden," in *Text im Kontext: Anleitung zur Lektüre deutscher Texte der Frühen Neuzeit,* ed. Alexander Schwarz and Laure Abplanalp (Bern: Peter Lang, 1997), 69–78. The brevity of the article does not allow a discussion of other texts by Wickram, but similar situations can be found in *Nachbarn*. Amelia is first overheard by her father and later witnesses a conversation between her father and Lasarus. The characters look for privacy, for a space reserved for the invited, while at the same time aware of the importance of openness and the dangers of secrecy. The private room is at the same time desired and feared, closed off and open. The behavior of Amelia's father makes clear that he feels uncomfortable with the thought of having heard something not intended to be heard by anyone. He can only be excused for having heard his daughter speak to herself because she has opened windows and doors to let the clear morning air into her room (89). This in turn shows the vulnerability of privacy. The danger of being heard is great when space is limited. See Frei, "Das Zufallen der Türen," 72.

[52] "So wollend wir unser speys / . . . / mit uns tragen / unsere magt mit uns furen / damit sie nit hiezwischen etwan ein rumor anfangen / in unserem abwesen" (So we will carry our food with us and bring our maids so that no rumor is started in our absence, 132).

[53] The passage discussed here stretches over pages 128–39. On women and citizenship, see Wiesner, *Gender, Church and State,* 114–25.

[54] "Oh my daughter, just as it ill suits a woman to receive company in the absence of her husband, it is just as inappropriate for a woman in her husband's absence to leave her house to visit someone. . . . therefore it is more proper for me, oh dear daughter, to stay at home and take care of my house," 131.

[55] "Es aber / liebe muter / hat ein andre gestalt / umb dich unnd dein liebe und getrewe Lucia / dieweil ir so liebe nachbeurin und von wegen ewer grossen liebe und trew / wol schwestern genant mügen werden" (But dear mother / that which you and your dear and faithful Lucia have / is something different. / Since you are such dear neighbors and because of your great love and fidelity / you might be called sisters, 131). For a discussion of spiritual kinship, see Maurice Aymard, "Friends and Neighbors," in *A History of Private Life: Passions of the Renaissance,* vol. 3, ed. Roger Chartier (Cambridge: Belkamp Press, 1989), 466. Aymard refers to anthropological terminology, using spiritual kinship for relationships modeled on the family. Pia Holenstein in her study of Fischart's *Geschichtklitterung* talks of the use of "Freundschaft" (friendship) and "Verwandtshaft" (kinship) as synonymous until the sixteenth century: *Der Ehediskurs der Renaissance in Fischarts Geschichtklitterung: Kritische Lektüre des fünften Kapitels* (Bern: Peter Lang, 1991), 138–41. Wickram makes a clear distinction between the words in *Nachbarn* but the intention is to incorporate friends with the family through marriage and thus to transfer "friends" to "family."

[56] "Ich gehe davon aus, daß die weibliche Ehre am Körper oder besser am Gebrauch der Körper von Frauen durch Männer festgemacht wurde, daß also Sexualität von

unverheirateten und verheirateten Frauen zusammenhing" (I assume that the female honor connected to the body, or rather to the usage of the body, was determined by men, and that the sexuality of married and [that of] unmarried women were connected): Susanna Burghartz, "Rechte Jungfrauen oder Unverschämte Töchter? Zur weiblichen Ehre in 16. Jahrhundert," in *Frauengeschichte — Geschlechtergeschichte,* ed. Karin Hausen and Heide Wunder (Frankfurt/New York: Campus, 1992), 174.

[57] A psychoanalytic study of the female characters in *Nachbarn* has to my knowledge not yet been published, but the door between the two families and the single door to the outside community are details that might benefit from psychoanalytic methods.

[58] Some of many well-known examples are Albrecht von Eyb's very popular *Ehebüchlein* (Little Book on Marriage, 1472), Hans Sachs's *Das künstlich frawen-lob* (The Artistic Praise of Women, 1562), and Johann Fischart's *Das philosophisch Ehezuchtbüchlein* (Philosophical Treatise on Marital Discipline, 1578).

[59] The rape of Lucretia as told by Livy, *History of Rome,* book 1.57–60. Livy's history of ancient Rome — a mix of historical and mythological characters and events — holds a number of portrayals of women to illustrate different sides of what is considered female virtue and vice. Cf. Lühe, "Hin ist Hin," 416–21.

[60] See Heide Wunder, "Geschlechtsidentitäten: Frauen und Männer im Späten Mittelalter und am Beginn der Neuzeit," in *Frauengeschichte — Geschlechtergeschichte,* ed. Karin Hausen and Heide Wunder (Frankfurt/New York: Campus, 1992), 52, and Burghartz, "Rechte Jungfrauen oder unverschämte Töchter?" 173.

[61] Cf. Lühe, "Hin ist Hin," 421.

[62] Erika Rummel has edited an excellent edition with texts by Erasmus that present his view of women: *Erasmus on Women* (Toronto: U of Toronto P, 1996).

[63] For more on this, see Wåghäll, *Dargestellte Welt — Reale Welt,* 55–79.

[64] Wickram mentions this in the preface of the *Knaben Spiegel* and discusses it in length in the text *Eine Wahrhafftige History von einem ungerathenen Son in ein Dialogum gestellet* (A True Story of a Prodigal Son Presented in a Dialogue, 1554 or 1555).

[65] On the dichotomy Mary-Eve, see Lorenz, "Vom Kloster zur Kirche."

Illustrations from Fischart's *Geschichtklitterung*.

3: Woman, Wife, Witch?: The Representation of Woman in Johann Fischart's *Geschichtklitterung*

> Vnnd welche Salomon in seinen Gleichnussen vnd Parabolen nennt das Weib: Da er sagt/ daß keine Bosheit vber eines Weibs Bosheit seie: Vnd bißweilen nennt ers ein Hure/ die alle Männer annimmet/ als die Matery aller formen/ . . . .[1]

THE IMAGE OF THE WOMAN as an evil creature — wet and slippery and hence difficult to grasp — meets the reader of Johann Fischart's German translation (1581, 1586) of Jean Bodin's *De Démonomanie des sorciers* (1580), a well-known witch tract of its time.[2] Expressing the common fears that men have of women, the text is in no way unusual for a time when many women were prosecuted and sentenced to death for what was considered witchcraft and the use of evil powers. Having studied law Fischart certainly was familiar with witch trials as well as family feuds, prostitution, and other cases that brought women before court. But it has not been possible to find arguments in his own texts or other documents that explain why he chose to translate a misogynist text in the tradition of Heinrich Institoris's *Malleus maleficarum* (1486) and to publish a new edition of the infamous *Hexenhammer* (Hammer of Witches, 1582).[3] A strong believer in the Reformation, he also engaged in transmitting the ideas of the reformers in his writings. His *Philosophisch Ehezuchtbüchlein* (Philosophical Treatise on Marital Discipline, 1578) is one of many marriage tracts of the time, based on ancient and medieval texts and published to emphasize the importance of marriage for humanity. Oscillating between fear, hatred, and songs of praise Fischart thus does not differ from his contemporaries in his ambiguous attitude towards women, on the one hand calling attention to their disposition to witchcraft and magic, on the other hand stressing their importance as the companion to man within marriage. It is therefore not surprising that a person like Fischart who published a great number of texts chooses to take different standpoints in various genres, even though his decision to translate and publish witch tracts might appear dubious to the modern reader.[4] Also, when he employs comical effects, as in *Flöh,*

Hatz, Weiber Tratz (Hunting of Fleas, Defiance of Women, 1573), the female sex takes a central role as a creature of evil. The text is an adaptation — possibly of a text by Mathias Holtzwart — but Fischart feels no obligations towards the original.

The comical turns into the grotesque in the *Geschichtklitterung,* a translation and adaptation of François Rabelais's *Gargantua* where Fischart once again uses an existing text for his own purposes.[5] An abiding interest in women, especially in their position as opposites to a predefined man whose own position never seems questioned — not even when threatened — thus characterizes a number of texts by Fischart. His close ties to the prosecution of witches puts him in a position quite different from the other authors discussed here.[6] He is a learned man, fluent in several languages that give him access to foreign people and cultures. Fischart published his texts about twenty to thirty years later than Frey, Montanus, and Wickram, when the reform movements had given way to consolidation, the Counter-Reformation had brought Catholicism back to some areas in Germany, and the witch-hunts were a grim reality in many parts of Europe. The variety and diversity of Fischart's work make it impossible to even attempt a comprehensive study of the role women take in his texts — as agents of the plot or as the object of discussion.[7] My attention will therefore be centered on the fifth chapter in one of his most complex works, the *Geschichtklitterung,* Entitled "Mit was wichtigem bedencken unser Held Grandgauchier zu der Ehe hab gegriffen und sich nicht vergriffen" (With What Important Reflections Our Hero Grandgauchier Decided to Marry), it is a chapter on marriage Fischart has added to his translation of Rabelais's book.[8] Focused on the importance of marriage to man, it contains imponderable statements on the role of woman in general and the role of the wife within marriage in particular. I have chosen this text because it shows the disparity and ambiguity inherent in Fischart's work in its concept of "woman." This makes it an interesting but highly difficult text when looking for possible changes in the discourses of sexuality, marriage, and family life and their significance for the shaping of "woman."

It is beyond the scope of my study to involve myself in the discussions that have been carried out among scholars on language and style in Fischart's work.[9] The phonological, morphological, and etymological experiments on the one hand deter the scholar of literature from investigating the text because of its linguistic complexity; on the other hand they challenge the curiosity to search for some kind of inner logic or structure, since coherence is not a word one generally associates with the *Geschichtklitterung.* The seemingly free association of words hides jumps and bumps and makes sentences end in contradictions and dichotomies that say the opposite to what the reader has expected. It is almost impossible to tell if Fischart is serious or joking; the reader feels fooled no matter what interpretation is chosen. Seemingly serious statements are followed by words or sentences that make the reader doubt every word said so far in the text. A study of the *Geschichtklitterung* can thus never be anything but a play on Fischart's terms and an attempt to find reason in chaos. Despite the risk of falling prey to relativity I would claim that this is what makes his work especially interesting when investigating the position of woman in the text. The *Geschichtklitterung* takes twists and turns that other texts do not dare, and it says what many times remains unspoken,[10] yet without completely transgressing conventional norms.[11]

The text with its hyperbolic construction of words and endless paratactic sentences, its stylistic complexity and allusions to ancient mythology, history, literature, and philosophy, is a discourse on marriage and gender relations.[12] Already the title of the chapter — "Mit was wichtigem bedencken unser Held Grandgauchier zu der Ehe hab gegriffen und sich nicht vergriffen" — indicates an impossible mission, a desire to confront the reader with a topic as vast as the size of the main characters: how to find the right spouse. It tells of how the protagonist Grandgauchier is able to marry successfully and to avoid marrying the wrong wife due to his wisdom.[13] The discussion that follows in Fischart's text is a vivid example of the complexity of human relationships and the different approaches found within the discourses of marriage, sexuality, and family life at the end of the sixteenth century. Like most other texts on marriage Fishart's focuses on men and women of the urban middle class who are wealthy enough to have servants but not so wealthy that they do not partake in the daily work of the household. The text gives copious examples of good and bad behavior, of historic, mythological, and literary figures that have been victims of their own desire and thus have been incapable of controlling their instinct.[14]

Focused on the significance of women in a world inhabited by eccentric giants, Fischart in his fifth chapter writes on the characteristics of women and their "natural" attachment to men:

> Wie solt Weibern solch natürliche geschicklichkeit dem man zu dienen, . . ., umbsonst zugestanden sein? warumb wer sie also plöd geschaffen, ohn daß sie sterckeren zusatz und beistand bei dem man het zuerheben unnd zusuchen?[15]

The mental and physiological weakness of woman is the argument for her as a natural companion to man. She is made frail in order to serve him in exchange for protection. The logic behind the argument is clear to the reader; a strong woman is a contradiction in herself. She has to be weak in order to be a woman. The weakness thus appears as a necessary defect. The perfect human being is a man "by nature." Only he is strong and capable of protecting others. The topic no doubt was dear to Fischart, and by letting Rabelais's text "host" a plea for marriage he could treat it with great freedom by letting giants take the part of husband and wife. It is, however, noteworthy that the narrator seems to change pace when coming to what commonly has been called the "praise of marriage" (Ehelob).[16] Some of the sentences are shorter, the accumulation of words, phrases, and examples at times less extensive, just to be followed by yet another digression. This starts with Grandgauchier's decision to take a wife, but the narrator cannot deter himself from regular excursions in the world of literature (89). He has a hard time resisting long chains of examples, but he returns to his main topic — the value of marriage and family life to the man and hence the value of forming the wife in accordance with male desires.[17] The fifth chapter has been considered more serious than other chapters of the book,[18] but I would suggest that it is a matter of content; the substance of what is being told being more important than the telling itself. A "message" is transmitted to the reader more overtly than can be found in long passages of pure digression — they may be the accumulation of examples or a simple play with words. It is thus not so much the seriousness of the topic in chapter five as the greater emphasis on content that gives parts of the text a slightly more coherent appearance. This can be seen in correspondence with the perception of literature in the later part of the sixteenth century as has been suggested by Josef K. Glowa:

> The novel's primary concern now is with language and the narrative process rather than its message. This becomes evident when Fischart's novel is compared with the works of the other best-known sixteenth-century German prose author Jörg Wickram, whose novels are still strongly indebted to the tradition of didactic literature.[19]

Fischart was about forty years younger than Wickram, which makes for several differences in their work, but the didactic aspect is in no way absent in the *Geschichtklitterung*.[20] It may be more subtle and expressed by means of examples that are more ambiguous to the reader than the straightforwardness in many of Wickram's texts, but the *Geschichtklitterung* has not yet arrived at the point of the modern novel. There is, however, a great difference in narrative complexity between Wickram and

Fischart, showing the disparity in education and artistic ability as well as a later date of publication for Fischart's texts.[21]

It is unlikely that Fischart's work reached a large audience, considering the complexity of the text and the limited number of educated readers, but it was published in three different editions within fifteen years, each time with additions by Fischart that make Rabelais's original appear brief.[22] Fischart would most likely have chosen a different type of text had he wanted to write on marriage for a more general public. The conclusion to be drawn from this is that the *Geschichtklitterung* had mostly male readers when it was published but that the choice to write in the vernacular did not limit the text to learned academics.[23] Clearly turning to male readers Fischart states: "Kurtzumb wer kein Ehgesibete hat, ist halb tod" (whoever has no wife is half dead, 95). He shows no sign of wanting to address women and this could be an explanation for his moralizing comments regarding male sexuality and the relative lack of such comments in regard to women.[24] The fifth chapter is concerned with the importance of marriage from a male perspective. The narrator tells of women in their role as complementing men but addresses only Grandgauchier and other men. "Woman" is thus not understood as a reader of this book; she is part of what men talk of, someone they want to shape and own in order to control. The woman is hence merely of interest in her relationship to man. Male behavior is at stake, not female.[25] The text, being primarily interested in the construction of "man" in his role as husband and father, offers a clear contrast to most of Wickram's work, where marriage is described as an essential issue to men as well as to women, and thus where women are important as part of the readership as well as (characters that are) part of the plot.

The omnipresent narrator in the *Geschichtklitterung* does not take his eyes off the male protagonist in chapter five. He makes sure that Grandgauchier is presented with all negative aspects attached to life outside of marriage as well as with adultery, bigamy, and polygamy. He is not given a chance to choose a life in sin. Women are here only presented as the object of study, as a necessity for the husband to run the household properly, to be taken care of, and to give him offspring. This object is given a face and a body in the sixth chapter but only insofar as the reader is told what Grandgauchier does with his wife and how she reacts; she is described as swelling, a sign of the pregnancy that is the outcome of intercourse (109). Reading the text this way, female agency is reduced to passive reception, the female body to a container of male semen. "Woman" is at the center of discourse only in her complementary role to "man"; the fifth chapter discusses sexuality (sexual intercourse), marriage (to legalize intercourse), and family life (the result of legal intercourse, pregnancy and childbirth) in regard to "man." The aim is to find a way for "man" to claim his position and to gain control over what is essential for humankind: procreation. It would, however, be misleading to treat the text as misogynous in all parts and aspects. The *Geschichtklitterung* is more complex than that; it holds brief passages that point out female resistance to male dominance and it presents examples of male behavior at its worst, as will be seen below.[26]

Fischart — like many of his contemporaries writing on marriage — makes use of opposites when presenting marriage as the best and most natural way for men and women to arrange their lives. On the one hand the reader is bombarded with arguments concerning the importance of married versus unmarried life, fidelity and chastity versus adultery and sodomy, procreation and the importance of a family and good neighbors versus celibacy and other forms of life deviating from marriage, if marriage is defined as a heterosexual relationship sanctioned by the Catholic and reformed churches and secular law. On the other hand Grandgauchier seems to navigate straight ahead, circumventing all dangers and temptations, in his search for the perfect wife — personified by the equally enormous Gurgelmilta.[27] The necessity of marriage is made evident by turning norms upside down and depicting the dangers and problems surrounding physical and verbal contact with the other sex from the perspective of a man.[28] It would be dangerous to focus solely on misogynous images of women in this context; it would discourage the reader instead of encourage him. Instead of depicting a dichotomous relationship between man and woman built on female vice and male bravery, the text stresses the incompleteness of both man and woman and the complimentary roles assigned to them "by nature." The family is depicted as the smallest unit forming society and the foundation for its growth:

> Dann durch zusamenwachsung, unnd vernachbaurung einer gantzen Freundschafft wird ein gaß besetzt, auß vielen gassen ein Flecken, auß eim Flecken ein Statt, auß Stätten ein Land: auß Landen ein Königreich und Keyserthumb, auß Keyserthummen die Welt, auß der Welt das Paradiß.[29]

This image of the family expanding from a few people to the whole world is opposite to the closed-off sphere found in *Nachbarn*, but the idea is the same: the family is the center of the universe and necessary for upholding law and order, and the head of the family is without question the man. Marriage thus saves mankind from evil but it is also perceived as the way for a man to found his own "Herrschaft" (domain, estate).[30]

Men and women are assigned different tasks within the boundaries of married life and they are of equal importance for the survival of the family, but the existence of the woman is justified to the reader by her connection to the man as his natural companion. Fischart makes any objection to his claim unnecessary by turning to nature and to the Bible — to Adam and Eve. Woman belongs to man; he is not complete without her and Fischart asserts: "In summa, wer sich mit keiner Ehgehülffin behilffet, ob er schon der reichste wer, hat er doch nichts das recht sein ist" (In sum, a man who does not take a wife has nothing that is really his, even if he were the richest of men, 96). It is possible to argue that Fischart in this text emphasizes the importance of the woman — that she is necessary for the survival of the man[31] — but her value is to be seen in correspondence with her ability or willingness to subordinate herself to the man. The woman belongs to the man, she is "das recht sein."

The result is that unmarried women do not seem conceivable to the narrator unless they are recognized as future wives; they are not real women. The accent put on men in this text — their behavior ranging from outrageous, sick, and crazy to good, excellent, and marvelous — overshadows the women and female behavior. The context makes clear that anything considered improper male behavior includes a woman of equal sort since bad behavior is almost exclusively related to sexuality, but these women are not categorized as married or unmarried. They are simply prostitutes — and Fischart has as many names for them as for their male counterparts — with no further right of recognition or right to claim a position among "real" women.[32] They are whores, mares (in heat), sirens, and much more, but their civilian status is unrecognized. They are women only insofar as they have heterosexual intercourse with men. Their sex or gender is otherwise irrelevant because of their status as evil. A "real" woman equals wife, a person emotionally and legally attached to her opposite, her "Herrscher" (ruler, sovereign), the man. A "real" man — personified in the giant Grandgauchier — is hence the opposite of wife; he is the married man, the husband. An unmarried man is almost a dead man (95), left alone without friends (97). This is where the strongly emphasized mutuality ends. Husband and wife according to Fischart seem to live in a relationship that is built on mutuality and dichotomy at the same time. Husband is opposite to wife and vice versa, but the husband is superior to the wife and in charge of all decisions.[33] This includes delegating the right to decide in certain matters as well as assigning household duties to the wife.

The man is thus no less sinful than the woman, but this is not the point in this book full of giants, indulging themselves in the joys of life. The point to be made is rather that the strong emphasis on companionship actually reduces the options for women to act on their own despite the respect and responsibility they are given within the household. This is best expressed in the representation of woman as a "HaußSchneck," a snail always carrying her home with her (105).[34] Praised for her virtue and diligence, she makes sure that the household is run according to the norms set by the husband. Even though it is stressed over and over again in the text that love between man and woman has to be reciprocal, as is expressed in the word "Gegenlieb" (104), it is also said about the woman that she legally belongs to her husband: "ist sie auch von Rechtswegen schuldig sein Kuchenlump zusein" (103). The text further emphasizes that the money a wife spends belongs to her husband: "alles auß des Manns Gelt" (all money is taken from the man, 104), which shows her legal and economic dependency on the man. The legal aspect is taken to its extreme when it is claimed that it is easy to live with a good man but a virtue to live with an evil one: "Dann es ist kein tugend, mit eim guten Mann außkommen, sonder eim Bösen" (100). A woman who is willing to submit herself to the rule of an evil man is thus the most virtuous according to the text. The strong emphasis on mutuality and "Gegenlieb," however, as well as the statement that a man should treat his wife as his "Haußkönigin" (queen of the household, 90) and share his table and bed with her, reveal the ambivalence and ambiguity in the *Geschichtklitterung*.[35] The mutuality stressed in the text remains theoretical since one part is subordinate to the other instead of being treated as an equal.

The "praise of marriage" may be central to the fifth chapter of the *Geschichtklitterung* but the problems involved in a relationship between man and woman are not withheld from the reader. Brief comments that negate the otherwise positive view of marriage interrupt the torrent of words and make the image of the wife and thus woman more complex while at the same time indicating obstacles that need to be dealt with within marriage. Grandgauchier marries a woman of whom the reader is told that she is his perfect compliment, she is all that he is not, she knows what he wants before he does himself, she helps him when he asks for help, keeps quiet if not asked. The long passages praising the good wife mix jokes with wishful thinking and stress every imaginable advantage of having a wife while simultaneously showing the sources for conflict.[36] At the same time, the short passages of female resistance and refusal of complete subordination show that the narrator is aware of the tension inherent in a relationship that is not built on equality. Is there an undertone of fear in the lands of giants? No wife/woman will ever live up to the ideals described. No woman will accept or respect a stinking drunkard who beats her all the time. The husband is no God; if never questioned he turns into an idol that is worshipped on the wrong grounds. The text illustrates this kind of marriage by calling the bed of a married couple the altar of reconciliation or appeasement and the husband the idol. The shoes placed next to the altar/bed further contribute to the feeling of a sacred but not necessarily Christian act: "Er wird ihr Abgott sein, das Bett ihr Altar, darbei man die Schuh stelt, darauff alle versönung geschicht" (He will be her idol, the bed her altar, next to which one places one's shoes and on which reconciliation takes place, 99).[37] Later on in the text the husband is not only called the "Haupt" (head of the family, 103) but also the "Ehelicher Bapst" (pope of marriage, 103). In a Catholic context this statement could strengthen an argumentation that elevates the position of the husband and makes him the representative of God on earth, but Fischart's firm belief in the reformed Church and his severe attacks on Catholicism in other texts make it more likely that the phrase is another ambivalent twist of the text, insinuating irony but leaving the reader without clear guidance.[38]

The woman appears smarter than the narrator wants her to be: She clears the way for the husband when he comes home drunk so that he falls down the stairs more easily (100), she asks what he likes to eat and does not cook it (101), she pretends to miss him when he leaves home (102), and she fools her husband into thinking that she is faithful while he is gone (103). She is up with the sun like every efficient wife but is also called the "Lucifer of the house" (105). The narrator adds "God be with you" in a sudden fear of this woman/wife who is taking care of house and husband with tireless energy and a will much stronger than he expected or wanted.[39] The kingdom of the husband suddenly has a ruling queen despite the invocations of the opposite. Fischart obviously has a hard time finding a good example of a woman that could be used to illustrate the perfect wife. He quickly concludes that a wife as described by Jean Luis Vives cannot be made out of any woman he knows of. Going through different images of women as created by men since antiquity (98), he has to leave the question of the making of the perfect wife unanswered and ends with a sexual allusion. It indicates a view of the human being as imperfect since a result of sexual intercourse. It is thus impossible for man to make up the perfect woman in any other way than in his own mind.[40] The ideal woman only exists in theory.[41]

An indication of the danger of taking Fischart's text too seriously is his description of the person in charge — the man — as prone to dissipation. Grandgauchier may be a virtuous hero but he is at the same time enjoying an excessive lifestyle. This can only be explained by his exclusive position as a giant, since only those men who consider honor more important than instant satisfaction of the flesh are regarded as "real" men in this text. Masculinity is thus a result of virtue and honor, but the text at the same time allows us to question whether this is at all possible — as in the case with the ideal wife.[42] The virtuous giant Grandgauchier is confronted by a number of warning examples but is already convinced of the advantages of marriage. He does not long for more than one woman, well aware of the problems following infidelity;[43] he realizes the uselessness of risking his reputation for half a night with a woman,[44] and he never considers sharing his wife with other men.[45] Since intercourse outside of marriage is graphically depicted as causing illness, Grandgauchier is told to prefer an honorable life: "dann sein ehr war ihm lieber" (his honor was more important to him, 86). The representation of a "true" or "real" man as depicted in the text leaves no room for weakness: he is mentally and physically strong, takes care of his wife, children, and servants, and he does not even think of women other than his wife. He stays away from the sick, deformed, stinking, and stupid men and women who are unable to control themselves and who expose themselves publicly in excitement (85–87). The list of sinners is close to endless and their punishment not only limited to sickness: they risk having illegitimate children (88), their friends leave them, and they are the target of public ridicule (97). The narrator concludes: "Nun wolan, so wißt ihr nun, daß er nichts hielt auff die Heimdückische, gestolene, Nachtdiebische Kitzelfreud" (Now you know that he [Grandgauchier] did not think much of stolen nightly excitement, 88).

The (male) reader does not have a chance to doubt the importance of marriage when presented with such overwhelming evidence but he is nevertheless confronted with a myriad of arguments, indicating that this reader is not equipped with the same moral strength as the giant Grandgauchier.[46] At the beginning of chapter five the narrator claims to be puzzled by his vast knowledge, but an explanation is not presented.[47] He is ashamed of this familiarity with human sexuality at its worst — outside of marriage — but is nevertheless very outspoken. The brief passage seems more of a rhetorical statement used to excuse further digression into human sexuality. The narrator sets forth but stops once again to repeat the importance of marriage to man by claiming it natural.[48] The emphasis on natural dispositions takes the edge off any argument in this and other sixteenth-century texts. What is natural should not be changed by man (or woman); this in turn requires obedience and adaptability among humankind. Anyone who is trying to resist nature is punished by juridical instances or by God. The use of warning examples and the linking of them to natural forces thus make for strong evidence. By referring to men who deviate from the married norm as sick and deformed, a person physiologically categorized as an adult male is defective unless married. The text here makes no distinction between men and women.

Hence a man's gender identity can only be realized through marriage. The more accepting attitude towards extramarital affairs (among men) and male sexuality found in the chapbooks by Frey and Montanus is replaced by emphatic denial. The *Geschichtklitterung* rather expresses the same belief in marriage as was found in Wickram's *Knaben Spiegel* and *Nachbarn* with one important exception. Wickram's texts were found to suppress sexuality altogether as soon as they moved into the realm of marriage and family life. The discourse of sexuality in his texts takes its expression in silence. Only the children born show that intercourse must have taken place. Chapter five of the *Geschichtklitterung* on the other hand declares sexuality a disease outside of marriage — pushing it off to the discourse of medicine and pathology — but makes sex between husband and wife a natural given after the Fall of Man.

The sixth chapter of the book, "Von der Gurgelmilta von Honigmunda, des Grandgosiers Gemal schwangerem Leib, und ihrem Katzenreinen Weibergelüst, welchen sie mit Würsten, Kutteln und Pletzen hat gebüßt" (On Gurgelmilta von Honigmunda, the pregnant body of Grandgosier's wife, and her hunger which she satisfies by eating sausages, entrails, and cookies) graphically depicts how Grandgauchier and Gurgelmilta have sex; the narrator then turns to the pregnancy.[49] The text brings together what is kept apart in the other texts discussed here: sexuality, marriage, and family life.[50] Pregnancy is the immediate result of intercourse, children a blessing to their parents. Sexuality within marriage consequently does not need to be suppressed. It is a legitimate desire when expressed between spouses. The sexual act is a moment of reciprocity: Grandgauchier and Gurgelmilta unite in an act that ends in her pregnancy (109). The female body is allowed to take active part in intercourse; it is not reduced to function merely as a container of male semen. The metaphors and allusions used to describe the conception of Grandgauchier and Gurgelmilta's child do not, however, deviate from the language used for warning examples. Fischart makes use of the same images for portraying intercourse between the spouses as Montanus and Frey do when depicting adulterous couples. In the *Geschichtklitterung* husband and wife are allowed to have sex not only for the reason of procreation but for pure pleasure, but this does not make the sexual act in itself less sinful. It is only legitimized in marriage.

The inclusion of the discourse of sexuality in the discourse of marriage thus gives marriage even greater importance as the societal norm of living, and it allows for the woman/wife to enjoy intercourse without necessarily being regarded as a prostitute. But it also excludes all other forms of sexual intercourse by claiming them unnatural. Adultery has to be strictly forbidden since it threatens marriage. Sodomy and other forms of intercourse that do not comply with heterosexual coitus must be equally forbidden and are presented in the text in connection with diseases like syphilis. Intercourse practiced against the norm not only causes illness but is performed by sick people.[51] Homosexuality is not explicitly mentioned but undoubtedly on the list of forbidden sexual activities since the heterosexual relationship within marriage equals the "natural" norm in the text. Fischart writes:

> Da doch solche ehliche Weltsamung zu fördern, der höchstgedacht weisest Schöpffer dem Mann, so das ansehlichest unnd erstgestifftes vernünfftig geschöpff ist, nicht allein von außen ein standmäsige und zugelassene mitgefärtin und gespilin an dem Weiblichen geschlecht, sonder auch von ihnen im Hertzen ein Natürliche zuneigung und anmut zu derselbigen hat gebildet. (92)

Paraphrasing the text it is apparent that the man — the first and most important human being — has in the female sex found not only a companion who is his equal on the outside (legally and socially) but also a person to whom he feels natural attachment and affection. Nature not reason is the explanation for heterosexual love and the desire to marry. Any feelings that do not correlate with these can hardly be justified except for non-incestuous love between close relatives such as the love between parents and children.

The mixture of high and low and the emphasis on the grotesque and the comical permits the use of obscene language in the *Geschichtklitterung*. A narrator who claims to speak in the manner of "Rabelistigem Ernst" makes every additional attempt at an unambiguous interpretation fail.[52] He compares humans with animals and alludes to excess, indulgence, and disorder.[53] He gives the impression that even the best of husbands are ruled by their penises, and the best of wives take great interest in sex, but this is not a problem as long as sex is practiced within the boundaries of marriage. Does this indicate that the text allows a certain leeway within marriage after all, as was seen in some of the

Schwänke? Does the emphasis on marriage need a more pragmatic view when judging a single case? A woman sleeping with the servant when the man is gone or a wife who loves her husband so much that she does not mind if her husband has an affair with the maid (98) are plots for a chapbook and warning examples in a marriage manual, but the ambivalent status of the two episodes in the *Geschichtklitterung* is bewildering. There is a discourse on extramarital sex twice added to the passages praising marriage. These passages could be read as attempts to make behavior commonly regarded as impracticable and usually assigned the discourse of sexuality merge with the discourse of marriage. This reading of the text would correspond well with the finding that intercourse within marriage is given a status it does not have in any of the other texts discussed here. If marriage is to have the social dignity found in the *Geschichtklitterung* and other sixteenth-century texts, then to a certain extent it must be protected from outside threats as it was in the chapbooks, where adultery was not necessarily punished unless publicly known. It is thus possible to reject extramarital affairs in theory but to accept deviations from the norm if they do not lead to separation. The preservation of marriage — the preservation of social order — is more important than an occasional affair.

The conclusion seems plausible since divorce is considered unacceptable in the text: it is as if the sun would quit shining on the earth (91). Fischart gives a horrific picture of the death and desertion that awaits anyone considering divorce, and it is an effective tool for propaganda. The rhetorical question "Seind dann nicht alle geschöpff zu außbringlicher erhaltung des Menschen geschaffen und gesegnet?" (Are not all people created and blessed to preserve humanity? 91) exemplifies the importance of procreation within marriage. It also implies that a marriage without children is no true marriage and that the separation of a childless couple is no real divorce, thus opening up the possibility of remarriage.

If the prime reason given for marriage is procreation, then the inability to have children together dissolves any argument that promotes continued marriage. The text here follows Luther and Bucer's conception of divorce closely: If the marriage does not lead to a new family it cannot be justified.[54] It was, however, difficult to tell which of the spouses was the reason for the childless relation. Sixteenth-century medicine was not capable of diagnosing childlessness or of telling whether husband or wife or both were sterile for some reason. The only way to find proof for an argument was in a new relationship, as was seen in the Schwank by Wickram, where the husband has sex with the maid in order to prove his virility.[55]

The dignity given to children in the *Geschichtklitterung* is explained by their importance to man.[56] Since the text already has made clear that the wife by nature is subordinate to man and later is depicted as "his," it cannot be doubted that the offspring belongs to the father and that he is the one to suffer in case the marriage does not lead to children. Motherhood is at the same time presented as something naturally inherent in every woman/wife. She is physically as well as mentally well equipped for motherhood. Fischart refers to woman when rhetorically asking: "wer kan sie [die SpRößlin] aber besser auffzielen, als die von natur darzu geschaffene?" (who can bring up the children better than the person made for it by nature? 94). But the text also expresses hesitation with regard to women's disposition to be responsible for the upbringing of children. The same fear of female weakness appears as in the *Knaben Spiegel*.

Women are accused of spoiling their children and of bribing the schoolteachers to treat them with softness (95).[57] The explanation given for this is the mother's love of the child since it is of her flesh. She furthermore is said to love her children more than she loves her husband because of the biological ties and the knowledge that they can never betray her as he can (94–95). Probably unintentionally the text here points out the vulnerability of married women. At the same time it talks of the importance of woman for the well-being of the children and belittles her capacity to carry out what she is presupposed to do by nature. The close ties between mother and children make sure that the man has everything he needs around him. Since "nature" makes them stay with him, he does not have to fear a life in solitude and promiscuity, as stressed over and over again.[58] The fear of the woman at being left alone (with the children?) thus expresses her dependency on a man while securing his future. Her love of the children is transposed to the man, who has to be introduced to affection in order to voluntarily leave his freedom as a single man.[59] If "man" can only learn affectionate bonding through the woman, then her importance for the family is extremely important, but it also once and for all inscribes softness, weakness, and emotions as basic conditions for being considered female.

From what has been said above one can conclude that the text makes no attempt to compare the woman with the evil Eve, at least not so long as she is married and does not participate in extramarital, sodomitic, or homosexual intercourse. If "woman" equals "virtuous wife," then she does not equal "witch." Only an unmarried person of female sex or a person who is repetitiously adulterous and thus a "non-woman" resembles the witch as presented in the witch tracts. The fifth chapter of the *Geschichtklitterung* should not be compared with a book like Fischart's translation of *De Démonomanie* since it focuses exclusively on the positive effects of marriage to "man." When advocating marriage as a way for man and woman to reach salvation, the woman cannot be depicted as representing the only evil. The narrator thus does not further develop his comparison with the Bible after his introductory remarks in the fifth chapter, but he states:

> ... er ist die Sonn, sie ist der Mon, sie ist die Nacht, er hat Tagsmacht, was nun von der Sonnen, bei tag ist verbronnen, das kült die Nacht, durch des Mons macht, sie laßt keinen unwillen zwischen ihnen einwerffen.[60]

This passage at first appeared in Fischart's *Ehezuchtbüchlein*,[61] but it was added to the second edition of the *Geschichtklitterung*, thereby placing the book in genres very different from misogynous texts like the witch tracts and the "Frauenschelte" (women scolding) while at the same time stressing the importance of the discourse of marriage in Fischart's work. Heide Wunder in her study of Fischart claims that "Fischart thus did not understand the pairings of sun-moon and day-night merely as opposites, but also as phases in a cyclical process that gave each element its due in succession."[62] According to Wunder, Fischart tries to invalidate the dichotomy between man and woman as found in many texts discussing the relations between the sexes in the sixteenth century. She states further: "In this concept of gender relations there simply was no general subordination of the wife to the authority of the husband."[63] This is in my opinion a view that puts too much emphasis on the equality between spouses, as has been discussed above. Fischart uses traditional metaphors common to the sixteenth-century reader to describe man and woman. The woman represents the dark side of life, the night and the moon, and has no function in herself except as the companion of the man. The woman is given healing powers through the word "kühlen" (to cool) and the comparison of man and the burning sun stresses his destructive sides, but this only emphasizes her ability to give care while not demanding anything in return. She (the weak part) takes care of him (the strong part) so that he will temper himself. She helps him to perfection while receiving little in return. Even though this recognizes certain qualities inherent in woman, it does not abolish the dichotomy between man and woman. The life of the man is more complete when he has a woman at his side, but his identity and integrity are never questioned if he is by himself.[64] Woman as described in the *Geschichtklitterung* is a creature that is made only to accompany man. She can thus only be defined through the man and find her gender identity in opposition to him even when seen as his complementary companion. Even positive comments on women are consequently to be regarded as a comparison with the male standard. The woman is made understandable to men by men according to rules set by men.[65] The discourse of marriage not only narrows down the definition of woman to wife and makes it the norm; it also excludes unmarried persons of the female sex from finding a gender identity if solely based on the married standard. Their gender can thus be defined only in negation to the norm. A person of female sex is no woman unless married. If defined as opposite to "wife" she is a "nonwife," unable to bear legitimate children and hence prone to prostitution, bringing her closer to the witch.

The similarity to the other texts discussed here is obvious; the boundaries of female agency are very limited even if the woman is regarded as the companion to the man. The most powerful tool for a woman to use in her relationship to man is her ability to bear children, but this is also her weakest side. She can be the mother of important heirs, but also used, abused, raped, and left alone. The man alone has the right to make decisions concerning himself and the members of the household. He is the ruler and the king — "Haußfürst" and "Haußkönig" (89) — just to mention two of the words associated with the married man and his dominion.[66] He has to cultivate this kingdom like the farmer who has to take care of his lands and his animals (89) but he is also given the power to decide freely.

The *Geschichtklitterung* is a grotesque portrayal of giants that inhabit the world. Everything in the text is exaggerated to the point where the reader loses him- or herself in a vast flow of words. The excessive use of sexual metaphors and allusions through irony and satire[67] raises the question of whether the text is of any use for the study of the construction of woman. The answer must be that gender is shaped in and by all types of texts, that the autonomy of the literary text is a chimera, and that the literary text rather produces and represents gender systems while at the same time reproducing social norms and values.[68] The author of the *Geschichtklitterung* hides behind his words, making the reader exhausted and confused,[69] but the discourse of marriage found in this travesty of married life is an integral part of the sixteenth-century society. The world in Fischart's work is no longer only turned upside down — the *Geschichtklitterung* is much more complex than that — but the image of a "Narr" (the fool) telling the actual truth and unraveling the misdemeanors of the "sane" remains.[70] The ideal woman is the wife and the ideal wife an ideal that Fischart does not quite seem to dare believing in and thus has to restrict. The ideal woman is not only attractive to look at, she is sexually active within marriage in order to procreate and to satisfy her husband, yet chaste as a virgin in her thoughts,[71] a good mother and spouse, and she only talks if invited to do so by her husband.[72] What is different in this text in regard to the other texts discussed here — and this is important — is the right conceded to the married woman, in a text printed for mass publication, to enjoy sex with her husband.[73] And yet we must wonder whether she was able to enjoy this "ars erotica of marriage"[74] if she was restrained in the way presented in the *Geschichtklitterung*.[75]

Notes

[1] "And who Solomon in his allegories and parables calls the woman: because he says that no evil is worse than the evils of woman: and at times he calls her a whore who takes possession of all men like matter takes all forms . . .," Johann Fischart, *Vom Ausgelasnen Wütigen Teuffelsheer [1581]* (Graz, 1973), 3. The essence of the quote in its context is the absolute evil inherent in the female constitution, which Fischart explains in Platonic terms in that he ascribes it to the "liquid and elementary" material out of which woman was created.

[2] The belief that the human being was composed of wet, dry, cold, and warm humors goes back to antiquity and was the object of study among many scholars of the sixteenth century. "In keeping with the theory of the humors, physicians of this era recommended a different diet for men and women. Man was seen as warm and dry, woman as moist and cold." Heide Wunder, *He Is the Sun, She Is the Moon: Women in Early Modern Germany* (Cambridge: Harvard UP, 1998), 39–40.

[3] Fischart's lack of preference for a single type of text or genre allowed him to express his thoughts and ideas in many different ways. The genre can thus explain the difference in view concerning women in different texts, but it does not explain why he chose to translate or publish witch tracts.

[4] Cf. Maria E. Müller, "Schneckengeist im Venusleib. Zur Zoologie des Ehelebens bei Johann Fischart," in *Eheglück und Liebesjoch. Bilder von Liebe, Ehe und Familie in der Literatur des 15. und 16. Jahrhunderts*, ed. Maria E. Müller (Weinheim: Beltz, 1988), 159. Müller stresses the difference in genre as explanation for the wide span between Fischart's witch tracts and the *Ehezuchtbüchlein*. She also briefly reviews the research on the position of woman in Fischart's work. Cf. Tilmann Walter, *Unkeuschheit und Werk der Liebe. Diskurse über Sexualität am Beginn der Neuzeit in Deutschland* (Berlin: De Gruyter, 1998), 202. Walter Eckehart Spengler lists Fischart's works chronologically in a book that attempts to cover the life and work of the author, to discuss language and style in his work, and also to categorize Fischart and to place him in a literary tradition: *Johann Fischart, Gen. Müntzer. Studie zur Sprache und Literatur des ausgehenden 16. Jahrhunderts* (Ph.D. dissertation, Göppingen, 1969), 55–58. Spengler additionally lists the different editions of Fischart's works that were published at his lifetime or in the seventeenth century (435–36). Spengler's book is almost five hundred pages long and still an important source for anyone desiring an extensive overview of Fischart's life and work. Nothing similar is available in English.

Summaries, with commentaries, of Fischart's best-known titles can be found in Hugo Sommerhalder, *Johann Fischarts Werk. Eine Einführung* (Berlin: Walter de Gruyter, 1960).

[5] Rabelais wrote a series of five books (1532–64) of which this is known as the first, even though it chronologically is seen as the second book: Francois Rabelais, *Gargantua*, ed. Gérard Defaux (Paris: Le Livre de Poche, 1994). It has often been claimed that it is impossible to discuss Fischart's text without Rabelais's *Gargantua*, but this is to underestimate Fischart. The *Geschichtklitterung* is clearly written in the tradition of Rabelais's work, but far from being a mere translation it deserves the recognition of an independent work. For a brief and clear summary of the *Geschichtklitterung*, see Josef K. Glowa, *Johann Fischart's Geschichtklitterung: A Study of the Narrator and Narrative Strategies* (New York: Lang, 2000), 111–15.

[6] The accusation of witches was rare until the beginning of the 1550s, according to Lorna Jane Abray. She stresses that the city magistrates at times tried to downplay the accusations in order to avoid the problems occurring in other parts of Europe: *The People's Reformation: Magistrates, Clergy, and Commons in Strasbourg, 1500–1598* (Ithaca, NY: Cornell UP, 1985), 171–72. This did not, however, keep the city and its residents from believing in magic or from persecuting people for what they held to be witchcraft. Now thirty years old but still very interesting for the Strasbourg area is H. C. Erik Midelfort, *Witch Hunting in Southwestern Germany, 1562–1684: The Social and Intellectual Foundations* (Stanford, CA: Stanford UP, 1972).

[7] For further comments on the diversity of Fischart's work, see Pia Holenstein, *Der Ehediskurs der Renaissance in Fischarts Geschichtklitterung: Kritische Lektüre des fünften Kapitels* (Bern: Lang, 1991), 21–22. Holenstein concludes that the reader has to accept discrepancies in the various texts by Fischart and that this needs to be seen in relation to his use of irony and other stylistic and rhetorical tools to make the reader uncertain (24).

[8] Cf. Jan-Dirk Müller, "Texte aus Texten: Zu intertextuellen Verfahren in frühneuzeitlicher Literatur, am Beispiel von Fischarts Ehzuchtbüchlein und Geschichtklitterung," in *Intertextualität in der Frühen Neuzeit: Studien zu ihren theoretischen und praktischen Perspektiven*, ed. Wilhelm Kühlmann and Wolfgang Neuber (Frankfurt am Main: Lang, 1994), 149.

[9] For a comprehensive overview see the Introduction in Glowa, *Johann Fischart's Geschichtklitterung*. Glowa sums up much of the research done in this field. Little has been done recently, even less in English. Fischart continues to be relatively unknown outside a group of German-speaking academics despite the enormous number of his publications. No text is translated into English, but several of his works must also be regarded as almost impossible to translate. Hans-Gert Roloff has initiated a critical edition but only the first volume is so far published, while two more volumes are planned. Scholars thus still have to work with a patchwork of texts.

[10] A thorough comment on sexual metaphors and allusions in the fifth chapter of the *Geschichtklitterung* can be found in Holenstein, *Der Ehediskurs der Renaissance*. Holenstein is mainly concerned with the discourse on marriage but this includes a longer general discussion of the place of "woman" in sixteenth-century literature in the third part of the book, called "Ehediskurs und Realität" (Discourse of marriage and reality, 249–324). It is a good survey of different topics in regard to "woman"

in early modern literature — such as a catalogue of female vice as presented in literature (287–301) — but Holenstein does not discuss the *Geschichtklitterung* in depth in this last part. Her most interesting comments on the position of woman in the fifth chapter of Fischart's text can be found in her thorough commentary. It would have been of great help to the reader had she closed with a conclusion, even though the primary aim is to comment on single words, phrases, or passages in Fischart's work.

[11] Jan-Dirk Müller and Walter Haug have emphasized this ambiguity of the text in their study of the fifth chapter of the *Geschichtklitterung*. Müller refers to the ambiguity as characteristic of Fischart and points out that in the *Geschichtklitterung* he is able to pick out what is excluded from the marriage tracts and make it a central theme of his writing. Müller calls it a "counter discourse" (Gegendiskurs) that makes it possible for Fischart to say more than he would have been able to in the *Ehezuchtbüchlein:* Jan-Dirk Müller, "Von der Subversion frühneuzeitlicher Ehelehre. Zu Fischarts *Ehezuchtbüchlein* und *Geschichtklitterung,*" in *The Graph of Sex and the German Text: Gendered Culture in Early Modern Germany 1500–1700*, ed. Lynne Tatlock (Amsterdam: Rodopi, 1994), 134. See further 142–43 and 155–56. Haug sees a connection to the carnival as found in Bakhtin, the text oscillating between seriousness and absurdity and almost dissolving itself but always finding a way out through laughter: Walter Haug, "Zwischen Ehezucht und Minnekloster. Die Formen des Erotischen in Johann Fischarts *Geschichtklitterung,*" in Tatlock, ed., *The Graph of Sex and the German Text,* 170–72. For a critical discussion of Müller and Haug in regard to their readings of the *Geschichtklitterung* see 564–75 in Ulrich Seelbach, "Fremde Federn. Die Quellen Johann Fischarts und die Prätexte seines idealen Lesers in der Forschung," *Daphnis* 29, no. 3–4 (2000): 465–583.

[12] For a recent study of the sources to Fischart's work, see Seelbach, "Fremde Federn." Seelbach is one of the editors of the new critical edition of Fischart's work. Glowa comments briefly in his introduction to *Johann Fischart's Geschichtklitterung* on older research of the many sources that Fischart based his writing on.

[13] The English paraphrase does not show the play with the words "gegriffen" for having taken someone (here referring to the wife) and "vergriffen," meaning "taken the wrong one" (84).

[14] When Florence Weinberg in a discussion of Fischart's reception of Rabelais claims that Fischart in the *Geschichtklitterung* shows minimal interest in sex, she seems to disregard the fifth (and to a certain extent the sixth) chapter: "Fischart's Geschichtklitterung: A Questionable Reception of Gargantua," *Sixteenth-Century Journal* 3 (1982): 23–35. Weinberg's article is one of few publications in English on Fischart and it focuses on Fischart's reception of Rabelais. Unfortunately Weinberg does not see the originality in Fischart's work, regarding it as "irritating" because of Fischart's free use of Rabelais's original.

[15] "How could such a natural talent to serve the man have been given women for no reason? . . . Why should she be of such weak constitution, if she did not value and search for a stronger supplement and assistance in the man?" Johann Fischart, *Geschichklitterung (Gargantua). Text der Ausgabe letzter Hand von 1590. Mit einem Glossar,* ed. Ute Nyssen (Düsseldorf: Karl Rauch Verlag, 1963), 93. This edition is used for all quotations of the *Geschichtklitterung* in this chapter, and is the reference

for all page numbers cited. For the most part I have chosen to paraphrase Fischart and to add the German original to the notes due to the extreme complexity of the language and in the absence of an official English translation. Ulrich Seelbach is very critical of the Nyssen edition, especially the glossary, but there is not yet a new critical edition of the *Geschichtklitterung* (Seelbach, "Fremde Federn," especially the pages 513–22). I have chosen to cite the Nyssen edition but to disregard the glossary in my discussion of the text. For a brief review of the dichotomy man=culture, woman=nature see Sigrid Weigel, "Geschlechterdifferenz und Literaturwissenschaft," in Tatlock, ed., *The Graph of Sex and the German Text*, 7–26.

[16] Holenstein (*Der Ehediskurs der Renaissance*, 74–75) divides the chapter into three parts of different length and dignity in accordance with the rhetorical structure of the text: a brief introduction, warning examples of other (sexual) relationships than marriage, and the praise of marriage, but she sees further subdivisions and also points to the relativity of any such classification. The complexity of the text with its constant digressions makes any grouping of text passages extremely difficult, but Holenstein's suggested division of the text into three is general enough to hold the essential parts: bad and good examples.

[17] Glowa summarizes his study of the narrator and narrative strategies in the *Geschichtklitterung:* "[T]he narrator is fully brought to life as an important character in the *Gkl.* and creates the fiction of being on the same time plane as his readers. From time to time, however, he also enters the fictional world of Gargantua, addresses its characters, and pretends to be witness to the events as they develop. His connection to the fictional realm, his dialogue with the readers, and his numerous comments on his writing activity create the impression that the narrative is not a finished artifact, but rather an event that is unfolding and developing before the reader's eyes" (*Johann Fischart's Geschichtklitterung*, 109).

[18] See Holenstein, *Der Ehediskurs der Renaissance*, 60.

[19] Glowa, *Johann Fischart's Geschichtklitterung*, 6–7.

[20] See Hans Geulen, "Johann Fischarts *Geschichtsklitterung:* Nachträge zu ihrer Bedeutung," *Germanisch-Romanische Monatsschrift* 39, no. 2 (1989): 149. Geulen claims that the *Geschichtklitterung* aims at a presentation of the loss of morals and order in the world and that it emphasizes distress with the current circumstances despite all the jokes and comic effects. Geulen's short article is an interesting comparison to Rabelais's original text, pointing out the differences in French and German literature and culture at the end of the sixteenth century. See also Erich Kleinschmidt's study of Fischart, "Gelehrtentum und Volkssprache in der Frühneuzeitlichen Stadt: Zur literaturgesellschaftlichen Funktion Johann Fischarts in Strassburg," *Zeitschrift für Literaturwissenschaft und Linguistik: Eine Zeitschrift der Universität Gesamthochschule Siegen* 37 (1980): 128–51. Cf. Müller, "Schneckengeist im Venusleib," 156.

[21] Clemens Lugowski's 1932 study of the development of the novel is still interesting in regard to early modern prose texts, especially because of his work on Wickram: Clemens Lugowski, *Die Form der Individualität Im Roman* (Frankfurt am Main: Suhrkamp, [1932] 1976). For a comment on Lugowski, see Armin Schulz, "Texte und Textilien. Zur Entstehung der Liebe in Georg Wickrams *Goldtfaden* (1557)," *Daphnis* 30, no. 1–2 (2001): 57. See also Geulen's comments on the intended

meaning inherent in the *Geschichtklitterung* in "*Johann Fischarts Geschichtklitterung.*" Geulen stresses that Fischart's work is written at a time of transition and suggests a reading of the text in accordance with Blumenberg's understanding of the world as presented in his work on the "Copernican turn": Hans Blumenberg, *Die Genesis der kopernikanischen Welt,* 3 vols., 3rd ed. (Frankfurt am Main: Suhrkamp, 1996).

[22] At the beginning of the book the reader is immediately drawn into the world of Rabelais as translated by Fischart by being directly addressed as a "pantagruelist" (7). Cf. Glowa, *Johann Fischart's Geschichtklitterung,* 2, and also his comment on the different editions of the text in note 8.

[23] Walter Haug comes to the same conclusion but argues somewhat differently by claiming an attitude based on the "qualitative consumption of the world" as typically male. Haug says further: "Aber es bleibt, zumindest historisch gesehen, doch festzuhalten, daß die Dialektik zwischen der Konstruktion von Ordnungen und ihrer befreienden Zerstörung in erster Linie eine Männerangelegenheit gewesen ist" (It should be stressed that the dialectic between the making of order and its liberating destruction, at least historically seen, has been an affair between men), ("Zwischen Ehezucht und Minnekloster," 175). It is in my opinion dangerous to define certain genres or types of texts as male or female, since it is very difficult to account for such a hypothesis objectively. More likely to me is the availability of texts to certain readers and the educational level of the audience. Since women with few exceptions were excluded from higher education up to the late nineteenth and early twentieth century they were also excluded from reading texts in foreign languages as well as stylistically or topically complex texts. See also Kleinschmidt, "Gelehrtentum und Volkssprache." Kleinschmidt discusses Fischart's role in the greater literary context of Strasbourg.

[24] Holenstein (*Der Ehediskurs der Renaissance*) in a similar way stresses that women usually were not directly addressed in written texts but rather were the objects of men's speech. This is of course not the case in texts specifically aimed at female readers that often were focused on female conduct, such as *Der Frawen Spigel in wellichem Spiegel sich das weyblich Byld / jung oder alt beschawen oder lernen / zu gebrauchen / die woltat gegen irem eelichen Gemahel* (Strasbourg: M. Flach II, 1520), or Hans Thanner, *Frawen Spiegl: Auf Erden ist khein Creatur so löblich als ain Weybes Figur die von Natur ist wollgestallt und sich in Eeren Frümbklich hallt (Ain Lied was ainer Eefrawen gebüret)* (Vienna: Syngriener, 1553), or the German version of Bonaventura, *Unser Frauen-Spiegel* (Basel: Furter, 1506). These texts have to be distinguished from the learned tracts on "woman" by the humanists and other learned men that often were written in Latin and hence not intended for female readers.

[25] Cf. Müller, "Von der Subversion frühneuzeitlicher Ehelehre," 150–51.

[26] Holenstein stresses the difference between the first and the third edition of the *Geschichtklitterung,* pointing to the growing excess in style and content: "Alles, was die These ironisiert, ist Zusatz, der gröbste ist in der letzten ausgabe dazugekommen, und erst dieser verläßt die Argumentationsebene" (Everything subject to irony in the thesis has been added. The crudest part has been added in the last edition and only this one diverts from the level of argumentation: *Der Ehediskurs der Renaissance,* 144–45).

[27] Gurgelmilta enters the story in chapter six, after Fischart thoroughly has presented the "pros and cons" of marriage.

[28] Maria E. Müller speaks of Fischart's concept of marriage as an "organic unit," that does not fit the idea of marriage as the center of the *familia* or *oikos*. It reduces the household to only man and woman; kin and servants have no place in this unit according to Müller ("Schneckengeist im Venusleib," 181–82). This resembles the idea of the family in Wickram's *Nachbarn* as a very small unit. Neither text is willing to fully accept servants as members of the household, even though Wickram emphasizes the importance of friends — male and female — for the existence of the family. He thus widens the concept as presented by Müller.

[29] "For through the merging and becoming-neighbors of an entire group of friends, a street becomes inhabited, many streets become a village, a village becomes a town, and the towns become a land, the lands become a kingdom and empire, the empires become the world, and from the world stems paradise," 91.

[30] Fischart uses the word monarchy (Monarchie) but also plays with the word by turning it into "Manherschi," thus indicating the sex of the person in charge — the man, 88. See also Holenstein, *Der Ehediskurs der Renaissance,* 126.

[31] See Haug, "Zwischen Ehezucht und Minnekloster," 157–77.

[32] See Holenstein, *Der Ehediskurs der Renaissance* for a thorough discussion of names, allusions, etc. Seelbach ("Fremde Federn," 568–75) discusses the names of infamous women in his comment on Müller and stresses the importance of a thorough reading of the text.

[33] Cf. Walter, *Unkeuschheit und Werk der Liebe,* 298–99. Walter points out that Fischart repeatedly stressed the equal importance of spousal mutuality and subordination of the woman without regarding this as contradictory — to the disadvantage of the wife.

[34] See Maria E. Müller's excellent article on Fischart's use of animals to describe the vice and virtue of woman, "Schneckengeist im Venusleib."

[35] See also Frank Schlossbauer, *Literatur als Gegenwelt: Zur Geschichtlichkeit literarischer Komik am Beispiel Fischarts und Lessings* (New York: Lang, 1998), 116. Schlossbauer's study of the comical in the *Geschichtklitterung* reveals the ambivalence inherent in the text very well; he refers to the difficult task of telling irony from seriousness in the *Geschichtklitterung* as a key to the work (117–18). Regarding the ironic ambivalence in the text, see also Haug, "Zwischen Ehezucht und Minnekloster," 173.

[35] The problems surrounding absent men and women left on their own is a common topic in literature. The *Geschichtklitterung* treats it with the humor found in the chapbooks instead of giving it the touch of serious concern found in Wickram's prose texts, but the greater context makes the reader wonder if this is yet another trap.

[36] *Geschichtklitterung,* 99–106. See also Haug, "Zwischen Ehezucht und Minnekloster," 166–77 and Müller, "Von der Subversion frühneuzeitlicher Ehelehre," 149–56. Both scholars call attention to the ruptures that develop from brief comments that contradict what previously was claimed.

[37] Cf. Haug, "Zwischen Ehezucht und Minnekloster," 171.

[38] For a presentation of Fischart's anti-Catholic writings see Stephen L. Wailes, "Johann Fischart (1546 or 1547–1590 or 1591)," in *German Writers of the Renaissance and Reformation: Dictionary of Literary Biography,* vol. 179, ed. James Hardin and Max Reinhart (Detroit: Gale Research, 1997), 55–62.

[39] Müller ("Von der Subversion frühneuzeitlicher Ehelehre," 153) comes to the same conclusion but has not noticed that the funeral mentioned is part of the warning examples directed to the unmarried man and not another image of the joking wife (96). Cf. Haug, "Zwischen Ehezucht und Minnekloster," 171.

[40] "Wie? treffen wirs nicht recht mit dem Ars ins kalt Wasser? Oui par messer: alsdann bleibt das gemecht beim geschlecht, unnd das geschlecht beim gemecht," 98. Cf. Müller, "Von der Subversion frühneuzeitlicher Ehelehre," 153–54. Holenstein (*Der Ehediskurs der Renaissance,* 192) does not specifically comment on this passage but gives the word "gemecht" the meaning of "sexual organ" as opposed to "geschlecht" (sex).

[41] Cf. Holenstein, *Der Ehediskurs der Renaissance,* 192.

[42] Helmut Puff claims that the concept of honor is less explicit in the fifth chapter of the *Geschichtklitterung* than in the *Ehezuchtbüchlein* and explains this by the explicit didactic intention of the latter work. This does not, however, exclude the importance of honor to Grandgauchier: "Die Ehre der Ehe — Beobachtungen zum Konzept der Ehre in der Frühen Neuzeit an Johann Fischart's *Philosophisch Ehezuchtbüchlein* (1578) und anderen Ehelehren des 16. Jahrhunderts," in *Ehrkonzepte der Frühen Neuzeit. Identitäten und Abgrenzungen,* ed. Sibylle Backmann, et al. (Berlin: Akademie Verlag, 1998), 105. Puff also stresses that honor is gender-specific, that male and female honor take different expressions (109). This is clearly the case in all texts discussed here while honor at the same time is made equally important to men and women.

[43] "Ließ sich auch an der einigen Fidel benügen, dieweil er auch nur einen Fidelbogen hat, dann was sollen zusamen vilerley Safft? Eins nimpt dem andern die krafft. . . . So heißts ja auch, wa sich uneinigkeit straußt, da wird zu eng das Hauß, unnd ziehet der stärckst dem schwächern den Harnisch auß" (85); "Benügt sich mit eyner, wie der Himmel mit der einigen großgebeuchten schwangeren Erd, die Sonn, dem einigen Mon: Lebt also on eifer, darff mit keim anderen umb die Henn gobelen, . . ." (97).

[44] ". . . ward kein Mundischer Isenpfaff drumb, daß er ins elend einer nacht halben komm" (86).

[45] "Noch viel minder kont er verdäuen des Platons Lacedemonisch Gartenbrüderisch Weibergemeynschafft, wiewol es inn den Decreten . . . gebillicht wird, weil unter guten Freunden all ding soll gemeyn sein" (88). This can be compared with the Schwank in *Das ander theyl der Garten gesellschaft* where Montanus depicts two men who solve an argument by each sleeping with the wife of the other: *Martin Montanus Schwankbücher (1557–1566),* ed. Johannes Bolte (Tübingen: Der literarische Verein in Stuttgart, 1899), 317–21.

[46] Cf. Holenstein, *Der Ehediskurs der Renaissance,* 125.

[47] "Es nimpt mich selber wunder, wie ich den Hurendantz weiß also zuerzelen" (87).

[48] "Sonder (damit ich ein mal abtruck) er schicket sich nach ordnung der natur zu einer ordenlichen Ehrennehrlichen, Nachbaurlichen, gesindfolgigen, gemeynnutzlichen, handlichen und wonhaftlichen Haußhaltung und eygenherd" (Fischart, *Geschichklitterung*, 88).

[49] Hugo Sommerhalder (*Johann Fischarts Werk*, 64) briefly comments on the body of Gurgelmilta and sees in it a "swelling of desires" (Aufschwellung der Triebe) and relates it to her specific beauty. Sommerhalder regards the giants in Fischart's work as opposites to the ascetic heroes of the Middle Ages, while Schlossbauer (*Literatur Als Gegenwelt*, 120) talks of the ambivalence inherent in the positive view of sexuality within marriage and the negative tone that characterizes the moment of conception after which women start swelling because of the poison injected in them by the penis, the "Erbsündigen Schlangenschwantz" (109). The *gigantic* appearance of Grandgauchier and Gurgelmilta can, however, also be seen in correspondence with their lives as giants. The manifestation of physical and mental characteristics has to be expressed in terms of the extraordinary large, so that the reader can visualize the size of the protagonists. See Robert W. Scribner on the "Eroticising of the Female Body" in the sixteenth century, *Religion and Culture in Germany (1400–1800)*, ed. Lyndal Roper (Leiden: Brill, 2001), 138. Scribner discusses what he regards as a change in literature and the visual arts in the second half of the sixteenth century: "the representation of the female body as an erotic object."

[50] This can be found in the brief question: "Seind dann nicht alle geschöpff zu außbringlicher erhaltung des Menschen geschaffen und gesegnet" (Are not all creatures made and blessed for the preservation of the human being?, 91).

[51] Fischart's excess in gruesome images is impressive as is Holenstein's commentary on the evils connected with sexual intercourse outside of marriage in *Der Ehediskurs der Renaissance*, 85–90; see also 124–25. On syphilis and prostitution, see Merry E. Wiesner, "Paternalism in Practice: The Control of Servants and Prostitutes in Early Modern German Cities," in *The Process of Change in Early Modern Europe: Essays in Honor of Miriam Usher Chrisman*, ed. Philipp N. Bebb and Sherrin Marshall (Athens: Ohio UP, 1988), 194–95.

[52] *Geschichtklitterung*, 94. A play on the words "Rabelais," "Rabe" (raven), and "listig" (cunning) makes the word "Ernst" (serious, earnest) lose much of its actual meaning and causes the reader to question everything said. Cf. Holenstein, *Der Ehediskurs der Renaissance*, 161, and Haug, "Zwischen Ehezucht und Minnekloster," 170. The "cunning" way of speaking fits well with an additional helper, the mythological figure Silenus. Cf. Geulen, "Johann Fischarts *Geschichtklitterung*," 148; Holenstein, *Der Ehediskurs der Renaissance*, 126; Müller, "Von der Subversion frühneuzeitlicher Ehelehre," 150; and Haug, "Zwischen Ehezucht und Minnekloster," 161–62.

[53] "Darumb gabe es auch nachmals so fein Kiefferwerck, daß sie einander den Speck dapffer einsaltzten, und spielten der faulen Brucken, unnd des Thiers mit zweyen Rucken: Also daß sie nachgehends anfieng sich gegen dem Mann auffzublähen" (109).

[54] See H. J. Selderhuis, *Marriage and Divorce in the Thought of Martin Bucer*, trans. John Vriend and Lyle D. Bierma (Kirksville, MO: Thomas Jefferson UP, 1999), esp.

the chapters on divorce: 20–24 and 257–326. The latter chapter deals exclusively with divorce in the theology of Bucer. A critical edition of Bucer's writings on marriage now is available: Martin Bucer, *Schriften zu Ehe und Eherecht,* ed. Stephen E. Buckwalter, Robert Stupperich, and Wilhelm H. Neuser, *Martin Bucers Deutsche Schriften,* vol. 10 (Gütersloh: Mohn, 2001): This will probably result in an increased interest in Bucer's work and more publications regarding the position he took as a mediator between Luther and Calvin.

[55] Georg Wickram, *Sämtliche Werke,* ed. Hans-Gert Roloff, vol. 7, *Das Rollwagenbüchlein* (Berlin: Walter de Gruyter, 1973), 17.

[56] This is made evident in the gruesome examples given to the reader to illustrate the result of illicit intercourse. Fischart not only mentions the defects these children will be born with but also gives examples of different ways of getting rid of illegitimate children (88). Cf. Müller, "Von der Subversion frühneuzeitlicher Ehelehre," 152, and Seelbach, "Fremde Federn," 568. See also Elisabeth Koch, *Maior dignitas est in sexu virili: Das weibliche Geschlecht im Normensystem de 16. Jahrhunderts* (Frankfurt am Main: Vittorio Klostermann, 1991), 142–48, on abortion.

[57] Holenstein, *Der Ehediskurs der Renaissance,* 168–71.

[58] The comment that there is a need for two parents — husband and wife — in case twins are born so that each child can be comforted by one parent each, must be another joke of Fischart's. The text does not prescribe male involvement in the care of babies at any other place. Hence, it does not seem to deviate from other sixteenth-century texts that give the mother full responsibility for the care of the children until they start their formal education — as was also depicted in *Knaben Spiegel* and *Nachbarn.* Cf. Haug, "Zwischen Ehezucht und Minnekloster," 170. Steven Ozment has published several texts that show that affection between spouses and parents and their children in no way was unusual: *When Fathers Ruled: Family Life in Reformation Europe,* Studies in Cultural History (Cambridge, MA: Harvard UP, 1983), *Three Behaim Boys: Growing up in Early Modern Germany: A Chronicle of Their Lives* (New Haven: Yale UP, 1990), *The Burghermeister's Daughter: Scandal in a Sixteenth-Century German Town* (New York: St. Martin's P, 1996).

[59] Holenstein comments that the men have a desire to have children but does not further discuss male-female bonding in *Der Ehediskurs der Renaissance,* 152–53.

[60] "He is the sun, she is the moon, She is the night, he the day's might, And what the sun burns by day, Is cooled at night by the power of the moon, [she does not allow any irritation arise between them]," 99. For the first part, I have used the translation as it appears in Wunder, *He Is the Sun, She Is the Moon,* 205. The last part, in square brackets, is my translation.

[61] The intertextual allusions to the *Ehezuchtbüchlein* are manifold in the *Geschichtklitterung.* See among others Jan-Dirk Müller, "Texte aus Texten," 63–109, here 127.

[62] Wunder, *He Is the Sun, She Is the Moon,* 206–7.

[63] Wunder, *He Is the Sun, She Is the Moon,* 206.

[64] Cf. Müller, "Texte aus Texten," 151–52. See also Karin Hausen and Heide Wunder, "Frauengeschichte — Geschlechtergeschichte: Einleitung," in *Frauengeschichte — Geschlechtergeschichte,* ed. Karin Hausen and Heide Wunder (Frankfurt/New York: Campus, 1992), 174.

[65] Cf. Claudia Brinkler-von der Heyde, "Der Frauenpreis des Agrippa von Nettesheim: persönliche Strategie, politische Invektive, rhetorisches Spiel," in *Text im Kontext: Anleitung zur Lektüre deutscher Texte der Frühen Neuzeit*, ed. Alexander Schwarz and Laure Abplanalp (Frankfurt am Main: Lang, 1997), 41. Brinkler-von der Heyde talks of an androcentric point of view that makes reading a process of male cognition.

[66] Words associated with earthly rule seem to have a more positive connotation than the expression "pope of marriage" mentioned above. They are also much more frequent in the text than are allusions with religious connotation.

[67] See Müller, "Texte aus Texten," 155.

[68] See Sigrid Brauner, "Gender and Its Subversion: Reflections on Literary Ideals of Marriage," in Tatlock, ed., *The Graph of Sex and the German Text*, 180, 190.

[69] Cf. Haug, "Zwischen Ehezucht und Minnekloster," 174–75.

[70] Cf. the preface where Fischart describes how learned men like Democritus laugh at the world for its inability to see the truth and instead thinking of foolishness as the "wise truth." He then quickly adds that this world needs difference — that one also needs people who paint white walls with soot (6) — thereby making for an ambiguity uncommon in older texts but that can be compared with the "mixed" characters in the *Knaben Spiegel*.

[71] "Maid" (Jungfrau) described both the young, unmarried woman and the virginal, "chaste" woman (Wunder, *He Is the Sun, She Is the Moon*, 24); see also Hausen and Wunder, "Frauengeschichte — Geschlechtergeschichte: Einleitung," 147.

[72] Cf. Müller, "Texte aus Texten," 153–54.

[73] It nevertheless seems to be an unequal pleasure since always initiated by the man. The text vividly describes all the places where intercourse can take place, but only as often as "he" wants it: "Ja im Bad, inn der Bütten, auff dem Scherpffbanck, inn der Sennften, inn der Kammer, mit welcher er ungehindert mag schertzelen, mertzelen, kützeln, kritzeln, schwitzeln, Pfitzelen, dützelen, mützelen, fützelen und bürtzeln, so offt es ihn gelust zustützelen und zuzustürtzelen" (102). Cf. Müller, "Von der Subversion frühneuzeitlicher Ehelehre," 154, and Walter, *Unkeuschheit und Werk der Liebe*, 244.

[74] Müller, "Schneckengeist im Venusleib," 187.

[75] I have chosen not to comment on Haug's discussion of the abbey Willigmuth as an example of perfect living conditions for man and woman since this already has been done thoroughly by Sigrid Brauner, "Gender and Its Subversion."

4: Polizeiordnungen: Taming the Shrew with Common Sense and the Law

Having discussed popular texts intended to be read for pleasure and with no other normative claims than a desire to portray good and bad examples of male and female behavior, I will now turn to decrees passed by the city council of Strasbourg to study a completely different type of text in search of the role(s) women play in these texts. The records discussed here are products of an almost exclusively middle or upper class male population, the "Bürger," and hence not representative for all residents of the city. These texts are, however, aimed at the same readership and audience that Frey, Montanus, Wickram, and Fischart address in their prefaces, and they are all written by men who express their view of women without ever letting the women make their own voices heard. The decrees passed by the city council depict problems as they were perceived by those in power, and they show what issues were important to the council and its members. By prescribing how these problems should be solved, they indirectly describe sources of conflict within the city and among its inhabitants. Some of these problems were clearly gender-related while others were not.

The Strasbourg Council was given the mandate of leading the city and ensuring that peace and order were maintained.[1] It was elected to act on behalf of all citizens and did not stand to benefit from passing any laws or decrees that would cause uprisings or riots. Rather, such regulations would have been regarded as counterproductive, since the loss of order would have resulted in a loss of control.[2] The men in power thus needed to ensure that any dissatisfaction among the inhabitants of the growing city was kept to a minimum. The size of the early modern city — that is, the space enclosed within walls — was in no way proportionate to the size of its population. Indeed, most cities were overcrowded and only the wealthy could afford spacious living quarters. Looking at the architecture of sixteenth- and seventeenth-century towns and cities — the road network and the architecture of the buildings — it is not difficult to imagine that the lack of space was a risk factor for those responsible for upholding law and order.

A fear of disorder on the part of the men in power and their striving to preserve the status quo and prevent social upheaval are confirmed in many ways by current research on women and gender relations in early modern Europe and its rather grim picture of women's legal rights.[3] Enough evidence has been found in court records and other documents to prove the inequality between men and women appearing in court, despite these ordinances' claim of applying to men and women equally. Differences occur in the description of various offenses, in the presentation of the penalties, and in the discussion of the offenders. The legal discourse thus appears highly gendered: there is not only a difference between men and women according to their biological sex, but the records show that distinctions were also made between male and female behavior and that the gender of the suspect influenced the verdict. The penalty imposed on someone can thus be regarded as typically male or female.

If marriage is regarded as a part of the legal as well as the religious discourse, then divorce, adultery, fornication, and so on become a part of this discursive field as well, expressing the negative sides of marriage/non-marriage. As a result of the Reformation, marriage was regarded as *the* connection between man and woman, the nexus of interpersonal relationships between the sexes, and as a reason for a gendered discourse focused simultaneously on mutuality and subordination. At the same time, however, as marriage gained in importance, celibacy lost importance as a way of life.[4] It is therefore unsurprising that sexuality is forced into the discourse of marriage and that deviance from the married norm is held to be unacceptable by the law. Marriage unites man and woman around the task of procreation, but their union is hierarchical. Martin Luther may have claimed that man and woman are equal before God, and judging by some decrees, a legal pseudo-equality did indeed exist in early modern society, but within the institution of marriage itself there was little equality.[5] In the following I will investigate the discourses of sexuality and marriage in the "Polizeiordnungen" (police laws) of the city of Strasbourg. Because of their status as public legal documents aimed at regulating the moral standards of the inhabitants, it is likely that they influenced the ways men and women in the city viewed themselves and others, and that these texts — like the others discussed here — contributed to the construction of "woman" and "man."[6]

The city archives in Strasbourg and the Biblioteque Nationale et Universitaire de Strasbourg (BNUS, the university library) contain an immense collection of documents from the sixteenth century on the city population and everyday life within the city walls. Due to wars, riots, and fires, especially in the seventeenth and eighteenth centuries, the city archives as well as the library have suffered severe damage on several occasions, making documentation of the sources extremely difficult, according to Joseph Fuchs, former head of the archives.[7] Fuchs should know: he has spent years of his life trying to bring order into chaos, to systematize and to list the holdings. It is nevertheless a challenge to search for documents concerning a particular theme, topic, or time period. The indexes are close to innumerable, many of them saying more about the archivist than about the documents listed. Some of the records have been lost or misplaced in the wrong files, and some records have yet to be indexed.[8] The municipal archives vividly show the arbitrariness of documentation, and the difficulties of re-creating the past with the aid of incomplete sources. The immense work put into the organization of the holdings makes the scholar acutely aware of the impossibility of writing the definitive history of the city and its inhabitants. Nevertheless, it is impressive that so much has been saved from fires and wars for later generations to read.

Having said this, it is evident that any study of archival material must be incomplete and selective at the same time. For this book, I have chosen to focus on texts found in series R (Mandats et Reglements), decrees regulating the lives of Strasbourg's inhabitants on an everyday basis. Like many literary works of their time, these texts tell a story of decay and moral deterioration while giving solutions and prescribing "correct" behavior: a life lived in accordance with the laws of God and the city council. First and foremost, it should be emphasized that matters regarding gender by no means constitute the greater part of the regulations issued in Strasbourg in the fifteenth and sixteenth centuries. There are, however, a number of Polizeiordnungen that deal with marriage, adultery, divorce, and prostitution, topics of great importance for the preservation of order in the city. Like decrees regulating commerce and trade and the activities within and between the guilds, the marriage and divorce tracts were aimed at controlling interpersonal relationships and preserving a traditional hierarchy and an established order while also legitimizing the existence of an urban middle class on the rise. The sheer numbers of ordinances issued indicate that the magistrate felt that the social order was threatened, but also — as will be discussed below — that revisions of existing ordinances were necessary to better deal with changes that had occurred over time.[9]

The selection of texts can always be called into question. Here the choice was based on the assumption that the decrees exhibit discursive practices similar to those of the literary texts discussed above. Considering the importance of local legislation in Germany, I have chosen to focus on the city to which all the authors discussed above had connections and where they all had published at least some of their work. It is easy to find similarities between the legislative and the literary texts: a set of rules are imposed from above — either by the magistrates (as authors of the decrees) upon the citizens, or by the author upon his text. Authors of legal documents and authors of literary texts both produce an imagined society based on their lived or experienced reality; they hope for a new and better world, but are products of the world they live in; they often claim that their rules apply to everyone, but there are clear differences between men and women and between people of different classes. And they all seem to fear change while striving to preserve a (God-)given order. But to consider only the similarities would most likely be to discover only what was presumed or proposed and little else. It therefore seems more important to look at the various ways of describing and regulating what is regarded as typically male and female and to search for social and cultural functions ascribed to "man" and "woman" in the Polizeiordnungen.

Due to the impact of the Reformation on the city, one document has been selected from the period before 1520, and two from the 1520s. Then there is a leap to the second half of the century, when orthodox Lutherans took control over governance of the city. Martin Bucer was forced to leave Strasbourg at this time, and the willingness to compromise that was characteristic of the city's reformers in the 1520s and 1530s was replaced by stricter regulation of citizens, other inhabitants, and visitors. I will discuss two documents from this period: one decree from 1565, "die Ehe belangend" (on marriage), and another from 1570. The last of the decrees I will examine here was passed in 1594. The decrees from the second half of the sixteenth century were issued in print form after the publishing of Wickram's, Montanus's, and Frey's works in Strasbourg and also after these authors had died, but they were contemporaneous with Fischart's work and were part of a growing printed discourse on the relationship between man and woman.[10]

Legislation regarding marriage, divorce, adultery, fornication, and prostitution was nothing new to the sixteenth-century residents of Strasbourg. A look back into the fifteenth century is necessary for the discussion, since the Reformation of the city in the 1520s resulted in changes in the secular legislation that had implications for the status of married life and thus for the relationship between man and woman and the construction of gender. Emphasis here will be placed on a few selected documents, as many decrees are very similar — some even identical — and as exhaustiveness is neither possible nor of interest in this study.

Common to all these decrees is a brief statement saying who passed it, for what purpose, and its relation to older ordinances. This is often followed by a comment on the current state of affairs which motivated the renewal and revision of the decree. Some of the ordinances deal with individual issues, but frequently several topics are dealt with at the same time. Hence adultery can be discussed together with gambling and drunkenness, all problems that posed a threat to the civic order.

In general, the ordinances become longer and more specific over time, pointing to the increasing complexity of urban governance. When going back to the fifteenth century, one is struck not only by the brevity of many documents, but also by the crudeness of some of them: the distance between the common man and the men in power who were writing and passing the decrees grew in proportion to the increasing population. If one also takes into account the increased use of the printing press for mass publication, the dissemination of public information underwent great changes at the beginning of the sixteenth century, and as a result, more people could be reached much faster. As early as 1889, Johann Brucker in a publication of selected manuscripts from the municipal archives pointed out that "Zunft- and Polizeiordnungen" (guild and police laws) were not printed in large numbers or circulated widely until after 1500, and that older ordinances are hard to find.[11] While many documents have of course been lost — the older the rarer — the dearth of ordinances also results from the fact that written tracts were not printed until a demand for them had arisen, printing presses and distribution channels had come into existence, and literacy rate among the population had increased. As a major German city with a quickly growing population, Strasbourg needed an efficient municipal administration to organize city affairs and maintain control over its residents. The increasing number of "inwohner," people who resided and worked in the city without having sworn the civic oath, was especially a source of problems for the city council. Obedience, a key word to the administrators, was achieved through psychological and corporal punishment, and it was a commonly accepted notion that discipline could be maintained only in a morally sound population. The Polizeiordnungen hence became more detailed as city life came to require stricter regulation in the eyes of the authorities, and at the same time, the punishments grew harsher as well.[12] Corporal punishment seems to have been a central part of the fifteenth-century penal system.[13] It becomes evident from the ordinances that the common man did not live up to the expectations of the mayor and the council; many of the documents start with complaints regarding the moral deterioration of the population.

Brucker claims that his selection of ordinances from the fifteenth century is "culturally interesting." This statement of course makes a dangerous generalization, especially since he does not specify how the texts were collected, how they were selected, or to what extent they have been edited. Many of them can still be found in the municipal archives, but it is difficult to find the original source without clear references in the edited text. The scarcity of printed material from this time nevertheless makes Brucker's collection interesting, and a comparison between a few of Brucker's texts and the sources in the municipal archives shows that he must have worked there. Brucker has unfortunately left out some parts of the documents, such as the stereotypical introductions, but he does not seem to have made any other changes in regard to content. The edited texts deviate from the original records mainly in spelling and punctuation.[14] His edition includes decrees concerning adultery, concubinage, procuration, and prostitution along with other documents on the moral condition of the city and its inhabitants.

A large part of the ordinances from the second half of the fifteenth century dealing with the relationships between men and women were specifically aimed at regulating the lives of prostitutes: they prescribed where the prostitutes were allowed to live, where they could conduct their "business,"[15] what they should or should not wear,[16] and what activities they were welcome to participate in.[17] Even though the prostitutes were surrounded by restrictions, prostitution in itself was not questioned or prohibited in these documents if practiced as regulated by the local legislation.[18] Prostitutes were mentioned by name and address — even those who did not describe themselves as prostitutes in hopes of escaping the list.[19] These women had little chance of keeping their work a secret, but as long as their activities were regarded as a profession that was legal, albeit immoral, they did not have to. A decree from 1473 mentions four burghers who had been elected to inspect the brothels in the city.[20] The brothel inspectors, who are mentioned again in a decree from 1496,[21] are presumably respected men from the middle and upper classes. It is not stated in the decree exactly what they are to inspect, but a decree from 1471 prohibits married men from visiting brothels,[22] and states that men who do are to be punished, as are the prostitutes with whom they are found. In 1493 it is stated that girls who have not reached puberty should be punished if found working as prostitutes,[23] obviously a law passed not only to protect young girls but also to save the honor of the men. It is, however, not made clear what kind of punishment awaited the sinning man.

It is apparent from the legislation surrounding prostitution that the male authorities tried to restrict prostitution in the course of the fifteenth century and that they regarded it as a kind of "Notlösung" (makeshift solution) to what were regarded as male needs. Not until the latter part of the century were married men singled out from the general group of "men" and prohibited from visiting the brothels, indicating that the importance of fidelity within marriage was increasingly stressed in the city. With the exception of young girls, female prostitutes and the conditions of their lives seldom appear to have been the subject of much interest; the regulations were passed to protect men from falling prey to their own desires and from the resulting loss of self-control — a secular as well as religious problem. By restricting the areas where prostitution could be practiced as well as the areas where the prostitutes were allowed to move about outside of the brothel, they could be made less visible to the population in general. The function of the prostitute was thus not so much to offer pleasure as to help men avoid sins that were considered worse than buying sex from an official prostitute. By channeling male sexuality outside of marriage to the municipal brothel (so it was reasoned), respected women in the city (non-prostitutes) were less likely to become the victims of illicit sex. The prostitute can hence be regarded as, on the one hand, helping men to engage in legal — but immoral — sexual intercourse, while on the other hand, preventing other women from involving themselves in illegitimate relationships. The prostitute was sexually depraved because she was sexually active outside of marriage, but nevertheless she had an accepted, though disrespected, function in fifteenth-century society. This function was taken away from her in the early and mid-sixteenth century, when sexuality was limited completely to marriage and officially rendered illicit and unacceptable at all other times.

It should be noted that most ordinances from the late fifteenth century that are kept in the municipal archives and the BNUS deal with trade and commerce and the regulation of various professions. They do not concern themselves primarily with the moral standards of the residents, thus illustrating that prostitution was treated as one trade among many. Many professions were regarded as gender-specific and reserved for either men or women, but gender is not the major issue in these decrees. Regulations concerning marriage only seldom appear in secular legislation in Strasbourg before the 1520s, and rules regarding commerce focus on the correct handling of goods rather than on the person handling them. The public inspections of the brothels can consequently be seen both in the light of a growing interest in the morals of the city's inhabitants and as the necessary inspection of a public institution.[24] The lists, naming the prostitutes as well as the inspectors, show the public nature of the brothels. However, there is a fundamental difference between the men and the women in this legislation. While the men are appointed to inspect the women, and are in charge of deciding who should be called a prostitute — designating who is permitted to help men find sexual satisfaction without endangering their social status — the women in the end are made social outcasts. They do not even deserve to be called women even though they work "for the good" of the city.

Decrees in the municipal archives as well as in Brucker's anthology indicate that aside from the aforementioned regulations regarding prostitution, moralizing comments and detailed prescriptions for male-female relationships were rather rare until the time of the Reformation. In the sixteenth century, legislation concerning marriage becomes extensive and is often combined with issues of female conduct, such as the wearing of improper jewelry and clothes. The female body is the main target of interest, but the ordinances do not exclusively criticize women; rather, they express concern for the lives of both male and female residents. According to a decree from 1514 "Wider Eebruchen Üppigkeit vnd ander süntlich Wergk" (against adultery, luxury, and other sinful acts), men as well as women should be punished for committing adultery.[25] No distinction is drawn between the sexes: the severer the crime, the severer the punishment, regardless of the sex of the offender.[26] The decree does not even refer to "man" or "woman" specifically, but uses the gender-neutral "who." One exception can be found in the writings regarding a relationship between a man and a nun. In 1514 such a relationship was punished by fines, while a few years later German reformers took pride in marrying nuns, "saving" them from a life in sin. The main issue of the decree is consolidation: the reunion of the estranged couple is its ideal outcome. This is a plausible reason for the focus on fines instead of on physical punishment for lesser crimes. The 1514 decree is one of only a very few ordinances that do not mention corporal punishment in connection with adultery. Divorce is not yet openly discussed, but "teylung" (separation) is mentioned as regulated in the book of the "Sübener."[27]

Even though prostitutes are mentioned as cunning women who take the money from boys and men,[28] and homeless prostitutes are doomed to imprisonment, the decree states that men should be punished as procurers when they force their wives or children into prostitution. If they do not live in accordance with existing rules and regulations, they can be banished from the city. Men are thus recognized as active in the business of prostitution, not only as inspectors but also as pimps, selling the bodies of their wives and children.[29] Underage prostitutes seem to have been a problem in the city. This decree from the early sixteenth century stresses what was said in the 1493 decree: girls are not allowed to work as prostitutes before they reach puberty — that is, before they have breasts or "other things."

> Wo ouch döchterlin funden wurdenn/ es were by tag oder by nacht die libs halb zu dem werck nit geschicke/ sunder zu junge werent/ Also das sie weder brüste/ noch anders hetten das dazu gehört/ die sollent mit der Kütten darumb bestroffet/ unnde dazu der Stat verweisen werden by libes stroffe/ So lange biz sie zu irem billichen alter kommen.[30]

The phrasing indicates that in the sixteenth century, clear distinctions were drawn not only between men and women but also among women at different stages of their lives.[31] "Anders" probably refers to menstruation, a physiological function necessary for procreation and indicating that a girl was reaching adulthood. Male prostitution is not mentioned anywhere in this or other documents. It does not mean that it did not exist, but it is of no importance in fifteenth- and sixteenth-century city ordinances.[32] The prostitution of women, the domestication of the "Sponziererin," was the key issue. She was the person responsible for releasing sexual tension in unmarried adult men — upon request — with few rights of her own. The growing animosity against the widespread practice in the Catholic priesthood of living in concubinage, and the growing importance of married life as opposed to celibacy at the dawn of the Reformation decreased the social value of the prostitute even more. Hence the increased interest in regulating her life, and keeping her away from other women.[33]

Forced to wear special clothing and restricted to certain areas, the prostitute became a social outcast in the course of the sixteenth century; she no longer had a profession to practice legally, and there was consequently no place for her at all in early modern society. She was slowly marginalized in the legal records. Few ordinances released after the 1520s discuss prostitution at length. They focus on illicit sex outside of marriage and do not distinguish prostitution from other forms of "Unee" (adultery and fornication). Prostitution was officially prohibited in Strasbourg at the time of the Reformation and an ordinance from 1594 bans all "Sponziererin" from the city.[34] It regulates that any prostitute caught within the city will be arrested, kept in prison and fed only water and bread until banished.

> Es sollen auch alle Sponziererin vnd die so offentliche Bulschafft treiben / weder in vnserer Statt / noch dero Burgbann vnd Obrigkeyt ge-

duldet / sonder da sie befunden vnd ergriffen / in vnser hafft eingezogen / mit wasser vnd brot gehalten / vnd als dann vnserer Statt vnd Obrigkeyt verwiesen werden.[35]

This change in the treatment of the prostitutes in the city can be traced to ordinances issued during the turbulent years of the Reformation in Strasbourg. "Constitution und Satzung, eins loblichen Raths/ der fryen statt Straßpurg/ Wie das Gotslestern/ fluchen/ vnd Ehebruch/ Nodzog/ Jungkfrawen schwechen/ hurerey vnd Copplerey/ in irer Statt vnd Oberkeit gestrafft werden soll" from 1521 does not mention prostitution specifically but gives a more detailed description of the punishment for adultery and fornication than the decree from 1514.[36] The person committing adultery not only has to pay a fine but is also imprisoned. The first offense results in four weeks in jail (im Thurn) with only water to drink and bread to eat, and the fine amounts to five pounds (fünf pfund pfennig). At the second offense, the penalty is doubled, and the third time, the offender is shown to the public and then banished from the city. In these cases, the same punishment is imposed upon men and women, but if a person has been pardoned and commits adultery yet another time, he or she is sentenced to death, and the method used depends on the sex of the accused: men are decapitated and women drowned. There is clearly a reason for this differentiation. Drowning was often used in witch trials and other trials where the majority of the persons persecuted were women. Decapitation, on the other hand, seems to have been reserved for men. The gendering of capital punishment is meaningful only in a culture whose structure is based on difference in sex and gender. What at first sight seems equal — the death sentence applying to both men and women — is in fact not, since there is a difference in value regarding the way the punishment is carried out.[37] It can thus be expected that it would be humiliating to a man to be drowned since it was a "female" punishment.

The 1521 decree further states that if a single resident male has a relationship with a married woman, he should be punished, but the type of punishment is not specified in detail. However, if the offender is a non-resident, he should be imprisoned immediately and pay a fine. Men without the means to pay the fine have to spend more time in jail: one week for every pound they owe the city. They are then banished from the city together with the woman they have been seen with, and neither one of them is allowed to return without the permission of the council. The same applies to an unmarried woman who has an affair with a married man. The difference is that women also lose their right to wear gold or silk; there is no similar restriction regarding men's clothing. The offense of the woman is thus made visible to everyone in the city. She bears the stigma of the prostitute by being restricted in her jewelry and dress, as can often be seen in decrees aimed at prostitutes. Adulterous women are also banned from attending dances and weddings and may not visit honorable gatherings, "eerliche gesellschafften," another rule that shows great similarities with those dealing with the prostitutes in the fifteenth century.[38] Adulterous men, on the other hand, are no longer allowed to hold official posts in the city after 1521. The adulterous husband in the *Rollwagenbüchlein* who feared losing his position as a respected member of society (see page 33 above) thus had predecessors of flesh and blood. It is evident that sixteenth-century men did not have to fear new dress codes but did stand to lose an integral part of their everyday public life: the right to hold public office. Women did not have to fear such a change, since they could not hold an office anyway, but their ties to the household and family sphere are only further emphasized by the fact that they were permitted to appear in public only at dances, weddings, and other festivities not related to the professional world. Weddings and many other festive occasions were, on the other hand, public celebrations in their own way, and as a result of the Reformation, the wedding had to be public in order to legitimate the marriage. Unlike the virtuous women in Wickram's *Nachbarn,* women in real-life Strasbourg were not completely restricted to the private, domestic sphere.[39]

It can be questioned whether these laws and their differentiations were of any relevance to the men and women at the very bottom of society. The lower classes were most likely occupied with pure survival and had little or no money to spend on pleasures, but the document from 1521 nevertheless makes clear that men and women had different positions and functions and thus different status in the city, and that this was an essential part of their everyday lives. Adulterous men who lost their rights to hold public office also lost a social function regarded as specifically male. In a strictly gendered society built on differences that are characterized as typically male or female, the loss of this right to hold office can also denote the loss of masculinity for the upper- and middle-class man. He is banished from the group of people with whom he identifies himself. It does not necessarily imply that he falls to a lower social class but that he is simply regarded as less trustworthy. Similarly, adulterous women are estranged from their likes. Their offense makes them "lesser" women and brings them closer to the women at the very bottom — the prostitutes. The difference between men and women is thus that the woman experiences a punishment related to her as a person, while the man experiences a penalty directed towards his function. The city ordinances indicate that women were accused in their role *as women* but men were deprived their office, and it has often enough been proven that it is easier to regain a position or an office than to regain other people's respect for one as a person.

The decree from 1529 builds on and further expands the ordinance from 1521.[40] Again, adultery, fornication, rape, and procuration appear in the same decree with other moral offenses like drinking, gambling, and cursing. The mayor together with the council express great concern that previous decrees have not achieved the desired result: proper conduct among the people. The tone, therefore, is sharper and the punishment more severe. The council undoubtedly understands itself as representing God in earthly matters and writes:

> ... nit allein als von der Oberkeit / zu erhaltung gemeins friedens / Erbarer polici vnd wesens / angesehen vnd bekant / Sunder auch dem heyligen wort Gottes / dweil das selbig teglich / vnnd offenbar / wider der gleichen laster gepredigt würt / gehorsamlich erschynen sein.[41]

The aim is to enforce what is believed to be divine order on the citizens; secular laws and regulations are not passed for the good of the council or the residents of the city, but in the name of God. This makes it nearly impossible for the citizens to question any decree that is passed, much less to question the idea of a "natural," God-given order. It further explains the need to place the decree in a long tradition. The crimes are categorized according to older decrees, but there is an increasing differentiation in punishments imposed for the same crime.[42] Not only does this ordinance show more interest in distinguishing between residents and non-residents of the city, it also judges an unmarried resident women who has a relationship with a married man exactly as it does a non-resident man. An unmarried adulterous male resident is punished like a married resident, but his female counterpart, who receives the same punishment as the non-resident man, has to pay a higher fine and spend more time in jail. If she repeats her crime, she is ultimately banished from the city permanently. The unmarried woman evidently has become a greater threat to the city than in older decrees. There is no single explanation for these changes, but when brothels and convents were closing in the course of the sixteenth century, the number of unmarried adult women at least initially increased in the city. Unmarried women had few opportunities to support themselves in a time of high inflation and the growing restrictions surrounding most professions in the sixteenth-century city. With few rights and many obligations, the single woman was regarded as a burden to the city officials, who preferred for her to marry and thus obtain financial support and legal protection through her husband.[43] In the case of the truly impoverished, the difference was again superfluous: people with no property or money had to go to jail and to work for the city — whether they were men or women.

> Were yemands der Eebrüchigen also arm / das es obgemelt gelt straff / nit zu bezalen hette / oder die sach seiner halb / also gestalt were das ein Rath erkennen möchte / das durch abnemung solcher gelt straffen / nitt allein er / sunder vil meer / das ander vnschuldig eegemecht / vnd ir beder kinder / gestrafft / vnd also mangel an ir notdurfftigen narung / leiden möchten. So sol solch geltstraff in einander leibstraff / ye nach gelegenheit der personen / verwendt / oder aber verordent werden / dz sollich gelt / mit arbeiten / an vnser statt werck / wett machen kann.[44]

It was, however, very important to the city officials that neither the betrayed man or woman nor their children should suffer financial losses because of the new family situation. Support for those left behind was of great concern, especially since the women had few opportunities to support their children and themselves. This is contrary to many of the stories in chapbooks, where adultery is usually regarded as a problem caused by both spouses, the combined result of men's inability to control themselves and their wives and the weakness ascribed to women. In a way, the Schwänke give a more plausible view of an adulterous relationship than the ordinances do. Considering the fact that moral offenses were made public in the early modern village and town, there was little chance for a betrayed spouse to shield him- or herself from the comments of other residents, and gossip was probably no less difficult to prevent in the sixteenth century than it is today.

The city officials no doubt wanted married people to stay together for reasons of material support, morality, and the private and public social order.[45] All ordinances dealing with adultery or fornication leave open the possibility of a reunion. The adulterous partner had to be punished, but the city wanted husband and wife to stay together. The betrayed partner did, however, have the right to be separated — divorced — from his or her spouse and to receive financial or other support if the adulterous husband or wife had any assets that allowed for this.[46] Gifts given to the bride by her husband after the wedding night — the "Morgengabe" — had to be returned to the husband if the wife was unfaithful. Other gifts that were meant to grant security if one of the spouses died had to be returned in the case of adultery.

Yet, even if the decree prefers to discuss adultery without mentioning "men" or "women," words such as "Morgengab" and "widum"[47] demonstrate that the decree was directed mainly towards adulterous women, who were denied the public support often granted to women on the death of their husbands.[48] If a woman left her husband for someone else, she thus lost her legal right to the assets reserved for her. If he left her for someone else, she could claim her part and — depending on the amount — hopefully have enough to survive for a while. This was again of no importance to the great majority of people who did not have any assets and whose main concern was to find food for the day in order to survive. The ordinance only addresses people who risked losing money, goods, or land to the spouse. The increasing number of restrictions on female labor in the sixteenth century — as has been described in depth by, among others, Merry Wiesner-Hanks and Heide Wunder — must have been a great problem to the administrators when husbands deserted their wives and children. If the goal was control, then other means of exerting this control had to be found. If a husband was left by his wife, the loss of a spouse was just as difficult for him, but the man was not as limited like the woman in his search for support. As the head of the household, he was usually in greater need of a person to take care of the children than of financial aid, since he was usually accustomed to providing for his family financially himself.

Despite ambivalence in the legal records in regard to female conduct, the council clearly was aware of the dangers women were exposed to in the city. The decree from 1529 allows no leeway in the case of rape: the rapist will be sentenced to death.[49] Men were also punished for "Junckfrawen schwechen" (seducing virgins) if they did not immediately agree to marry the woman they had — secretly — been involved with. This in turn required the consent of her parents. If the man decided to leave the woman, he had to pay fines to the city, but he also had to pay the woman — unless he was too poor, in which case he had to spend ten weeks in jail. Married men were also obliged to pay a fine to the city, and to pay the seduced woman and her family for lost honor. They were then additionally punished for adultery as described above. If the relationship had been consummated in sexual intercourse or had even resulted in pregnancy, the punishment was more severe; it appears that a death sentence was possible, although not always carried out.[50]

While the decree states that in the eyes of the law, men and women share the responsibility for illegitimate relationships, in actual practice, the council did indeed try to identify one party as the guilty one. It refers to seductive women who encourage men and cunningly trick them into something they would otherwise never have thought of. In such cases, the woman has herself to blame and must be punished. The possibility that a combination of different factors are sometimes involved — for example, with one party being the seducer and the other more than willing to play the game — is not mentioned. Such a scenario would, of course, lead to marriage in most, but not all, cases. Clearly, a scapegoat needed to be found, and it is questionable whether women were able to defend themselves and claim their innocence if the accused man was of higher social standing or otherwise regarded as more trustworthy because of his status as a man. The council speaks of underage women — girls who, at very young age, "in die freuelkeit kommen" (become sinners) and need to be imprisoned to learn their lesson. On the one hand, the council regards this as something that happens only to some girls. The members of the council do not seem to think that certain girls have actively chosen prostitution as their profession. Their behavior can therefore not be regarded as biologically determined — as something inherent in every woman. The seductive nature of woman is, on the other hand, taken for granted.[51]

The attitude towards prostitutes is harsh in the 1929 decree, but the council still leaves a door open for them: they are asked to seriously reconsider their behavior and to find a better way of living, a rather difficult undertaking for these women who were often poor and thus rarely had a choice. The more open these women were about their profession, the severer the punishment. According to the decree, they normally had to leave the city. There is a clear difference between this document and the decrees from the fifteenth century where prostitutes were frowned upon, but still a part of the community.

Procuration, finally, seems to have been much more of a problem among women than among men. Even if men and women were dependent on their parents in their choice of spouse, especially if they belonged to the upper class, women were almost always dependent on someone else: their parents, husbands, or guardians. Women were consequently easy targets for procurers, who could be members of the woman's own family or complete strangers. Judging by the city ordinances, "trafficking," which was referred to as "kupplery" (procuration), was not at all unknown to sixteenth-century men and women.[52]

After the beginning of the Reformation in the 1520s, the Church and the city council together made a recommendation that men and women marry. However, marriages in which the spouses were not interested in each other or had been forced into matrimony benefited no one. The 1529 decree vividly shows the struggle to uphold law and order in the growing city. The council addresses all residents of Strasbourg: "Wann auch yemans / es sey frembd oder heimisch / ledig oder in der Ee / wer der wölle / nymands vßgenommen. . . ." (If somebody, be he a stranger or a native, single or married, whoever he may be, without exception . . .). No one is excluded from helping the council to maintain secular and divine order. Everyone, burghers and other residents alike, are responsible for the well-being of the city:

> So sollen menigklich / burger / inwoner / vnd hindersossen / geistlich und weltlich / weib vnd mann / beyderley geschlechts / zu fürderung der eer gots / auch pflantzung christlicher zucht / vnd erbarkeit / vß christlicher pflicht / damit sy alle Gott / dem Allmechtigen / vnd einander selbst verwandt syndt . . . .[53]

Thus breaking the law meant acting against the will of God, the worst offense imaginable.[54]

This communal responsibility in earthly matters before God moreover calls attention to the significance of continuity. "Eins Ersamen Raths der Statt Straßburg Decret / die Ehe belangend" (A decree from the honorable council of the city of Strasbourg / on marriage) from 1565 again refers to older decrees in order to establish its own legitimacy and demonstrate its rootedness in tradition: "Von Ehesachen. Vnd lautet mehr anzogne unserer Vorfahren / vnd vnser vor Jaren außgangne vnd jetzo ernewerte / vnd zum theil verbesserte Constitution / wie volgt."[55] The text makes evident that the legitimacy of official decrees is of growing importance, and it emphasizes that the decree is distributed "offentlich publiciert vnd in Truck" (officially published and in print). Like earlier decrees concerning marriage, it stresses that all residents of the city are made equally responsible, and that no one is excluded.[56] Additionally the city's responsibility for marital matters is expanded. A marriage court consisting of five men holding administrative positions in the city had been formed already in 1529 to hear all cases reported.[57] The growing population and the shift in responsibility from Church to city must have resulted in an increasing number of cases dealing with marriage, but also opened up the possibility to apply for divorce in some cases.[58] The city thus needed an organization large enough to handle all cases. The growing control of secular powers over marriage did not, however, result in a loss of belief in the divine order: the council never questioned "the holy estate of matrimony." The decree states: "Dieweil vnd aber der Ehestand / von Gott dem Allmechtigen vnserm HERRN selbst verordnet / vnd hernach durch Jesum Christum vnsern Erlöser bestätigt worden . . ." (While matrimony has in fact been ordained by

God the Almighty our LORD himself and hereafter endorsed by Jesus Christ our savior . . .). The connection between the council, the city, and God is established.

Major issues to the reformers were the problems related to clandestine marriages.[59] Most agreed that secret marriages should be regarded as illegitimate; they did not become legally binding until registered and made public. According to Lutheran theology, it was not possible for a man and a woman to claim that they were married only on the grounds that intercourse had taken place between them in the past. This had been a legitimate argument in the Middle Ages, even though intercourse was regarded as fornication before the Church officially had sanctioned the marriage. Ideal and reality here seem to have clashed. Old traditions lived on for a long time side by side with more modern ideas, and court cases dealing with broken promises and lost honor are common in the reformed parts of Europe.[60] The differences between Roman and canonical law further complicated the legislation on marriage.[61] A problem often associated with clandestine marriages was the legal age of marriage. According to the canonical law, boys were allowed to marry at the age of twelve and girls at the age of fourteen. Although marriages between very young people were rare among common people because of the need for money or property to start a family, they still occurred, especially as part of the marriage politics of the nobility. It was in the interests of the city council to prevent such marriages; as they saw it, the reason for marriage was primarily procreation, the building of a stable family that would not cause problems to the city administration but rather contribute to the wealth and growth of the city. Without a secure income, the young family would be dependent on others, something that had to be avoided at a time when a great majority of the population was struggling to survive. The ordinance not only emphasizes the seriousness of marriage, and the importance of staying together for better or for worse but also advises the couple that maturity is needed to make the marriage last.

The city council tries to come to terms with these problems in the 1565 decree. What had not yet been developed in the 1520s is given a great deal of attention here. No marriages are to be arranged without the consent of the parents or guardians. Neither girls nor boys who are still dependent on their parents are allowed to "one vorwissen vnnd bewilligung derselbigen / in die Ehe begeben vnd versprechen mögen" (marry without the knowledge and consent of the parents). Clandestine marriages are declared invalid, disobedient, and illegal according to divine law (vnordentlich / vngehorsamlich vnd vngöttlich). Anyone helping young people to marry is to be punished as an accomplice and according to the degree of involvement. However, children over the age of twenty-five may act on their own, even if the parents or guardians oppose the marriage for whatever reason.[62] This can be seen as a drastic contrast to canonical law, but it probably is more realistic. It was not uncommon that men were close to thirty years old before marrying, a result of the strict regulations often imposed on income and other assets. Secure living conditions were here more important than instant love, and marriage of utmost value to those upholding law and order. It becomes very clear that in the reformed cities, marriage is to be regarded as an obligation. According to the decree, parents who keep their children from marrying will be punished. The resemblance to the conversation between Amelia, her mother, and their friend in Wickram's *Nachbarn* is striking (see page 116 above). Amelia has to marry if she wants to live a life as ordained by nature and God, but she is only allowed to do so after consulting her parents first. The parents, in turn, are not allowed to promise their children to anyone unless they discuss this with the children first.

The Strasbourg council is, however, well aware of the problems underlying these issues. Feelings and emotions always come into play in such cases and reason therefore has to go before law. The marriage court should act according to the law and the Bible, but the annulment or annihilation of invalid marriages should be avoided if the couple and the parents stand to suffer more than they will benefit from the separation: "Es weren dann dermassen vmbstend . . . vorhanden / Das die Annulation oder vernichtigung der Ehe / den Kindern vnd Eltern mehr zu nachtheil vnd verkleinerung / dann zu vortheil vnd wohlfart gelangen möcht."[63] No distinctions are made between men and women in the decree, but we would probably find that distinctions were made in practice if we looked at actual cases brought before the court.

Divorce remains a dilemma to the council. Even though the problems surrounding the separation of a married couple in the Catholic Church were abolished when marriage was secularized in the sixteenth century, divorce was a last resort and not accepted by all secular and religious authorities. Despite already strict regulations, the city council tries to tighten the rules regarding separation in the 1565 decree: a deserted person cannot bring charges against the spouse until one year has passed since he or she left, regardless of the offense (adultery or other unspecified reasons), and no one is allowed to remarry without the consent of the marriage court. No distinction is made between men and women. The importance of documentation is obvious: as with weddings, which have to be preceded by the announcement of the forthcoming marriage and the notification of the marriage court, a separation must be made legally binding before either party may remarry.⁶⁴ A wedding ceremony held at the church is not enough; secular powers have to be involved: "So wöllen wir das alle Ehe / vor vnd ehe dann sie mit dem Kirchgang / vnd Einsegnung bestetigt werden / offentlichen auff der Canzel zu dem wenigsten Zweymal sollen außgeruffen vnd verkündiget werden."⁶⁵

Five years after this decree was issued, the council passed another declaration on fornication, this time specifically addressing young, unmarried women — Junckfrawen.⁶⁶ It is short and deals only with one topic: sex before marriage. It is not the first time the council singles out one group to assume responsibility for a problem, but most decrees up to this time dealing with sexuality have addressed men *and* women. Here the virgin is the addressee as well as the problem. The first half of the decree makes her solely responsible for not respecting secular and divine law or "the holy matrimony" (dem heyligen Ehestande). To the dismay of the council, not only do some women have sex before marriage, some are even pregnant at the wedding and give birth shortly afterwards.⁶⁷ The decree further addresses those daring women who still claim to be virgins after having had intercourse and hence lost their virginity, and who wear clothes and other attributes specifically reserved for a virgin. Men are not mentioned at all in this part, even though they are obviously intimately involved in the defloration of the young women. The importance of "purity" and chastity for young women does not apply in an equivalent manner to young men. Interestingly, when prohibiting fornication, the decree then changes from addressing only women to speaking to men and women alike:

> Demnach so Mandieren / gebietten vnd verbietten wir allen vnd jeden vnsern Burgern / jnwohnern / hindersassen / zugehörigen vnd verwandten inn Statt vnd Land / Das sie sich / bey vermeidung vnserer ernstlichen / Straff / fürterhin obangeregter vnnd anderer dergleichen Vnzucht / gäntzlich vnd aller dings enthalten.⁶⁸

The council is apparently aware of the fact that intercourse involves two people, but by returning to the young women who do not follow the decree, it on the one hand makes clear that both men and women should be punished for fornication, but on the other hand stresses that the woman is nevertheless at fault.

> Im fall aber eyniche dochter oder Junckfraw vber diß vnser Christlich vnd wolmeinend Mandat / fürthin jrer Junckfrawlichen ehren so gar vergessen / vnd vor dem ordenlichen Kirchengang sich deren berauben lassen würde / So Ordnen vnd wöllen wir hiemit / jetzt alß dann / vnd

> dan alß jetzo. Das dieselbig / neben vnser fernern straff / die wir gegen jr vnd jrem vertrawten / vnnachläßig fürzunemmen gedencken / ... / sonder also von den andern Erbarn vnd Ehrlichen Junckfrawen abgesündert sein vnd bleiben.[69]

The woman is depicted as the active party, the individual who takes the initiative, and the man thus becomes the victim. Needless to say, this could have been the case at times, but the opposite was probably just as common.

Turning to a decree from the last decade of the sixteenth century, the importance of tradition and continuity is once again emphatically asserted. With reference to earlier decrees, the document from 1594 points to the moral decay of the population and the need for harsher punishments.[70] Theory and practice seem to diverge: the decree states that fines have been imposed more often than imprisonment. This may have been a result of efforts towards reconciliation instead of separation or divorce — if a couple had agreed to stay together, imprisonment was probably not the best way of making the marriage work. However, according to the city officials, the fines had not produced the desired effect, and thus the law needed to be rewritten and enforced. According to the new decree, a first offender has to spend two weeks in jail for committing adultery. If a married man leaves his wife for a virgin, he has to pay her dowry. If he is poor, he is banished from the city until an agreement between him and the young woman has been reached. In accordance with older decrees, the adulterous man has to step down from any public offices he holds. Women experience the same increase in time served in prison; otherwise the punishment corresponds with older decrees. The betrayed party has the right to request that the adulterous spouse leave the city for at least one year. In cases of severe abuse — most likely men abusing their wives, even though this is not stated — this could have made the lives of betrayed spouses somewhat easier. At the second offense, the guilty party is not only to be imprisoned but put out to public ridicule and then banished from the city for life. Anyone trying to return without the permission of the city council is to be sentenced to death, man by "the sword" (decapitation), and woman by drowning. This differentiation between man and woman remains intact throughout the century:

> Der oder Die sollen nach erkundigung begangenen lasters / mit Vrtheyl vnnd Recht vom leben zum todt / da es ein Mann mit dem Schwerdt / da es aber ein Fraw / mit dem Wasser gerichtet vnd ertrenckt werden.[71]

The punishment for an unmarried man who has had a relationship with a married woman is the same whether he is a citizen, resident, non-resident, or foreigner, probably because fines had proven to be insufficient. The differentiation between men and women seen in older decrees is thus abolished here, maybe due to the increasingly harsh penalties. The offender has to spend fourteen days in prison and is then banished for life. Corporal punishment awaited anyone returning without permission. The worst offenses from the perspective of the city officials seem to have been when husband and wife committed deliberate actions to obtain a separation or divorce or when both committed adultery with other individuals.[72] Both offenses result in a death sentence; this is regarded as a crime as serious as rape.[73] Unmarried men who enter a relationship with a virgin without the intention to marry but with her consent have to pay her dowry, with the amount depending on her social status. They also have to spend two weeks in prison and have to leave town if too poor to pay. Single women convicted of the same crime could either be ordered to pay a fine or be sentenced to corporal punishment. The council seems to judge this on a case-by-case basis, but makes a clear distinction between rape and fornication, even though it must often have been difficult to tell if a woman had been raped or simply talked into something she did not want. The decree states:

> So sollen dieselben Weibspersonen / vmb solchen fräuel ohngebührlich vnd leichtfertig fürnemen an jhrem Leib oder Gut / der geschicht vnd jhres begangenen handelns halben / nach eynes Rahts erkantnuß / jederseits gestrafft werden.[74]

As in the Schwänke, which frequently describe maids having sex with their masters, the relationship implied in these official texts is one of complete dependency. The woman had little chance to defend herself, and turning down the head of the household could easily result in her losing her job. Even though the council grants her an official hearing, her chances there must have been slim. As is often the case even today, only in very clear cases of rape — if there were trustworthy witnesses, for example — did the woman have a fair chance to defend herself.

If the woman had not yet had reached puberty, the situation was slightly different. The penalty for men who had sex with minors (girls) varies according to the offense: from fines and loss of public office to corporal or capital punishment. The decree does not specify the penalty for the girls; it only states that they should be punished. This could mean it was recognized that the adult had to take on responsibility, but the decree is not clear on this point.

> Wann auch ein Ehemann / oder ein Lediger ein junge Tochter so vnter jhren jaren / mit guten worten oder verheyssungen zu seinem willen beredt vnd zu fall brächte / der soll der that nach / so am Leib / Leben / ehr oder Gut gestrafft werden. So auch solche junge Meydlein so vnter jhren jaren in die fräuelheyt kommen / das sie in ein solch laster fielen / trieben oder übten / die sollen nach erkantnus eynes Rahts gestrafft werden.[75]

The phrasing in the document shows that the opposite problem — older women having sex with boys — was of little or no significance to the council since it is not mentioned at all. Prostitutes obviously existed — they are mentioned in one paragraph in the decree — but they are not dealt with at length or in detail as they were in the records of the fifteenth century. It is only stated that they should be imprisoned and then banished. They are no longer asked to quit their sinful behavior and live honorably; rather, these women are simply not wanted within the city walls at all: "sonder da sie befunden vnd ergriffen / in vnser hafft eingezogen / mit wasser vnd brot gehalten / vnd als dann vnserer Statt vnd Obrigkeyt verwisen werden."[76]

Procuration remains a crime, and any father, mother, or husband found guilty is condemned to drowning. This is interesting since drowning was reserved for women in older decrees, and procuration does not seem to have included women, with the exception that "mothers" are mentioned a few times. One cannot but ask if the men accused of procuration thus sank to the level of women of the same social class. One does not find explanations as to why certain methods are used for certain crimes in the decrees, although convention surely played an important role, and decrees like the ones discussed here remain ambivalent throughout the sixteenth century in their treatment of men and women. A connection does, however, seem to exist between certain offenses and the loss of male (and in some cases female) honor. The city officials on the one hand wanted to see that everyone who committed a crime was punished, and on the other drew distinctions among the punishments for a given kind of crime depending on gender, social class, and residential status. The 1594 decree illustrates this in the concluding passage, which is taken from an older decree. It talks of the double standards of women who act as if they still were virgins but who actually have lost their virginity long ago. Even though they should be punished together with their lovers, they are regarded as worse offenders than the men. Men are not discussed further in the decree; they have nothing to lose since their loss of virginity can hardly be proven.

It is at times easy to forget the contexts of these decrees. I have emphasized that the aim of the council was to uphold law and order, that this was not an end in itself but a way of managing life in the early modern city. Famine due to wars or years of bad crops, epidemics, and natural disasters were a part of everyday life. The city walls could be a blessing as well as a curse for the inhabitants: at times they locked the residents in with no way out, at times they protected them from outside aggression. It was therefore of utmost importance that uprisings be brought to an end quickly, and that disagreements and other problems be solved rapidly. Any source of conflict endangered the lives of many people and had to be repressed. The scholar of the twenty-first century need not agree with the means used by those in power in the sixteenth century to grapple with the problems of the time or the measures implemented to solve them. He or she must nevertheless try to understand the very different living conditions of men and women in the early modern city that form the context for these measures.

One decree regulating weddings and other festivities from 1570 vividly demonstrates the very different understanding of cause and effect at that time.[77] The city had been suffering from famine, bad wine harvests, and wars, and the decree suggests that this is a result of misbehaving citizens who have aroused the wrath of God.[78] It continues with a detailed description of what may be consumed by whom on different occasions, how many days a wedding may last, who may be invited to the festivities, and so on. The distinctions drawn between rich and poor probably seemed just as natural to the residents of the city as they did to the council. The council thus emphasizes that proper behavior among all members of society — commensurate with their social status — will alleviate the problems addressed in the decree. Moral issues are hence brought into close connection to natural disasters in a way only possible in societies where people believe in a divine order.

The needs identified for the city are claimed to be identical with what is regarded as God's will. The individual's sex or gender has to be seen in this context as well. It makes the sex/gender system divinely ordained and thus impossible to change. The confusion among the sixteenth-century residents of Strasbourg in how to address issues of gender seems to stem from God himself, who gave them the contradictory images of Eve and Mary in the Bible. These images cannot be explained by class, race, or confession only, but cut across the female population in a way that is very difficult for "man" to cope with.[79] By reinforcing conventional images of women in written discourse while at the same time creating new stereotypes — for example, the Protestant housewife — "woman" changes in appearance when "man" is at her side. In the city ordinances, however, she is never associated with the witch-like figures that appear in the chapbooks but is given the opportunity to defend herself.

Notes

[1] The city council played a major role in the introduction of the Reformation in Strasbourg. For a thorough study of the ruling class in Strasbourg at the time of the Reformation, see Thomas A. Brady, *Ruling Class, Regime, and Reformation at Strasbourg 1520–1555* (Leiden: Brill, 1978). Brady gives a brief introduction to the structure of the city governance (42–43). See also Thomas A. Brady, *Communities, Politics and Reformation in Early Modern Europe* (Leiden: Brill, 1998) on the Reformation in Strasbourg (51–274). Cf. Lorna Jane Abray, *The People's Reformation: Magistrates, Clergy, and Commons in Strasbourg, 1500–1598* (Ithaca, NY: Cornell UP, 1985), 11. See also Abray's presentation of the city officials on the day of the civic oath (Schwörtag, 50). In her study, Abray investigates the impact of the Reformation on different social groups in the city. Besides Thomas Brady, Miriam Usher Chrisman is probably the best-known historian who has published in English: *Strasbourg and the Reform: A Study in the Process of Change* (New Haven: Yale UP, 1967) and *Lay Culture, Learned Culture: Books and Social Change in Strasbourg 1480–1599* (New Haven: Yale UP, 1982). There are a number of scholarly works in French on the Reformation in Strasbourg. One of the most important texts is Francois Rapp, *Réformes et Réformation a Strasbourg. Église et société dans le diocèse de Strasbourg (1450–1525)* (Paris: Editions Ophrys, 1974).

[2] The city officials clearly preferred pragmatism to a dogmatic stance in matters of public morality. As long as someone did not act in a way that would threaten the local social order, he or she would not have to fear severe punishment. Cf. Abray, *The People's Reformation*, 197.

[3] Wunder calls attention to the difference between the civil law, which mainly dealt with economic matters such as inheritance and property and which allowed women few rights, and the criminal law, which treated women as equal legal persons: Heide Wunder, *He Is the Sun, She Is the Moon: Women in Early Modern Germany* (Cambridge: Harvard UP, 1998), 188–91. See also Merry Wiesner, *Gender, Church and State in Early Modern Germany* (Harlow: Longman, 1998), the introductory chapter on women's public role as well as the fifth chapter on the legal position of women. Wiesner points out that both Roman and German law stressed the inferiority of women and justified the exclusion of women from a number of legal functions. Cf. Elisabeth Koch, *Maior dignitas est in sexu virili: Das weibliche Geschlecht im Normensystem de 16. Jahrhunderts* (Frankfurt am Main: Vittorio Klostermann, 1991), 69–74. Koch stresses that only unmarried women enjoyed a certain degree of legal independence. This means that in addition to gender, civilian status as well as social class were determining factors in legal matters. For a detailed discussion of the Protestant legislation of marriage, see Hartwig Dieterich, *Das protestantische Eherecht in Deutschland bis zur Mitte des 17. Jahrhunderts* (Munich: Claudius, 1970). Dietrich

focuses on legal changes up to 1650. For the social implications for the marriage reform in sixteenth-century Germany, see Joel F. Harrington, *Reordering Marriage and Society in Reformation Germany* (Cambridge: Cambridge UP, 1995).

[4] For a brief but interesting comment on the Reformation in Strasbourg and its impact on women, see Miriam Usher Chrisman, "Women and the Reformation in Strasbourg 1490–1530," *Archiv für Reformationsgeschichte: Internationale Zeitschrift zur Erforschung der Reformation und ihrer Weltwirkungen* 63 (1972): 143–67. Chrisman stresses that the Reformation did not lead to any fundamental changes of the position of woman in society but that the enhanced status of marriage resulted in the decreasing value of celibacy (166).

[5] Cf. Chrisman, "Women and the Reformation." For a discussion of "The Impact of the Reformation on Daily Life," see R. W. Scribner, *Religion and Culture in Germany (1400–1800)*, ed. Lyndal Roper (Leiden: Brill, 2001), 275–301.

[6] One important, albeit old, publication on marriage in Strasbourg in the sixteenth century is published in French: Francois Wendel, *Le mariage a Strasbourg a l'epoque de la Réforme 1520–1692* (Strasbourg: Imprimerie Alsacienne, 1928). It presents the views on marriage held by reformers as well as Catholics, and discusses different issues related to marriage. It also includes a number of German documents from the time of the Reformation.

[7] Joseph Fuchs, *Inventaire des archives de la ville de Strasbourg antérieures á 1790. Série I (Ancienne Série I.D.G.) et supplément de la Série AA* (Strasbourg, 1954).

[8] See Chrisman, *Lay Culture, Learned Culture*. Chrisman has cataloged *printed* sources in Strasbourg from the time of the Reformation and published an invaluable volume on this material. It is not complete but covers material from the municipal archives as well as from the BNUS.

[9] Susanna Burghartz's interesting study of marriage and sexuality in Basle discusses a number of examples and cases in regard to different aspects of marriage and sexuality as found in sixteenth-century documents. The emphasis on individual cases makes for a wide array of examples: *Zeiten der Reinheit — Orte der Unzucht: Ehe und Sexualität in Basel während der Frühen Neuzeit* (Paderborn: Schöningh, 1999).

[10] Ordinances strictly focusing on the celebration of weddings cannot be discussed in depth here. They appear within a more general discussion of the social construction of husband and wife, of the married couple. They set the limits for the size and thus cost of the wedding and are more often focused on social class than gender.

[11] Johann Brucker, *Strassburger Zunft- und Polizei-Verordnungen des 14. und 15. Jahrhunderts* (Strasbourg: Karl J. Trübner, 1889), xi.

[12] The term "Stadtordnungen" in Brucker's edition seems to correspond to series R in the municipal archives, but some of the decrees have been renumbered, which is why I here prefer to only refer to Brucker's anthology when citing texts from it. I have not been able to find all of the texts Brucker has transcribed. Some of them seem to be lost, but most of them can be found in the holdings of the municipal archives: Brucker, *Strassburger Zunft- und Polizei-Verordnungen*. The following texts are of interest when looking at the position of women in the fifteenth century. I have chosen not to translate them but to still include them in the notes, since the texts are hard to come by.

Vol. 19, folio 8b, 15th century: Unser herren sint überein komen, wer ein elich wip het und der gat und sü lat sitzen und ein ander unelich wip zu huse setzet, der bessert fünf jore von dirre stat. Dete och es ein wip, die einen elichen mann hette und von dem ginge und bi eime andern unelichen manne seze, die bessert och fünf jore. Were och ein ehlich wip hette und einre andern die ee gelobte und sie domitte also betrüge, der bessert zehen jor von dirre stat. Dete och es ein wip, die einen elichen mann hette und eime andern die ee gelobte, die bessert och zehen jor.

Vol. 28, folio 369, 17.3.1472: Verordnung gegen wilde Ehen. Heinrich Bisinger, Lienhart Ameister und Hans Burckhart. Als inen entpfohlen ist zu rotslahen von der personen wegen die öffentlich zur unee sitzent, so haben sie gehört lesen die ordenunge wie es vormals geordnet worden ist, und bedunket sie geroten sin das man solicher ordnunge fürbas nochgange und die ur ein nuwes gebiete zu halten, uf das sich die die mit solichen unelichen sachen (umbgon) und ouch die spontziererin wissen zu hüten vor der pene die darauf gesetzet ist. So beduhte ir ein teil geroten sin das man den rotherren und den meistern uf jeglicher stubenentpfehlen solt, wo sie jemans, der uf ir stube gehörte, wustent odern erfüren das er ofenlich zur unee sesse, das sie den für sich besanten und im gütlich setien von solicher uneeu ston; wolt er dann das nit nit tun, das sie im dann ir stube verbieten und es ouch verkünden sollen den sübenzühtern; die sollen inen dann darumb öffentlich rehtvertigen und fürnemen umb die besserung. Die rete und XXI haben dis erkantzu tun. . . .

Vol. 28, folio 242, 15th century: Verordnung wider Kupplerei und Ehebruch. Welicher dienende knecht, dinstjungfowe, maget oder kellerin jeman dem sie dienen und in deshuse und costen sie sint, ir kinde oder ir fründe kinde oder soliche kinde der vogt ein mann were, anherwirbet oder hindergat zur ee oder zur unee, inen selbs oder andern luten verkuppeltent one der nehsten fründe wissen und willen, die kinde sient zu iren tagen kommern oder nit, dete es ein knecht den soll man ertrencken, dete es aber ein solich wip, als vor geschriben stot, der soll man die ougen uszstechen, und soll darzu nyemer me gon Straßburg kommen, so solich geschicht geclaget und in der worheit erfunden würt. Were ouch das dhein dienender knecht sime herren, jungherren oder meister, in des muse und brot er wer, sin elich wip beslofet und geschendet oder ob ein solich knecht oder dienstjungfrowe, megede oder kellerin oder ander gesinde, wie die genant werent, ein solich frowe jeman verkuppeltent, kommet das in klage für und findet sich kuntlich in der worheit, dem oder den sol man ir zwene rechten finger abhouwen und das bistum ewiclich verbieten. Fünde ouch ein soliche herschaft solich ir knecht an frischer gedat by irem wiben, was den uf der gedat widerfüre, do engat kein besserunge noch. Wer hynnanfürder jeman sin kint, es sy knabe oder dochter, anherwirbet das es im die ee gelobet, oder zu der ee neme, do der knabe oder die dochter under zwentzig joren alt were (es sy deann mit vatter oder muter willen, oder der nehsten fründe wille, ob die kinde nit vatter oder muter hettent), wurt das meister und rat inklage fürbrocht in jores frist, nachdem vatter und muter oder die nehsten fründe, ob kinde vatter und muter nit enhettent, das empfindet, das soll nymer gon Straßburg kommen, one vatter und muter oder der jinde nahsten, als vor stot, wissen und willen. Und soll das kint das also die ee hinweg gelopt hette, sin erbezal das es von vatter und muter zu erbe kommen mag verloren haben; es sy dann das vatter und muter oder eins noch des andern tode es im mit gutem willen wider gebe und es im benomet das es zu erbe gon solt an irem gut. Wer sich berümet und ustut das im einer oder eine die ee gelobet habe und das geschieht von hinderunge den lüten zu tun oder von rumes wegen, und sich nit findet das soliche wort ergangen sienr die zu einer ee trefen mogent, der oder die sollent nymer me gon Straßburg kommen on des gnade dem soliches geschee, ob er das in clage fürbringe.

[13] Brucker, *Strassburger Zunft- und Polizei-Verordnungen*. One undated decree mentions drowning, poking out the eyes of the offender, and cutting off two fingers on the right hand. Brucker refers to vol. 28, 242 and dates it to the fifteenth century (it is undated).

[14] The latter is also the case with the editions of Frey's and Montanus's work from the nineteenth century. Bolte generally seems to prefer to adapt the texts to the spelling of his own time.

[15] Mandats et Reglements [hereafter M&R], R/2, 131–32, 1493, Archives municipales de Strasbourg [hereafter AMS], mention Bieckergasse, Klappergasse, Groibengasse, and Hinder die Muren. Prostitution was thus limited to these streets.

[16] M&R, R/2, 78v–79, 1471, Von den Spontzierern, AMS, prohibit prostitutes from wearing jewelry worth more than one florin.

[17] On the growing control of the city prostitutes, see Merry E. Wiesner, "Paternalism in Practice: The Control of Servants and Prostitutes in Early Modern German Cities," in *The Process of Change in Early Modern Europe: Essays in Honor of Miriam Usher Chrisman*, ed. Philipp N. Bebb and Sherrin Marshall (Athens: Ohio UP, 1988), 179–99.

[18] For a general study of prostitution and the brothels, see Peter Schuster, *Das Frauenhaus. Städtische Bordelle in Deutschland 1350–1600* (Paderborn: Schöningh, 1992) and Beate Schuster, *Die freien Frauen. Dirnen und Frauenhäuser im 15. und 16. Jahrhundert* (Frankfurt am Main: Campus, 1995). See also Lyndal Roper, *The Holy Household: Women and Morals in Reformation Europe* (Oxford: Clarendon, 1989), 89–131 in regard to prostitution in Augsburg.

[19] See M&R, AMS, R/2, 70, 1469, Von den Hushelterinnen und Sponziererinnen, AMS and M&R, R/2, 71v–72, 1469, AMS. By listing women who tried to hide from the authorities and did not want to be recognized as prostitutes, the city officials made them public examples of negative behavior. Even though prostitution was legal, it was thoroughly monitored by the authorities. While this is similar to the control the guilds carried out to protect guild members, there is also a crucial difference: prostitution was regarded as immoral despite being legal, and the list was intended to make prostitutes known to the residents of the city so they could be avoided.

[20] Stephan Storm, Hans Berlin, Jacques Muge, and Heinrich Bisinger; M&R, R/2, 85v, 1473, Gesselin und Husere . . . Den Spontziererin zu irem Gewerbe Gelogen, AMS.

[21] M&R, R/2, 137, 1496, AMS.

[22] "Von den Spontzierern."

[23] M&R, R/2, 131–32, 1493, AMS.

[24] An interesting study by Otto Winckelmann from 1922 describes the changes in the public welfare system at the time of the Reformation. The charitable work carried out by the Catholic Church was replaced by a system organized by the city administration in the mid-1520s: *Das Fürsorgewesen der Stadt Straßburg vor und nach der Reforma-*

tion bis zum Ausgang des sechzehnten Jahrhuderts. 2 Vols. (Leipzig: M. Heinsius Nachfolger, 1922).

[25] The differentiation of the fines is precise and dependent on the marital status of the offender rather than on sex/gender: "Wo aber zwey offenlich/ und hüselich zur unee sitzent/ die beide ledig sindt/ die sollent jeglichs by xxx.ß pfennig in acht tagen von einander kömen/ oder aber einander zur ee nemen. Do aber zwey offentlich/ und hüselich zur unee sitzent/ do eins inn der Ee ist/ und das ander lidig/ das ist Eebruch/ die sollent yeglichs by iij.lib.pfennig in acht tagen von einander kömen. Item wo zwey beyde inn der Ee sint/ und offenlich/ und hüselich in der unee by einander sitzent/ das ist der gröste Eebruch/ die sollent yeglichs by v.lib. pfen. in acht tagen von einander kommen. Item wo ein man by siner Eelichen hußfrowen sitzet inn der Ee/ und doch süntlich mit einer andern Bulschafft trybt/ der besser iij.lib.pfen. so dicker das verbricher. Item wo ein man mit einer Klosterfrowen inn Bulschafft wise zu sschaffen hat/ der ledig/ und lere ist/ der bessert v.lib.pfen. Wer aber inn der Ee ist/ der bessert x.lib.pfen" (M&R, R/3, 47, 1514, Zu Offenen Eebruchen Üppigkeit und Ander Süntlich Wergk, AMS).

[26] An excellent study of women and crime is Ulinka Rublack, *The Crimes of Women in Early Modern Germany* (Oxford: Clarendon Press, 1999).

[27] The "Sübener" or the "Siebenzüchter" was a subdivision of the city council, established in the fifteenth century to handle cases regarding misconduct.

[28] "und knaben / und männer täglichs lassent zu inen gon / und sie umb ir gelt nemen" (and they let boys, and men come to them every day, and they take their money from them, "Zu Offenen Eebruchen Üppigkeit und ander Süntlich Wergk").

[29] A decree from 1501 prohibits prostitution by individuals. It further restricts the activities of the prostitutes to certain houses (M&R, R/3, 9verso–11, 1501, Von der Hausshelterinnen und Spontziererinnenn Wegen, AMS).

[30] "Were little girls to be found, be it by night or by day, whose bodies were not meant to do the work, but were too young, that is, that they had neither breasts nor other things that come with them, they should be punished severely because of it, and also be banished from the city and sentenced to death if they return, until they come into their allowed age" ("Zu Offenen Eebruchen Üppigkeit und ander Süntlich Wergk"). Cf Wiesner, "Paternalism in Practice," 191–92. Wiesner sarcastically comments that girls were regarded as too young for prostitution but old enough to take care of themselves if driven out of the city. The city magistrates clearly did not care what happened to these girls after they had left the city and thus were no longer able to disrupt the social order.

[31] This corresponds to the division of "woman" into different categories in juridical matters as has been shown by Wiesner, *Gender, Church and State,* 85–87.

[32] Elisabeth Koch claims that homosexual prostitution was completely suppressed in sixteenth-century legal discourse and makes it appear to have been a conscious choice among the lawmakers (*Maior dignitas,* 131). However, I believe more research is needed in this field before a general statement can be made. There is too little written on the topic, and various aspects still need to be scrutinized.

[33] Records show that the prostitute was allowed to attend church — probably in the hope that she would abandon her profession and become a "respectable" woman —

but that she had to be separated from other women, in regard to both what she could wear and where she could sit in church.

[34] On the closing of the brothels, see Schuster, *Das Frauenhaus. Städtische Bordelle in Deutschland 1350–1600,* 182. Koch sees a clear correspondence between the ban on prostitution and the beginning of the Reformation. See the chapter on prostitution: in *Maior dignitas,* 131–41. H. J. Selderhuis comes to the same conclusion in *Marriage and Divorce in the Thought of Martin Bucer,* trans. John Vriend and Lyle D. Bierma (Kirksville, MO: Thomas Jefferson UP, 1999), 25–26. It is, however, evident that the dissatisfaction in the congregations with the low morality of the clergy contributed to the growing restrictions on prostitution despite the reformed theology.

[35] "No streetwalker or other person who commits fornication in public shall be tolerated in our city or within its jurisdiction, but shall be found and arrested, taken into our custody, kept on water and bread, and thereafter banished from our city and its surroundings" (M&R, R/5, 187, 1594, Straff des Ehebruchs, AMS).

[36] "Constitution and statute from the praiseworthy council of the free city of Strasbourg on how blasphemy, cursing, adultery, rape, the seduction of virgins, prostitution and procuration should be punished in their city and its surroundings" (M&R, R/3, 164, 1521, Wie das Gotslestern / Fluchen & Ehebruch / Nodzog / . . . Gestrafft Werden Soll, AMS).

[37] According to Wunder, drowning was regarded as a "milder" form of execution, as was being buried alive (*He Is the Sun, She Is the Moon,* 188). On the difference in penalties, see Koch, *Maior dignitas,* 159–65.

[38] See Susanna Burghartz on female honor, "Rechte Jungfrauen oder unverschämte Töchter? Zur weiblichen Ehre im 16. Jahrhundert," in *Frauengeschichte — Geschlechtergeschichte,* ed. Karin Hausen and Heide Wunder (Frankfurt/New York: Campus, 1992), 173–83.

[39] Cf. Chrisman, "Women and the Reformation," 143: "The German world was more masculine. Men dominated business, trade and manufacturing activities and the political life of the city as well. Social affairs tended to be addenda to politics — gatherings of the guilds in their meeting houses in taverns, ceremonial dinners for a particular political committee or religious confraternity. Women had no part in this public life; their function was a private one, within the family and the household." Chrisman then states that the widowed woman at times was able to live more independently than the married woman, but she does not mention other exceptions. Her statement is based on the lives of the middle and upper class. The lower classes did not have access to public functions in the city. It was reserved for citizens, men who had sworn the civic oath.

[40] M&R, R/3, 162–63, 1529, Straff des Ehebruchs, AMS. See also "Wie das Gotslestern / Fluchen & Ehebruch / Nodzog / . . . Gestrafft Werden Soll." This decree is almost identical to "Straff des Ehebruchs," but nothing is said about how to divide property in the case of a separation: "Verwirckung und theilung ir beider syts güter" (forfeit and dividing of the goods of both sides).

[41] ". . . not only known and constituted by the authorities to maintain public peace and honorable decrees, but also obediently established in accordance with the Holy

Word of God, since this is daily and clearly preached against such crimes" ("Straff des Ehebruchs").

[42] Categories discussing the relationship between men and women are: punishment for adultery (straff des Eebruchs), rape (nodtzog), seducing virgins (Junckfrawen schwechen), illegitimate relationships (zur unee sitzen), and procuration (kupplery).

[43] The German text states:

> So ein lydiger / sich mit einer Eefrawen sich vermischet / ist der ein burger / der soll gleich ein Eeman / laut voriger ordnung / gestrafft werden / ist er aber nit burger / der soll gefencklich angenommen / vnd v. pfundt pfenning bessern / hat er dz gelt nit zugeben / soll er v. wochen / in thurn gelegt vnd jm nichts anders dann wasser vnd brot geben werden / also das er alle woch ein pfundt pfennig / wett machen soll / vnd demnach diser statt vnd des Bistumbs verwisen / vnd bey der selbigen Eefrawen leben / vnd nach der selbigen todt / on sunder vnser erlaubnüß / Meister vnnd Raths / nit darein gelassen / noch begnadigt werden. Gleicher gstalt / soll es mit einer ledigen frawen person / so sich mit einem eeman vermischet / so sy Burgerin oder frembd ist / gehalten werden / wie obstat ("Straff des Ehebruchs").

[44] "Thus, if it is recognized by the council that one of the adulterers is poor and unable to pay the set fine, or his half of the household's costs, making the collection of such a fine a punishment not only to him, but also to the innocent spouse and children, and that they would thus have to suffer lack of their necessary nutrition, then such a fine shall be commuted to corporal punishment, according to the situation of the person in question. He who is able to shall work off the money for our city" ("Straff des Ehebruchs").

[45] Harrington (*Reordering Marriage*, 271) stresses that there is little difference in the regulation of marriages in Catholic and reformed parts of Europe. The enforcement of legislation can be found all over Germany in the course of the sixteenth century. Harrington's chapter on "sexual discipline and domestic stability" is a good survey of sixteenth-century public morality (215–71).

[46] Wa aber das unschuldig/ im solchs nit nachgeben/ sonder die scheidung begeren/ und auch sie erlangen wirde/ so soll das schuldig/ zusampt voriger uffgelegter straff/ der statt unnd Bistumb verwisen/ und nit wider harin/ so lang das ander unschuldig in leben ist/ gelassen werden. Es were dann sach/ das sy sich bederseits versunten/ und einander eelich beywonung thun wolten/ und wir unsern gunst und willen/ zum inlassen geben (If the innocent party does not tolerate it, but demands and is granted a divorce, then the guilty party shall, in addition to the previously imposed punishment, be banished from the city and the diocese, and not be allowed to return, as long as the other is still alive and innocent. It would, however, be recommendable that they be reconciled and live together as married, and that we would give our blessing and approval, "Straff des Ehebruchs").

[47] The assets reserved for a woman when her husband died before her: Alfred Götze, *Frühneuhochdeutsches Glossar* (Berlin: De Gruyter, 1967), 230. See also Koch, *Maior dignitas*, 45–46. Koch discusses the legislation regarding husband and wife if one abandons the other or dies (41–55). See also Wendel, *Le mariage a Strasbourg*, 166–69.

[48] "Wann ein eegemechte brüchig an dem andern wirdt/ und sy sich/ nit wider versünen/ so soll es irer güter halb/ volgender gstalt/ gehalten werden. Namlich so

soll dz brüchig eegemecht/ die morgengab/ die ihm von seim eegemahel/ an dem es brüchig vermacht worden/ verwircket haben/ und die/ den unschuldigen eegemecht/ zugehören/ und verfallen sein. Dergleichen/ wa die eegemecht/ einander Brutlauff oder nachwidem/ gemacht haben/ da sollen die widems niessung/ dem unschuldigen Eegemecht/ allein sein leben lang/ zu empfahen unnd zu nützen/ on verhinderung des andern brüchigen eegemechts/ verfolgt werden. Wo auch das unschuldig eegemecht/ vor dem brüchigen eegemecht/ todts abgieng/ so soll doch sollichs widems niessung/ oder eigenschafft dem brüchigen eegemahel/nit zugehören/ dann er des gar entsetzt oder beraubt sein soll / sonder solliche neissung an die kinder von inen beden erboren / wo sy vorhanden / fallen. Wo aber kein kinder vorhanden / so soll die neissung dem gemeinen casten der armen by uns / syn des brüchigen leben lang zugehören / vnnd nach seinem todt / die eigenschafft / syn des brüchigen nechsten erben / verfangen vnd zugehörig sein" ("Straff des Ehebruchs"). More details follow this but need not be cited here.

[49] It is mentioned that older ordinances dealing with rape have been lost, which makes it difficult to be precise on this point: "innhalt der artickel in unserm Raths buch vergriffen" (the contents of the article in the book of our council lost, "Straff des Ehebruchs"). The dangers surrounding women servants have been discussed by, among others, Eva Labouvie in connection with unwanted pregnancies: *Andere Umstände. Eine Kulturgeschichte der Geburt* (Cologne: Böhlau, 1998), 50–64. See also Koch, *Maior dignitas,* 100–104. Koch points to the difficult situation of the woman but also to the severe punishment for rape if a man was found guilty.

[50] The decree states: "der soll der that nach / so am leib leben / eer / oder gut / gestrafft werden" (he shall, according to the deed, be punished corporally, by death, by the loss of honor, or by the confiscation of goods, "Straff des Ehebruchs").

[51] It was a completely different case with adult men and women who more or less openly carried on a relationship without marrying. This was not uncommon among the lower classes of society, where money and other assets were rare. If caught, they were nevertheless forced to marry or separate. Even if they did marry, they were not able to escape fines or avoid imprisonment — which they must often have experienced since they were poor.

[52] Koch (*Maior dignitas,* 110) stresses that the often severe punishments for procuration were a result of the fear among the magistrates that it would cause disorder.

[53] "So shall all, burghers, citizens, and crofters, religious and worldly people, woman and man of both sexes (work), for the promotion of the honor of God, also (for) the fostering of Christian discipline, and honor, out of Christian duty, so that they all be like God the Almighty and each other . . . ("Straff des Ehebruchs").

[54] The need for coordination between towns, cities, and villages within one area is shown in a Polizeiordung from 1552, issued by the emperor (M&R, R/5, 8, 1552, Policey / Auch Deren Halben in Vergangnem Einvndfünffzigsten Jare . . ., AMS). It tries to cover all kinds of moral offenses and to regulate trade and commerce. A category "Von Leichtfertigen Beywonern" (on easygoing inhabitants) briefly summarizes what is being discussed in depth in the local ordinances: that illegitimate relationships and sex outside of marriage should be punished. The punishment itself is not specified; it is left to the local council and court to judge on a case-by-case basis.

⁵⁵ "On things concerning marriage. And so reads the constitution developed by our forefathers further, and outdated for years and now renewed and partly improved as follows" (M&R, R/5, 54, 1565, Die Ehe belangend, AMS).

⁵⁶ "allen vnsern Burgern / Einwohnern zugehörigen vnnd verwandten in Statt vnd Land" (all our burghers, dependents of our citizens and relatives in the city and in the country, "Die Ehe belangend").

⁵⁷ The marriage court in Strasbourg was a secular organization instituted by the great council. A marriage code followed it in 1530. See further, Selderhuis, *Marriage and Divorce*, 76, and Abray, *The People's Reformation*, 188–90.

⁵⁸ See chapter six of Selderhuis, *Marriage and Divorce*, 257–326. Selderhuis gives the background to the legislation regarding divorce in Strasbourg and stresses that Bucer regarded divorce only as a last resort, even though his writings on divorce are controversial. Selderhuis stresses the view held by Bucer that marriage was a "personal relation" and that the marriage has "ceased to exist" if the personal ties are broken (287). He then goes on to discuss reasons for separation as found in the work of Bucer: adultery, desertion or banishment, psychological and physical factors, the Pauline privilege, abuse, and criminal grounds. True divorce as opposed to separation of bed and board can only be granted if one spouse enters a monastery or convent. Selderhuis also gives a brief overview of the legal aspects of divorce at the time before the Reformation (20–24). The focus on Bucer in Selderhuis's study makes it especially interesting in regard to the secular legislation in Strasbourg. Cf. Thomas Max Safely, *Let No Man Put Asunder: The Control of Marriage in the German Southwest: A Comparative Study, 1550–1600* (Kirksville, MO: Sixteenth Century Journal Publishers, 1984) for a comparison with other southwestern cities.

⁵⁹ For an interesting study on consensual marriage and the view held by officials regarding secret marriages, see Jacqueline Murray, "Individualism and Consensual Marriage: Some Evidence From Medieval England," in *Women, Marriage, and Family in Medieval Christendom*, ed. Constance Rousseau and Joel T. Rosenthal (Kalamazoo: Western Michigan UP, 1998), 121–51.

⁶⁰ See Harrington, *Reordering Marriage*, on the demand for public approval of marriage vows. Cf. Roper, *The Holy Household*, 194–205.

⁶¹ Roman law generally makes a greater distinction between men and women than is found in the canon law. See further, Selderhuis, *Marriage and Divorce*, 9–24.

⁶² Age is only one parameter in the legislation surrounding marriage. Blood relationships were strictly regulated in the Catholic Church and they remained important to the reformers, even though the ties were loosened somewhat. However, there has been very little scholarly work done on incest, as Ublinka Rublack points out in an interesting article, Ulinka Rublack, "Viehisch, frech, vnd onverschämpt. Inzest in Südwestdeutschland, Ca. 1530–1700," in *Von Huren und Rabenmüttern. Weibliche Kriminalität in der Frühen Neuzeit*, ed. Otto Ulbricht (Cologne: Böhlau, 1995), 171. Incest was mainly directed towards women and occurred when men felt threatened and feared the loss of power or virility, according to Rublack. The linking of incest to "unnatural" behavior and the harshness of the punishment made families keep quiet, fearing that the situation would be even worse if the offender were taken to court (204–5).

[63] "There would then exist such circumstances in which the annulment or abolition of the marriage would be more of a disadvantage and weakening factor to the children and parents than it would be to their advantage and well-being ("Die Ehe belangend").

[64] "Deßhalben so wöllen wir vnd gebieten / das hinfürter keiner vnser Burger / Einwoner / Hindersaß vnnd angehöriger / es sey Mann oder Frawe / so in sollichem Fall erfunden würdt / vnerlangt von vnseren verordneten Eherichtern / einicher rechtlicher Ehescheidung / oder deren bewilligung / sich in ein ander nachgende Ehe begeben / oder verbinden soll / oder mag / Dann wer hierwieder handeln würde / soll der gebür nach / vnd erkandtnuß vnserer verordneten Eherichtern gestrafft werden" (We therefore want and demand that from now on, not one of our burghers, citizens, crofters or relations, be it a man or a woman, who has been a party in such a case, should or may, without having been asked to do so by our appointed marital judges, through a legal divorce, or through their approval, enter another subsequent marriage or promise himself for one. Thus whoever acts against this should be punished according to his crime and the decision of our appointed marital judges, "Die Ehe belangend").

[65] "And so we demand that all marriages be publicly proclaimed and announced twice from the pulpit before they are confirmed through the church ceremony and the blessing" ("Die Ehe belangend"). This is still the case in Germany where it is common that one ceremony is held in church and one at the registry office.

[66] M&R, R/5, 73, 1570, Junge Döchter nicht allein vor dem ehelichen . . ., AMS.

[67] Labouvie, *Andere Umstände*, 44–50, on planned pregnancies. The parents were not always married but had different reasons for desiring a pregnancy despite the illicit relationship.

[68] "We command and forbid each and every one of our burghers, citizens, crofters, dependents and relatives, in the city and in the country, that they, in order to avoid receiving serious punishment, from now on, completely and under all circumstances, keep away from the above-mentioned and other forms of similar bawdiness" ("Junge Döchter nicht allein vor dem eheliche").

[69] "Should, however, a girl or a young woman, in spite of our Christian and well-meant decree, from now on so completely forget about her virginal honor and let herself be robbed of it before having walked down the aisle in a church wedding, we hereby order and demand, in the present as in the past, and in the past as in the present, that in addition to our other punishment, which we will inevitably impose on her and her partner . . . that she also be set apart from the other honorable and honest virgins and remain so" ("Junge Döchter nicht allein vor dem eheliche").

[70] Referring to adultery, fornication, and prostitution the decree states: "das auch angeregte Laster mehr dann zuuor zugenommen. . . . Damit nuhn dergleichen mit ernst abgeschafft / vnnd menniglich dauon abgehalten würde / So seind wir [the city representatives] obangeregte veraußgangene Mandata nachuolgender massen zuernewern / zuscherpfen / vorgedachtem vbel vorzusein / vnd dasselb offentlich zu verkünden verursacht worden" (that such crimes have also increased more than in the past . . . so that these are now seriously abolished and people are prevented from committing them. Thus we have been forced to add necessary precautions to the

above-mentioned outdated mandates, to make them more severe, to foresee premeditated evil, and to announce it in public, "Straff des Ehebruchs").

[71] "He or she shall, after the investigation of the crime committed, having received a sentence and due course of law, be killed, if a man with the sword, but if a woman she shall be executed with water and drowned" ("Straff des Ehebruchs").

[72] This is in accordance with the view held by Bucer. Cf. Selderhuis, *Marriage and Divorce*, 259.

[73] The 1529 decree was very brief in the discussion of rape and stated: "innhalt der artickel in vnserm Raths buch *ver*griffen." The prefix of the verb indicates that the content has been lost in modern German, that it has been "taken away," but the decree from 1594 uses the same phrasing with one exception. It says: "Innhalt der Articul im Ratsbuch *be*griffen" (content of the articles are included in the book of the council; italics mine). It is unclear why the first decree uses "vergriffen," when both texts must refer to the same text.

[74] "So shall these females, if thoughtlessly committing such crime, always be punished corporally or through the confiscation of goods, depending on the act committed, after the acknowledgment of a council" ("Straff des Ehebruchs").

[75] "If a husband, or a single man, causes — with good words or promises — an underage young girl give in to him, bringing on her downfall, he shall be punished according to the deed, corporally, with death, or the loss of honor or confiscation of goods. So also such young girls that become sinners as underage persons, commiting such crimes, shall be punished according to the verdict of a council" ("Straff des Ehebruchs").

[76] ". . . but that they be found and arrested, taken into our custody, kept on water and bread, and thereafter banished from our city and its surroundings" ("Straff des Ehebruchs").

[77] M&R, R/5, 94, 1573, Wie es mit den Hochzeiten, uberflüssigen Essen, Trinken unnd anderem fürther gehalten werden soll, AMS. No new decree regarding adultery, fornication, or prostitution is passed at this time, but in the ordinance from 1573, the council states that previous decrees on these matters are still valid.

[78] "alles das jhenig damit der Allmechtig belaidigt / zu Zorn bewegt / vnnd der nächst geergert würde" (everything with which the Almighty was insulted, moved to rage, and then annoyed, "Wie es mit den Hochzeiten, uberflüssigen Essen, Trinken unnd anderem fürther gehalten werden soll").

[79] Although discussing English texts, Constance Jordan's investigation of social "class" as an important factor in the study of early modern women is also interesting for German texts: "Renaissance Women and the Question of Class," in *Sexuality and Gender in Early Modern Europe: Institutions, Texts, Images,* ed. James Grantham Turner (Cambridge: Cambridge UP: 1993), 90–106.

Conclusion

THE AIM OF THIS BOOK has been to investigate the function of the category "woman" in sixteenth-century chapbooks and other prose texts, as well as in legal documents, Polizeiordnungen, from sixteenth-century Strasbourg. What conclusions, if any, can be drawn from the discussion of the various texts? In the introduction it was assumed that there are ruptures in the representation of woman — despite the seemingly clear dichotomy between man and woman in these texts — and that this can only be shown clearly by looking at the representation of woman in her relation to man.

The relationship between man and woman as described in Wickram's Schwänke is focused on the communication between spouses. The female characters make their voices heard and are allowed to do so, but only in order to serve "man" better. Their prime function is to help the male characters to become better men. While these stories also stress the negative aspects of their female characters, the women are not presented as representative for all womankind. "Woman" is thus not necessarily evil, nor does she bear all the blame for her disagreements with "man." She is given the power to make herself heard and makes use of her rights without always misusing them. The stories found in Montanus's and Frey's chapbooks focus on sex, but the women — who are constantly talking, nagging, gossiping — are not allowed a language that makes communication with the other sex or the expression of feelings or desires possible. Their imperfect language shows their inferiority as human beings,[1] but silence can also express something else. Honor can be saved in cases of pre- or extramarital sex only when nobody besides husband, wife, and lover — those immediately involved — finds out what has happened. When it becomes official, when the secret is no longer a secret but the subject of open discussion, the social order is threatened. Silence can therefore be seen as a way of communicating the unspeakable in the Schwänke.

Wickram is not interested in detailed descriptions of human sexuality. He strives toward a harmonious world by presenting good and bad examples.[2] Frey and Montanus, however, seem to have abandoned hope. They claim to show the world as it is, but in reality describe the world that they fear. By doing so they not only preserve gender stereotypes, which Wickram does as well, but also create new stereotypes. In Montanus's texts, women are given the features of the sexually obsessed witch who threatens to dominate man if not kept under constant male control.[3] Frey, on the other hand, seems more concerned with "man's" inherent weakness: if he were able to control himself, he would also be able to maintain control over his wife or daughter. The chapbooks do not describe the material reality of the sixteenth-century man and woman but show the problems that were common and important among readers and audiences of that time. Neither men nor women were as "bad" as they appear in these texts, but female sexuality and male power over the self and over women, and the preservation of a patriarchal world order are themes of major concern to the chapbook authors. The men become blinded by the deceitfulness of the women and this in turn weakens and fetters male strength, reducing male power and transferring it to the woman, a process that has as its outcome a world turned upside down. In the chapbooks by Frey and Montanus there is a constant battle of the sexes that seems impossible to end. The conventional power relations are disrupted and no one is able to conquer the other sex in a way that would end the open fight. The woman is always dangerous, always opposed to man and thus foreign. She very clearly represents the "other," which is defined in reference to the norm: the man.[4] If it were not for her crucial function in procreation, she would seem superfluous. The message these texts convey to women is hard to misinterpret: obey and you will be praised in a society dominated by men; rebel and you will be cursed.

The woman who thinks and acts individually but without being punished exists no more in Wickram's texts than she does in Frey's or Montanus's. In most of Wickram's prose works, she accepts her earthly subordination before higher authorities, possibly consoled by her equality with men before God. Montanus's women, however, use their equality before God as an excuse for acting independently in their everyday lives; they are then severely punished and subjected to the control of male authority. When describing male-female relationships, Wickram closely adheres to Luther's concept of marriage — even more than Montanus does — as interpreted by Sigrid Brauner:

> Luther replaces the voracious sexuality of woman as eternal temptress with another side of her nature, her moral virtue and talent for piety, qualities reserved in the medieval view to the exceptional few women who lived celibate lives in religious retreat.... Nevertheless, Luther adopts the medieval clerical view of woman as physically and intellectually inferior to men. Although he maintains that men and women are spiritually equal before God, Luther assumes that they are unequal on earth.[5]

This characterizes most of the texts written by authors who were influenced by the German reformers, and Brauner has elsewhere added: "in a way Luther's ideal Christian woman is a nun turned housewife."[6] Such are the women in the *Nachbarn,* who live a life more sheltered than many nuns in their cloisters. The female characters in Wickram's prose work are potentially dangerous but often well integrated into (an ordered) society. For the most part they act and react according to male norms and traditions and willingly submit themselves to male rule. They restrict themselves to the private sphere with few occasions to move about freely, but they fulfill important functions in the community — they are mothers, wives, and daughters of exemplary men. The exception may be found in the character Concordia in the *Knaben Spiegel:* a good wife but weak mother, ready to give her life for the happiness of her son. Not until after her death does the son return home, ready to atone for his sins and live a life in compliance with secular and religious laws. Concordia causes the dissolution of the family and is responsible for great economic losses, but she is also an example of a woman who acts on her own without completely losing her good reputation. She demands that the school teacher be lenient with her son, she obviously has access to money to send to the son, and her husband treats her respectfully until her death. None of the women in the *Nachbarn* are this independent. This may be why Concordia has to die while the women in Wickram's last work seem to voluntarily give up all claims to independence.

The image of the ideal woman in Fischart's *Geschichtklitterung* does not really deviate from the female characters in the *Knaben Spiegel* or the *Nachbarn* with the exception that "woman" exclusively equals "wife." Fischart chooses a different type of text, a different genre, but not even when it turns toward the grotesque do the gender roles change. He scrutinizes and criticizes human behavior and human interaction, questions the moral standards of men and women alike, but leaves the social and sex/gender hierarchy intact. In this respect his text resembles the chapbooks, but with the difference that the complexity of Fischart's text makes the reader extremely hesitant and often confused. Neither the chapbooks nor Wickram's novels challenge their readers as the *Geschichtklitterung* does; they do not awaken hesitancy, doubt, or uncertainty about their intentions. Fischart, however, playfully contradicts himself within one and the same text.[7] The *Geschichtklitterung* shares in common with the chapbooks explicitly sexual language and an interest in human sexuality, but the difference is significant. The fifth chapter of the *Geschichtklitterung* is a plea for marriage that at the same time does not deny the problems involved in the marital relationship between man and woman. Here, marriage is no longer a necessary but evil state, as portrayed in the chapbooks or embodied in the hesitancy of Friedbert and Felix in the *Knaben Spiegel*. It appears as the only path to salvation, but in order to make this possible, Fischart has to complete what Wickram started: he must incorporate sexuality into the discourse of marriage. Wickram did so by suppressing the discourse of sexuality, while Fischart brings the explicit language of the chapbooks into the discourse of marriage and makes it acceptable. Intercourse remains a sin, but one that is needed for procreation and is thus a necessary evil. In the *Geschichtklitterung*, man and woman are allowed to enjoy their sexual attraction to each other. The woman, however, enjoys sex only to please the man; she can be justified as a person only in her relationship to the man. The woman is thus complete only in her role as wife. What sets her apart from man is clear: he is a man even when unmarried. His life may be incomplete without a wife but his existence is never questioned.

Does this apply to legal texts as well? Above all, the city ordinances of Strasbourg express great concern for human behavior. This is the reason for their existence, but the city council provides the scholar with rich material in matters regarding gender with its numerous decrees that treat men and women differently. As is the case with the texts by Frey, Montanus, Wickram, and Fischart, the city ordinances deal with two sexes that are regarded as "natural" and are defined in relation to each other, claiming the man as the norm and the woman as his "complimentary opposite." There is an escalation in the publication of ordinances regulating marriage and anything that can be considered a threat to the married couple in the course of the sixteenth century. This is the result both of dissatisfaction with the Catholic clergy and of the work of the reformers in the city, primarily Martin Bucer. It is not possible to identify the same change in the works of Frey, Montanus, Wickram, or Fischart, probably because of the legislative character of the city ordinances and the entertainment value of all the other texts discussed here. In the fictional texts, "woman" at times resembles the female witch in the witch tracts. Woman is regarded as evil by nature, as possessing magic powers, and as sexually obsessed. This view cannot be found in any of the "Polizeiordnungen" I have looked at. Woman is different from man; she does not enjoy the same rights since she is not quite his equal, but she is nevertheless a person who has a value even if unmarried. In the discourse of sexuality the woman is presented as initiating and engaging in illicit sexual practices, but the man is in no way innocent. In the discourse of marriage, both sexes are assumed to be responsible for the success of the undertaking, but when it fails, the type and severity of the penalty is often gender-specific. The discourse of family life is only indirectly expressed in the city ordinances. Children are not an issue unless illegitimate as defined by law.

In summary, it can be stated that the exaggerated sexual desire ascribed to women in the chapbooks and in the *Geschichtklitterung* is moderated by the city ordinances. The restrictions imposed on female agency in the *Nachbarn* seem to represent a male desire rather than an actual grim reality of sixteenth-century women: women were clearly allowed to move about more freely in reality than they were in the novel. It can thus be said that the common "division between women as victims and women as agents is a false one: women have always been both victims and agents."[8] The mismanagement of the family as expressed in the *Knaben Spiegel* would probably never have occurred if Gottfrid had followed the Strasbourg Polizeiordnungen. The woman's function according to the decrees is clearly to grow up and get married — to be a wife. This is her prime role, and when the adult woman plays any other role it is a deviation from the norm that makes the authorities issue strict regulations in order to keep her under male power.

Is there a change in discourse in the sixteenth century? Looking at the texts discussed here the city ordinances of Strasbourg clearly show that gender was an important category in the classification of the residents in the sixteenth century. Ingrid Bennewitz has somewhat provocatively claimed that the literature of the Middle Ages knew of only one sex/gender (Geschlecht), since the man was not defined by his sexuality but rather by other qualities.[9] This is no longer the case in the sixteenth century, to judge by the texts discussed here. Men and women are assumed to identify with certain characteristics that inscribe "man" or "woman" in their bodies. This growing awareness of one's gender identity applies to both men and women.[10] The fictional texts show that there is a difference in discourse not only between "fact" and "fiction," but also between texts of different genres, although I would like to suggest that the perceived dichotomies not only concern a divide between men and women but that there is an ambivalence in discourse within each category "woman" and "man." On the one hand "woman" and "man" can hold different social functions; on the other hand all texts express a desire to limit the man to husband and father and the woman to wife and mother. Virginity is practiced within marriage in Wickram's work while sex is given room within Fischart's marriage. This seems to be the crucial point in the narrative and it does not seem possible to reverse the chronology: the virgin may have sex within marriage and enjoy it. The city ordinances prove that this did not quite work in the lived reality of sixteenth-century Strasbourg.

Notes

[1] See Elfriede Moser-Rath on the discussion that has lasted for centuries as to whether or not woman can be seen as a human being: *"Lustige Gesellschaft." Schwank und Witz des 17. und 18. Jahrhunderts in kultur- und sozialgeschichtlichem Kontext* (Stuttgart: J. B. Metzler, 1984), 101.

[2] Genre is no doubt of importance for the construction of woman in discourse. In Wickram's short text *List der Weiber* (Cunning of Women), a shrove tide play, he writes completely in the tradition of misogynist literature with no intention to praise any female virtues: "List der Weiber," in *Georg Wickram: Sämtliche Werke*, ed. Hans-Gert Roloff, vol. 2, *Kleine Spiele* (Berlin: De Gruyter, 1997), 258–76.

[3] Sigrid Brauner, *Fearless Wives and Frightened Shrews: The Construction of the Witch in Early Modern Germany*, ed. Robert H. Brown (Amherst: U of Massachusetts P, 1995), 29–50. Gerhild S. Williams summarizes the *Malleus:* "The detailed frequently cumbersome structure contrasts sharply with the simplicity of the stated theme: how to identify, try, and judge the most elusive, perpetually growing, dangerous crime, witchcraft, and how to capture and control its principal agent, woman": Gerhild S. Williams, *Defining Dominion: The Discourses of Magic and Witchcraft in Early Modern France and Germany* (Ann Arbor: U of Michigan P, 1995), 71.

[4] Gerhild S. Williams, "On Finding Words: Witchcraft and Discourses of Dissidence and Discovery," in *The Graph of Sex and the German Text: Gendered Culture in Early Modern Germany 1500–1700*, ed. Lynne Tatlock (Amsterdam: Rodopi, 1994), 65; Barbara Becker-Cantarino, "Dr. Faustus and Runagate Courage: Theorizing Gender in Early Modern German Literature," in Tatlock, ed., *The Graph of Sex and the German Text*, 42.

[5] Brauner, *Fearless Wives and Frightened Shrews*, 60; see also Sigrid Brauner, "Martin Luther on Witchcraft," in *The Politics of Gender in Early Modern Europe*, ed. Jean R. Brink, Allison P. Coudert, and Maryanne C. Horowitz (Kirksville, MO: Sixteenth Century Essays & Studies, 1989), 35.

[6] Brauner, "Martin Luther on Witchcraft," 37.

[7] Hans-Jürgen Bachorski and Werner Röcke have investigated the proper nouns in the *Geschichtklitterung* from a psychoanalytical perspective, based on the research by Karl Bertau on Wolfram von Eschenbach. Summarizing Bachorski's article, it can be said that Bachorski and Röcke define groups of words related to the name Fischart (or pseudonyms used by him), and that this enables them to trace patterns that explain changes in the sixteenth-century mentality in regard to gender relations and the ambivalence in the perception of desire: Hans-Jürgen Bachorski and Werner Röcke, "Weltbilder: Ordnungen des Wissens und Strukturen der literarischen Sinnbildung," in *Weltbildwandel: Selbstdeutung und Fremderfahrung im Epochenübergang vom Spätmittelalter zur Frühen Neuzeit*, ed. Hans-Jürgen Bachorski and Werner Röcke (Trier: Wissenschaftlicher Verlag, 1995), 7–17. It is an interesting method, even though the emphasis on Norbert Elias's and Max Weber's view of the sixteenth-

century society in my opinion focuses it too much on change, despite Bachorski's claim to emphasize ambivalence.

[8] Judith M. Bennet, "Feminism and History," *Gender and History* 3, no. 1 (Autumn 1989): 262.

[9] Ingrid Bennewitz, "Der Körper der Dame: Zur Konstruktion von 'Weiblichkeit' in der Deutschen Literatur des Mittelalters," in *"Aufführung" und "Schrift" in Mittelalter und Früher Neuzeit,* ed. Jan-Dirk Müller (Stuttgart: J. B. Metzler, 1996), 223.

[10] See Heide Wunder, "Geschlechtsidentitäten: Frauen und Männer im Späten Mittelalter und am Beginn der Neuzeit," in *Frauengeschichte — Geschlechtergeschichte,* ed. Karin Hausen and Heide Wunder (Frankfurt/New York: Campus, 1992), 131–36, on the topic of gender identity. Wunder too points to the discrepancy between discourse and lived reality, 135.

Works Cited

Archival Records

Mandats et Reglements, R/2, 70. 1469. Von den Hushelterinnen und Sponziererinnen. Archives municipales de Strasbourg.

Mandats et Reglements, R/2, 71v–72. 1469. Archives municipales de Strasbourg.

Mandats et Reglements, R/2, 78v–79. 1471. Von den Spontzierern. Archives municipales de Strasbourg.

Mandats et Reglements, R/2, 85v. 1473. Gesselin und Husere . . . Den Spontziererin zu irem Gewerbe gelogen. Archives municipales de Strasbourg.

Mandats et Reglements, R/2, 131–32. 1493. Archives municipales de Strasbourg.

Mandats et Reglements, R/2, 137. 1496. Archives municipales de Strasbourg.

Mandats et Reglements, R/3, 9v–11. 1501. Von der Hausshelterinnen und Spontziererinnenn wegen. Archives municipales de Strasbourg.

Mandats et Reglements, R/3, 47. 1514. Zu offenen Eebruchen Üppigkeit und ander süntlich Wergk. Archives municipales de Strasbourg.

Mandats et Reglements, R/3, 164. 1521. Wie das Gotslestern / Fluchen & Ehebruch / Nodzog / . . . gestrafft werden soll. Archives municipales de Strasbourg.

Mandats et Reglements, R/3, 162–63. 1529. Straff des Ehebruchs. Archives municipales de Strasbourg.

Mandats et Reglements, R/5, 8. 1552. Policey / Auch deren Halben in vergangnem einvndfünffzigsten Jare. . . . Archives municipales de Strasbourg.

Mandats et Reglements, R/5, 54. 1565. Die Ehe belangend. Archives municipales de Strasbourg.

Mandats et Reglements, R/5, 73. 1570. Junge Döchter nicht allein vor dem ehelichen. . . . Archives municipales de Strasbourg.

Mandats et Reglements, R/5, 94. 1573. Wie es mit den Hochzeiten, Uberflüssigen Essen, Trinken unnd anderem Fürther gehalten werden soll. Archives municipales de Strasbourg.

Mandats et Reglements, R/5, 187. 1594. Straff des Ehenbruchs. Archives municipales de Strasbourg.

Primary Sources

Bonaventura. *Unser Frauen-Spiegel*. Basel: Furter, 1506.

Bucer, Martin. *Schriften zu Ehe und Eherecht*. Edited by Stephen E. Buckwalter, Robert Stupperich, and Wilhelm H. Neuser. Martin Bucers Deutsche Schriften, vol. 10. Gütersloh: Mohn, 2001.

Fischart, Johann. *Geschichklitterung (Gargantua). Text der Ausgabe letzter Hand von 1590. Mit einem Glossar*. Edited by Ute Nysssen. Düsseldorf: Karl Rauch Verlag, 1963.

———. *Vom Aussgelasnen Wütigen Teuffelsheer [1581]*. Graz, 1973.

Der Frawen Spigel in Wellichem Spiegel Sich das Weyblich Byld / Jung oder Alt Beschawen oder Lernen / zu Gebrauchen / die Woltat Gegen Irem Eelichen Gemahel. Strasbourg: M. Flach II, 1520.

Frey, Jakob. *Jakob Freys Gartengesellschaft (1556)*. Edited by Johannes Bolte. Tübingen: Literarischer Verein, 1896.

Luther, Martin. *Vom Ehelichen Leben und andere Schriften über die Ehe*. Edited by Dagmar C. G. Lorenz. Stuttgart: Reclam, 1978.

Montanus, Martin. *Martin Montanus Schwankbücher (1557–1566)*. Edited by Johannes Bolte. Tübingen: Der literarische Verein in Stuttgart, 1899.

Pauli, Johannes. *Schimpf und Ernst*. Edited by Johannes Bolte. Berlin: H. Stubenrauch, 1924.

Rabelais, Francois. *Gargantua*. Edited by Gérard Defaux. Paris: Le Livre de Poche, 1994.

Thanner, Hans. *Frawen Spiegl: Auf Erden ist khein Creatur so löblich als ain Weybes Figur die von Natur ist Wollgestallt und sich in Eeren frümbklich hallt . . .; (Ain Lied Was Ainer Eefrawen Gebüret.)*. Vienna: Syngriener, 1553.

Wickram, Georg. *Knaben Spiegel — Dialog vom ungeratnen Sohn*. Vol. 3 of *Georg Wickram: Sämtliche Werke*. Edited by Hans-Gert Roloff. Berlin: De Gruyter, 1968.

———. "List der Weiber." In *Kleine Spiele*. Vol. 2 of *Georg Wickram: Sämtliche Werke*, edited by Hans-Gert Roloff, 258–76. Berlin: De Gruyter, 1997.

———. *Ritter Galmy*. Vol. 1 of *Georg Wickram: Sämtliche Werke*. Edited by Hans-Gert Roloff. Berlin: De Gruyter, 1967.

———. *Das Rollwagenbüchlein*. Vol. 7 of *Sämtliche Werke*. Edited by Hans-Gert Roloff. Berlin: Walter de Gruyter, 1973.

———. *Von guten und bösen Nachbarn*. Vol. 4 of *Sämtliche Werke*. Edited by Hans-Gert Roloff. Berlin: Walter de Gruyter, 1969.

Secondary Sources

Abray, Lorna Jane. *The People's Reformation: Magistrates, Clergy, and Commons in Strasbourg, 1500–1598.* Ithaca, NY: Cornell UP, 1985.

Algazi, Gadi. "Ein gelehrter Blick ins lebendige Archiv: Umgangsweisen mit der Vergangenheit im 15. Jahrhundert." *Historische Zeitschrift* 266 (1998): 317–57.

———. "Kulturkult und Rekonstruktion von Handlungsrepertoires." *L'homme. Zeitschrift für Feministische Geschichtswissenschaft* 1, no. 11 (2000): 105–19.

Amussen, Susan D. *An Ordered Society: Gender and Class in Early Modern England.* New York: Columbia UP, 1988.

Ariès, Philipp. *Centuries of Childhood.* London: Pimlico, 1996.

"Aufführung" und "Schrift" in Mittelalter und Früher Neuzeit. Edited by Jan-Dirk Müller. Stuttgart: Metzler, 1996.

Aymard, Maurice. "Friends and Neighbors." In *A History of Private Life. Passions of the Renaissance. III*, edited by Roger Chartier, 447–92. Cambridge: Belkamp Press, 1989.

Bachorski, Hans-Jürgen. "Diskursfeld Ehe: Schreibweisen und thematische Setzungen." In *Ordnung und Lust: Bilder von Liebe, Ehe und Sexualität in Spätmittelalter und Früher Neuzeit*, edited by Hans-Jürgen Bachorski, 511–45. Trier: Wissenschaftlicher Verlag, 1991.

Bachorski, Hans-Jürgen, and Werner Röcke. "Weltbilder: Ordnungen des Wissens und Strukturen der literarischen Sinnbildung." In *Weltbildwandel: Selbstdeutung und Fremderfahrung im Epochenübergang vom Spätmittelalter zur Frühen Neuzeit*, edited by Hans-Jürgen Bachorski and Werner Röcke, 7–17. Trier: Wissenschaftlicher Verlag, 1995.

Becker-Cantarino, Barbara. "'Dames des Lettres' und 'Die Ordnung der Geschlechter': Neue Forschung zu Frauen und Geschlecht in der Frühen Neuzeit." *Daphnis* 23 (1994): 469–81.

———. "Dr. Faustus and Runagate Courage: Theorizing Gender in Early Modern German Literature." In *The Graph of Sex and the German Text: Gendered Culture in Early Modern Germany 1500–1700*, edited by Lynne Tatlock, 27–44. Amsterdam: Rodopi, 1994.

———. "Feministische Germanistik in Deutschland: Rückblick und sechs Thesen." In *Women in German Yearbook 8*, 219–33. Lincoln, London: U of Nebraska P, 1993.

———. "Renaissance oder Reformation? Epochenschwellen für Schreibende Frauen und die Mittlere Deutsche Literatur." In *Das Berliner Modell der Mittleren Deutschen Literatur: Beiträge zur Tagung Kloster Zinna 29.9.– 01.10.1997*, edited by Christiane Caemmerer, et al., 69–87. Amsterdam: Rodopi, 2000.

———. "(Sozial)Geschichte der Frau in Deutschland, 1500–1800: Ein Forschungsbericht." In *Die Frau von der Reformation zur Romantik*, edited by Barbara Becker-Cantarino, 243–81. Bonn: Bouvier Verlag Herbert Grundmann, 1980.

———. "Vom 'Ganzen Haus' zur Familieidylle. Haushalt als Mikrokosmos in der Literatur der Frühen Neuzeit und seine spätere Sentimentalisierung." *Daphnis* 15 (1986): 509–33.

Becoming Visible: Women in European History. Edited by Reante Bridenthal, Claudia Koonz, and Susan Stuard. Boston: Houghton Mifflin, 1987.

Belsey, Catherine. "Reading Cultural History." In *Reading the Past. Literature and History*, edited by Tamsin Spargo, 103–17. Basingstoke: Palgrave, 2000.

———. *Shakespeare and the Loss of Eden: The Construction of Family Values in Early Modern Culture*. Houndmills: Palgrave, 2001.

Bennet, Judith M. "Feminism and History." *Gender and History* 3, no. 1 (Autumn 1989): 251–72.

Bennewitz, Ingrid. "Der Körper der Dame: zur Konstruktion von 'Weiblichkeit' in der Deutschen Literatur des Mittelalters." In *"Aufführung" und "Schrift" in Mittelalter und Früher Neuzeit*, edited by Jan-Dirk Müller, 222–38. Stuttgart: J. B. Metzler, 1996.

Das Berliner Modell der Mittleren Deutschen Literatur. Beiträge zur Tagung Kloster Zinna 29.9–01.10.1997. Edited by Christiane Caemmerer, et al. Amsterdam: Rodopi, 2000.

Beutin, Wolfgang. *Sexualität und Obszönität. Eine literaturpsychologische Studie über epische Dichtungen des Mittelalters und der Renaissance*. Würzburg: Königshausen & Neumann, 1990.

Blumenberg, Hans. *Die Genesis der Koperkanischen Welt*. 3 Vols. 3rd ed. Frankfurt am Main: Suhrkamp, 1996.

———. *Die Legitimität der Neuzeit*, 2nd ed. Frankfurt am Main: Suhrkamp, 1999.

Bock, Gisela. "Frauenräume und Frauenehre. Frühneuzeitliche Armenfürsorge in Italien." In *Frauengeschichte — Geschlechtergeschichte*, edited by Karin Hausen and Heide Wunder. Frankfurt am Main, New York: Campus, 1992.

Bogdal, Klaus-Michael. *Historische Diskursanalyse der Literatur*. Opladen: Westdeutscher Verlag, 1999.

Bogner, Ralf Georg. *Die Bezähmung der Zunge. Literatur und Disziplinierung der Alltagskommunikation in der Frühen Neuzeit.* Tübingen: Niemeyer, 1997.

Brackert, Helmut. "Zur Sexualisierung des Hexenmusters in der Frühen Neuzeit." In *Ordnung und Lust: Bilder von Liebe, Ehe und Sexualität in Spätmittelalter und Früher Neuzeit,* edited by Hans-Jürgen Bachorski, 337–57. Trier: Wissenschaftlicher Verlag, 1991.

Brady, Thomas A. *Communities, Politics and Reformation in Early Modern Europe.* Leiden: Brill, 1998.

———. *Ruling Class, Regime, and Reformation at Strasbourg 1520–1555.* Leiden: Brill, 1978.

Brandstetter, Alois. *Prosaauflösung. Studien zur Rezeption der Höfischen Epik im frühneuhochdeutschen Prosaroman.* Frankfurt am Main: Athenäum, 1971.

Brauner, Sigrid. *Fearless Wives and Frightened Shrews: The Construction of the Witch in Early Modern Germany.* Edited by Robert H. Brown. Amherst: U of Massachusetts P, 1995.

———. "Gender and Its Subversion: Reflections on Literary Ideals of Marriage." In *The Graph of Sex and the German Text: Gendered Culture in Early Modern Germany 1500–1700,* edited by Lynne Tatlock, 179–200. Amsterdam: Rodopi, 1994.

———. "Martin Luther on Witchcraft." In *The Politics of Gender in Early Modern Europe,* edited by Jean R. Brink, Allison P. Coudert, and Maryanne C. Horowitz, 29–42. Kirksville, MO: Sixteenth Century Essays & Studies, 1989.

Brinkler-von der Heyde, Claudia. "Der Frauenpreis des Agrippa von Nettesheim: Persönliche Strategie, politische Invektive, rhetorisches Spiel." In *Text im Kontext: Anleitung zur Lektüre deutscher Texte der Frühen Neuzeit,* edited by Alexander Schwarz and Laure Abplanalp, 31–48. Frankfurt am Main: Peter Lang, 1997.

Brucker, Johann. *Strassburger Zunft- und Polizei-Verordnungen des 14. und 15. Jahrhunderts.* Strasbourg: Karl J. Trübner, 1889.

Bunzl, Martin. "Theoretical Issues: The Construction of History." *Journal of Women's History* 9, no. 3 (Autumn 1997): 119–31.

Burghartz, Susanna. "Rechte Jungfrauen oder unverschämte Töchter? Zur weiblichen Ehre im 16. Jahrhundert." In *Frauengeschichte — Geschlechtergeschichte,* edited by Karin Hausen and Heide Wunder, 173–83. Frankfurt/New York: Campus, 1992.

———. *Zeiten der Reinheit — Orte der Unzucht: Ehe und Sexualität in Basel Während der Frühen Neuzeit.* Paderborn: Schöningh, 1999.

Burke, Peter. *Popular Culture in Early Modern Europe.* Aldershot: Wildwood House Ltd, [1978] 1988.

Butler, Judith. *Bodies That Matter: On the Discursive Limits of "Sex."* London: Routledge, 1993.

———. *Gender Trouble: Feminism and the Subversion of Identity.* London: Routledge, 1990.

Cannon-Geary, Irene S. *The Bourgeoisie Looks at Itself: The 16th Century in German Literary Histories of the 19th Century.* Göppingen: Kümmerle, 1990.

Chrisman, Miriam Usher. *Bibliography of Strasbourg Imprints 1480–1599.* New Haven: Yale UP, 1982.

———. *Strasbourg and the Reform: A Study in the Process of Change.* New Haven: Yale UP, 1967.

———. "Women and the Reformation in Strasbourg 1490–1530." *Archiv für Reformationsgeschichte: Internationale Zeitschrift zur Erforschung der Reformation und ihrer Weltwirkungen* 63 (1972): 143–67.

Christ, Hannelore. *Literarischer Text und historische Realität. Versuch einer historisch-materialistischen Analyse von Jörg Wickrams Knabenspiegel- und Nachbarn-Roman.* Düsseldorf: Bertelsmann, 1974.

Coudert, Allison P. "The Myth of the Impovered Status of Protestant Women: The Case of the Witchcraze." In *The Politics of Gender in Early Modern Europe,* edited by Jean R. Brink, Allison P. Coudert, and Maryanne C. Horowitz, 61–89. Kirksville, MO: Sixteenth-Century Essays & Studies, 1987.

Dallapiazza, Michael. *Minne, Húsere und das Ehelich Leben: zur Konstitution bürgerlicher Lebensmuster in spätmittelalterlichen und frühhumanistischen Didaktiken.* Frankfurt am Main: Lang, 1981.

Delumeau, Jean. *Sin and Fear: The Emergence of a Western Guilt Culture, 13th–18th Centuries.* New York: St. Martin's Press, 1990.

Desire and Discipline: Sex and Sexuality in the Premodern West. Edited by Jacqueline Murray and Konrad Eisenbichler. Toronto: U of Toronto P, 1991.

Deufert, Wilfred. *Narr, Moral und Gesellschaft: Grundtendenzen im Prosawerk des 16. Jahrhunderts.* Frankfurt am Main: Peter Lang, 1975.

Deutinger, Jean. *L'age de la Littérature en Alsace.* Mundolsheim: Deutinger Verlag, 1986.

Dieckow, Peter C. M. "Um Jetzt der 'Katzenborischen Art Rollwagenbücher' zu gedenken — zur Erforschung deutschsprachiger Prosaerzählsammlungen aus der zweiten Hälfte des 16. Jahrhunderts." *Euphorion* 90, no. 1 (1996): 76–133.

Dieterich, Hartwig. *Das protestantische Eherecht in Deutschland bis zur Mitte des 17. Jahrhunderts.* Munich: Claudius, 1970.

Dinzelbacher, Peter. "Die Gottesbeziehung als Geschlechterbeziehung." In *Personenbeziehungen in der Mittelalterlichen Literatur,* edited by Helmut Brall, Barbara Haupt, and Urban Küsters, 3–36. Düsseldorf: Droste, 1994.

———. "Mittelalterliche Sexualität — Die Quellen." In *Privatisierung der Triebe? Sexualität in der Frühen Neuzeit*, edited by Daniela Erlach, Markus Reisenleitner, and Karl Vocelka, 47–97. Frankfurt am Main: Peter Lang, 1994.

Dülmen, Richard van. *Kultur und Alltag in der Frühen Neuzeit: Dritter Band — Religion, Magie, Aufklärung 16.–18. Jahrhundert.* Munich: C. H. Beck, 1999.

———. *Kultur und Alltag in der Frühen Neuzeit: Erster Band — das Haus und seine Menschen 16.–18. Jahrhundert.* Munich: C. H. Beck, 1999.

———. *Kultur und Alltag in der Frühen Neuzeit: Zweiter Band — Dorf und Stadt 16.–18. Jahrhundert.* Munich: C. H. Beck, 1999.

Eder, Frank X. "'Sexualunterdrückung' oder 'Sexualisierung?' Zu den theoretischen Ansätzen der 'Sexualitätsgeschichte.'" In *Privatisierung der Triebe? Sexualität in der Frühen Neuzeit*, edited by Daniela Erlach, Markus Reisenleitner, and Karl Vocelka, 7–29. Frankfurt am Main: Peter Lang, 1994.

Eisenstein, Elizabeth L. *The Printing Press as an Agent of Change: Communications and Cultural Transformations in Early Modern Europe.* Cambridge: Cambridge UP, 1985.

———. *The Printing Revolution in Early Modern Europe.* Cambridge: Cambridge UP, 1993.

Emberson, Jane. "Of Good and Bad Neighbors: Middle-Class Life in the Work of Jörg Wickram." *The Sixteenth Century Journal* 26, no. 3 (1995): 533–45.

Engelsing, Rolf. *Analphabetentum und Lektüre: zur Sozialgeschichte des Lesens in Deutschland zwischen feudaler und industrieller Gesellschaft.* Stuttgart: Metzler, 1973.

———. *Der Bürger als Leser. Lesergeschichte in Deutschland 1500–1800.* Stuttgart: Metzler, 1974.

Englisch, Ernst. "Die Ambivalenz in der Beurteilung sexueller Verhaltensweisen im Mittelalter." In *Privatisierung der Triebe? Sexualität in der Frühen Neuzeit*, edited by Daniela Erlach, Markus Reisenleitner, and Karl Vocelka, 167–86. Frankfurt am Main: Peter Lang, 1994.

Febvre, Lucien, and Henri-Jean Martin. *The Coming of the Book: The Impact of Printing 1450–1800.* London: Verso, 1990.

Foucault, Michel. *The History of Sexuality I–III.* New York: Vintage Books/Random House, 1990.

———. *The Order of Things: An Archaeology of the Human Sciences.* London: Routledge, 2001.

Frei, Peter. "Das Zufallen der Türen, der Zufall: Raumdarstellung in Jörg Wickrmas Goldfaden." In *Text im Kontext: Anleitung zur Lektüre deutscher Texte der Frühen Neuzeit*, edited by Alexander Schwarz and Laure Abplanalp, 69–78. Bern: Peter Lang, 1997.

Fricke, Harald. *Norm und Abweichung: Eine Philosophie der Literatur.* Munich: Beck, 1981.

Friedrich, Wolfgang. "Bemerkungen zu den Romanen Georg Wickrams." *Wissenschaftliche Zeitschrift der Martin-Luther-Universität Halle-Wittenberg. Gesellschafts- und Sprachwissenschaftliche Reihe* 10, no. 4 (1961): 1037–42.

Fuchs, Joseph. *Inventaire des archives de la ville de Strasbourg antérieures á 1790. Série I (Ancienne Série I.D.G.) et supplément de la série AA.* Strasbourg, 1954.

Gadamer, Hans-Georg. *Truth and Method.* 2d ed. New York: Continuum, 1994.

Gadol, Joan Kelly. "Did Women Have a Renaissance?" In *Becoming Visible: Women in European History,* edited by Renate Bridenthal and Claudia Koonz, 175–201. Boston: Houghton Mifflin, 1977.

Gaebel, Ulrike. "Erzähler und Erzählkonzepte in Marquarts vom Stein *Der Ritter vom Turm.*" In *Erzählungen in Erzählungen: Phänomene der Narration in Mittelalter und Früher Neuzeit,* edited by Harald Haferland und Michael Mecklenburg, 393–409. Munich: Wilhelm Fink, 1996.

Garber, Klaus. "Umrisse der Frühen Neuzeit — oder: elegische Besichtigung von grossen Männern, grösseren Werken und unabsehbaren Torsi." In *Das Berliner Modell der Mittleren Deutschen Literatur: Beiträge zur Tagung Kloster Zinna 29.9.–01.10.1997,* edited by Christiane Caemmerer, et al., 443–68. Amsterdam: Rodopi, 2000.

Geerdts, Hans Jürgen. "Das Erwachen des bürgerlichen Klassenbewusstseins in den Romanen Jörg Wickrams." *Wissenschaftliche Zeitschrift der Friedrich-Schiller-Universität Jena* 2 (1952–53): 117–24.

Geertz, Clifford. *The Interpretation of Cultures: Selected Essays.* New York: Basic Books, 1973.

Geulen, Hans. "Johann Fischarts 'Geschichtsklitterung': Nachträge zu ihrer Bedeutung." *Germanisch-Romanische Monatsschrift* 39, no. 2 (1989): 147–55.

Glowa, Josef K. *Johann Fischart's Geschichtklitterung: A Study of the Narrator and Narrative Strategies.* New York: Peter Lang, 2000.

Götze, Alfred. *Frühneuhochdeutsches Glossar.* Berlin: De Gruyter, 1967.

Greenblatt, Stephen. *Shakespearean Negotiations: The Circulation of Social Energy in Renaissance England.* Berkeley: U of California P, 1988.

———. "Towards a Poetics of Culture." In *The New Historicism,* edited by H. Aram Veeser, 1–14. New York: Routledge, 1989.

Griesebner, Andrea, and Christina Lutter. "Geschlecht und Kultur. Ein Definitionsversuch zweier umstrittener Kategorien." *Geschlecht und Kultur. Beiträge zur historischen Sozialkunde* Sondernummer (2000).

Harrington, Joel F. *Reordering Marriage and Society in Reformation Germany.* Cambridge: Cambridge UP, 1995.

Haug, Walter. "Die Verwandlungen des Körpers zwischen 'Aufführung' und 'Schrift.'" In *"Aufführung" und "Schrift" in Mittelalter und Früher Neuzeit*, edited by Jan-Dirk Müller, 190–204. Stuttgart: J. B. Metzler, 1996.

———. "Zwischen Ehezucht und Minnekloster. Die Formen des Erotischen in Johann Fischarts *Geschichtklitterung*." In *The Graph of Sex and the German Text. Gendered Culture in Early Modern Germany 1500–1700*, edited by Lynne Tatlock, 157–78. Amsterdam: Rodopi, 1994.

Hausen, Karin. "Öffentlichkeit und Privatheit: Gesellschaftspolitische Konstruktionen und die Geschichte der Geschlechterbeziehungen." In *Frauengeschichte — Geschlechtergeschichte*, edited by Karin Hausen and Heide Wunder, 81–88. Frankfurt/New York: Campus, 1992.

Hausen, Karin, and Heide Wunder. "Frauengeschichte — Geschlechtergeschichte: Einleitung." In *Frauengeschichte — Geschlechtergeschichte*, edited by Karin Hausen and Heide Wunder, 9–18. Frankfurt/New York: Campus, 1992.

Heidemann, Kyra. "'Grob und teutsch mit nammen beschryben': Überlegungen zum Anstössigen in der Schwankliteratur des 16. Jahrhunderts." In *Ordnung und Lust: Bilder von Liebe, Ehe und Sexualität in Spätmittelalter und Früher Neuzeit*, edited by Hans-Jürgen Bachorski, 415–26. Trier: Wissenschaftlicher Verlag, 1991.

Hirschberg, Anna. "Darstellung der Frau in den Romanen Jörg Wickrams und Untersuchung des kulturgeschichtlichen Wertes der Schilderungen." Ph.D. dissertation, Greifswald, 1919.

Holenstein, Pia. *Der Ehediskurs der Renaissance in Fischarts Geschichtklitterung: Kritische Lektüre des fünften Kapitels*. Bern: Peter Lang, 1991.

Houston, Rob A. *Literacy in Early Modern Europe: Culture and Education 1500–1800*. London: Longman, 1988.

Infinite Boundaries: Order, Disorder, and Reorder in Early Modern German Culture. Edited by Max Reinhart. Kirksville, MO: 16th Century Journal Publishers, 1998.

Intertextualität in der Frühen Neuzeit. Edited by Wilhelm Kühlmann and Wolfgang Neuber. Frankfurt am Main: Peter Lang, 1994.

Jonas, Monika. "Idealisierung und Dämonisierung als Mittel der Repression: Eine Untersuchung zur Weiblichkeitsdarstellung im Spätmittelalterlichen Schwank." In *Der Widerspänstigen Zähmung: Studien zur bezwungenen Weiblichkeit in der Literatur vom Mittelalter bis zur Gegenwart*, edited by Sylvia Wallinger and Monika Jonas, 67–93. Innsbruck: Universität Innsbruck, 1986.

Jordan, Constance. "Renaissance Women and the Question of Class." In *Sexuality and Gender in Early Modern Europe: Institutions, Texts, Images*, edited by James Grantham Turner, 90–106. Cambridge: Cambridge UP, 1993.

Kleinschmidt, Erich. "Gelehrtentum und Volkssprache in der Frühneuzeitlichen Stadt: zur literaturgesellschaftlichen Funktion Johann Fischarts in Strassburg." *Zeitschrift für Literaturwissenschaft und Linguistik: Eine Zeitschrift der Universität Gesamthochschule Siegen* 37 (1980): 128–51.

———. "Jörg Wickram." In *Deutsche Dichter der Frühen Neuzeit (1450–1600): Ihr Leben und Werk,* edited by Stephan Füssel, 494–511. Berlin: Erich Schmidt, 1993.

———. *Stadt und Literatur in der Frühen Neuzeit.* Cologne: Böhlau, 1982.

Klinger, Cornelia. "Die Kategorie Geschlecht in der Dimension der Kultur." *Geschlecht und Kultur. Beiträge zur Historischen Sozialkunde* Sondernummer (2000): 3–7.

Koch, Elisabeth. *Maior dignitas est in sexu virili: Das weibliche Geschlecht im Normensystem des 16. Jahrhunderts.* Frankfurt am Main: Vittorio Klostermann, 1991.

Kraft, Helga. "Töchter, die Keine Mütter Werden: Nonnen, Amazonen, Mätressen." In *Mütter — Töchter — Frauen: Weiblichkeitsbilder in der Literatur,* edited by Helga Kraft and Elke Liebs, 35–52. Stuttgart: J. B. Metzler, 1993.

Kreutzer, Hans Joachim. *Der Mythos vom Volksbuch. Studien zur Wirkungsgeschichte des frühen deutschen Romans seit der Romantik.* Stuttgart: Metzler, 1977.

Labouvie, Eva. *Andere Umstände. Eine Kulturgeschichte der Geburt.* Cologne: Böhlau, 1998.

Laqueur, Thomas. *Making Sex: Body and Gender from the Greeks to Freud.* Cambridge: Harvard UP, 1990.

Lorenz, Dagmar. "Vom Kloster zur Kirche: Die Frau vor und nach der Reformation Dr Martin Luthers." In *Die Frau von der Reformation zur Romantik,* edited by Barbara Becker-Cantarino, 7–35. Bonn: Bouvier Verlag Herbert Grundmann, 1980.

Lugowski, Clemens. *Die Form der Individualität im Roman.* Frankfurt am Main: Suhrkamp, [1932] 1976.

Lühe, Irmela von der. "Wolan, hin ist hin: Brief und Exemplum in Wickrams 'Nachbarn-Roman.'" In *Erzählungen in Erzählungen: Phänomene der Narration in Mittelalter und Früher Neuzeit,* edited by Harald Haferland and Michael Mecklenburg, 411–23. Munich: Wilhelm Fink, 1996.

Luke, Carmen. *Pedagogy, Printing, and Protestantism: The Discourse on Childhood.* Albany: State U of New York P, 1989.

Marshall, Sherrin. "The Process of Change in Early Modern Europe: Urban Society, Intellectual Development, and Family Life." In *The Process of Change in Early Modern Europe: Essays in Honor of Miriam Usher Chrisman,* edited by Philipp N. Bebb and Sherrin Marshall, 9–15. Athens: Ohio UP, 1988.

Maynard, Mary. "Beyond the 'Big Three': The Development of Feminist Theory Into the 1990s." *Women's History Review* 4, no. 3 (1995): 259–81.

McDonnell, Ernest W. *The Beguines and Beghards in Medieval Culture with Special Emphasis on the Belgian Scene.* New Brunswick, NJ: Rutgers UP, 1954.

Mertens, Volker. "'Aspekte der Liebe': Ihre Semantik in den Prosaromanen Tristrant, Melusine, Magelone und Goldfaden." In *Personenbeziehungen in der mittelalterlichen Literatur,* edited by Helmut Brall, Barbara Haupt, and Urban Küsters, 109–34. Düsseldorf: Droste, 1994.

Midelfort, H. C. Erik. *Witch Hunting in Southwestern Germany 1562–1684: The Social and Intellectual Foundations.* Stanford: Stanford UP, 1972.

Moi, Toril. *Sexual/Textual Politics: Feminist Literary Theory.* London, New York: Methuen, 1985.

Monter, E. William. *Enforcing Morality in Early Modern Europe.* London: Variorum, 1987.

Moser-Rath, Elfriede. *"Lustige Gesellschaft." Schwank und Witz des 17. und 18. Jahrhunderts in Kultur- und Sozialgeschichtlichem Kontext.* Stuttgart: J. B. Metzler, 1984.

Moxey, Keith. *Peasants, Warriors, and Wives: Popular Imagery in the Reformation.* Chicago: U of Chicago P, 1989.

Müller, Jan-Dirk. "Texte aus Texten: Zu intertextuellen Verfahren in frühneuzeitlicher Literatur, am Beispiel von Fischarts Ehzuchtbüchlein und Geschichtklitterung." In *Intertextualität in der Frühen Neuzeit: Studien zu ihren theoretischen und praktischen Perspektiven,* edited by Wilhelm Kühlmann and Wolfgang Neuber, 63–109. Frankfurt am Main: Peter Lang, 1994.

———. "Volksbuch/Prosaroman im 15., 16. Jahrhundert: Perspektiven der Forschung." *Internationales Archiv für Sozial- und Literaturwissenschaft* Sonderheft 1 (1985): 1–128.

———. "Von der Subversion frühneuzeitlicher Ehelehre. Zu Fischarts *Ehezuchtbüchlein* und *Geschichtklitterung.*" In *The Graph of Sex and the German Text. Gendered Culture in Early Modern Germany 1500–1700,* edited by Lynne Tatlock, 121–56. Amsterdam: Rodopi, 1994.

Müller, Maria E. *Eheglück und Liebesjoch: Bilder von Liebe, Ehe und Familie in der deutschen Literatur des 15. und 16. Jahrhunderts.* Edited by Maria E. Müller. Weinheim: Beltz, 1988.

———. "Naturwesen Mann." In *Wandel der Geschlechterbeziehungen zu Beginn der Neuzeit,* edited by Heide Wunder and Christina Vanja. Frankfurt am Main: Suhrkamp, 1991.

Murray, Jacqueline, and Konrad Eisenbichler. *Desire and Discipline: Sex and Sexuality in the Premodern West.* Toronto: U of Toronto P, 1996.

Opitz, Claudia. "Mutterschaft und Vaterschaft im 14. und 15. Jahrhundert." In *Frauengeschichte — Geschlechtergeschichte*, edited by Karin Hausen and Heide Wunder, 137–53. Frankfurt/New York: Campus, 1992.

Osinski, Jutta. *Einführung in die feministische Literaturwissenschaft*. Munich: Erich Schmidt, 1998.

Ozment, Steven. *The Burghermeister's Daughter: Scandal in a Sixteenth-Century German Town*. New York: St. Martin's Press, 1996.

———. *Flesh and Spirit: Private Life in Early Modern Germany*. New York: Viking, 1999.

———. *Three Behaim Boys: Growing up in Early Modern Germany: A Chronicle of Their Lives*. New Haven: Yale UP, 1990.

———. *When Fathers Ruled: Family Life in Reformation Europe*. Cambridge, MA: Harvard UP, 1983.

Padgug, Robert A. "Sexual Matters: On Conceptualizing Sexuality in History." *Radical History Review* 1 (1979).

Pastenaci, Stephan. "Tragischer Liebestod versus sozialer Aufstieg in Georg Wickrams Prosaromanen *Gabriotto und Reinhard* und *Der Goldfaden* — zwei Verlaufsvarianten einer Novelle von Boccaccio." *Wolfenbüttler Renaissance-Mitteilungen* 19, no. 2 (1995): 49–58.

Peters, Ursula. *Text und Kontext: Die mittelalterliche Philologie zwischen Gesellschaftsgeschichte und Kulturanthropologie*. Wiesbaden: Westdeutscher Verlag, 2000.

———. "Zwischen New Historicism and Gender-Forschung: Neue Wege der älteren Gemanistik." *Deutsche Vierteljahrschrift für Literaturwissenschaft und Geistesgeschichte* 71 (1997): 363–96.

Pieters, Jürgen. "Facing History, or the Anxiety of Reading: Holbein's *The Ambassadors* According to Greenblatt and Loytard." In *Reading the Past Literature and History*, edited by Tamsin Spargo, 88–102. Basingstoke: Palgrave, 2000.

Puff, Helmut. "Die Ehre der Ehe — Beobachtungen zum Konzept der Ehre in der Frühen Neuzeit an Johann Fischart's *Philosophisch Ehezuchtbüchlein* (1578) und anderen Ehelehren des 16. Jahrhunderts." In *Ehrkonzepte der Frühen Neuzeit. Identitäten und Abgrenzungen*, edited by Sibylle Backmann, et al., 99–119. Berlin: Akademie Verlag, 1998.

Rapp, Francois. *Réformes et Réformation a Strasbourg. Église et société dans le diocèse de Strasbourg (1450–1525)*. Paris: Editions Ophrys, 1974.

Röcke, Werner. "Liebe und Melancholie. Formen sozialer Kommunikation in der *Historie von Florio und Biancefora* (1587)." In *Variationen der Liebe. Historische Psychologie der Geschlechterbeziehung*, edited by Thomas Kornbichler, 129–48. Tübingen: Diskord, 1995.

Roper, Lyndal. "Discipline and Respectability: Prostitution and the Reformation in Augsburg." In *Feminism and History,* edited by Joan Wallach Scott, 333–65. Oxford: Oxford UP, 1999.

———. *The Holy Household: Women and Morals in Reformation Europe.* Oxford: Clarendon, 1989.

———. "Männlichkeit und männliche Ehre." In *Frauengeschichte — Geschlechtergeschichte,* edited by Karin Hausen and Heide Wunder, 154–72. Frankfurt/New York: Campus, 1992.

———. *Oedipus and the Devil: Witchcraft, Sexuality and Religion in Early Modern Europe.* London: Routledge, 1994.

———. "Sexualutopien in der deutschen Revolution." In *Ordnung und Lust: Bilder von Liebe, Ehe und Sexualität in Spätmittelalter und Früher Neuzeit,* edited by Hans-Jürgen Bachorski, 307–36. Trier: Wissenschaftlicher Verlag, 1991.

Rose, Sonya O. "Introduction to Dialogue: Gender/History/Women's History: Is Feminist Scholarship Losing Its Critical Edge?" *Journal of Women's History* 5, no. 1 (Spring 1993): 89–101.

Rublack, Ulinka. *The Crimes of Women in Early Modern Germany.* Oxford: Clarendon Press, 1999.

———. "'Viehisch, frech, vnd onverschämpt.' Inzest in Südwestdeutschland, Ca. 1530–1700." In *Von Huren und Rabenmüttern. Weibliche Kriminalität in der Frühen Neuzeit,* edited by Otto Ulbricht, 171–214. Cologne: Böhlau, 1995.

Safely, Thomas Max. *Let No Man Put Asunder: The Control of Marriage in the German Southwest: A Comparative Study, 1550–1600.* Kirksville, MO: Sixteenth Century Journal Publishers, 1984.

Schlossbauer, Frank. *Literatur als Gegenwelt: zur Geschichtlichkeit literarischer Komik am Beispiel Fischarts und Lessings.* New York: Peter Lang, 1998.

Schnell, Rüdiger. "Die Frau als Gefährtin (Socia) des Mannes. Eine Studie zur Interdependenz von Textsorte, Adressat und Aussage." In *Geschlechterbeziehungen und Textfunktionen. Studien zu Eheschriften der Frühen Neuzeit,* edited by Rüdiger Schnell, 119–70. Tübingen: Niemeyer, 1998.

———. *Frauendiskurs, Männerdiskurs, Ehediskurs. Textsorten und Geschlechterkonzepte in Mittelalter und Früher Neuzeit.* Frankfurt am Main: Campus Verlag, 1998.

———. "Geschlechterbeziehungen und Textfunktionen. Probleme und Perspektiven eines Forschungsansatzes." In *Geschlechterbeziehungen und Textfunktionen. Studien zu Eheschriften der Frühen Neuzeit,* edited by Rüdiger Schnell, 1–58. Tübingen: Niemeyer, 1998.

———. "Geschlechtergeschichte, Diskursgeschichte und Literaturgeschichte. Eine Studie zu konkurrierenden Männerbildern in Mittelalter und Früher Neuzeit." *Frühmittelalterliche Studien* 32 (1998): 307–64.

———. "Liebesdisdurs und Ehediskurs im 15. und 16. Jahrhundert." In *The Graph of Sex and the German Text: Gendered Culture in Early Modern Germany 1500–1700*, edited by Lynne Tatlock, 77–120. Amsterdam: Rodopi, 1994.

———. "Text und Geschlecht. Eine Einleitung." In *Text und Geschlecht. Mann und Frau in Eheschriften der Frühen Neuzeit*, edited by Rüdiger Schnell, 9–46. Frankfurt am Main: Suhrkamp, 1997.

Schulz, Armin. "Texte und Textilien. Zur Entstehung der Liebe in Georg Wickrams *Goldtfaden* (1557)." *Daphnis* 30, no. 1–2 (2001): 53–70.

Schuster, Beate. *Die freien Frauen. Dirnen und Frauenhäuser im 15. und 16. Jahrhundert.* Frankfurt am Main: Campus, 1995.

Schuster, Peter. *Das Frauenhaus. Städtische Bordelle in Deutschland 1350–1600.* Paderborn: Schöningh, 1992.

Schwitzgebel, Bärbel. *Noch nicht genug der Vorrede. Zur Vorrede volkssprachiger Sammlungen von Exempeln, Fabeln, Sprichwörtern und Schwänken des 16. Jahrhunderts.* Tübingen: Niemeyer, 1996.

Scott, Joan Wallach. "Feminism and History." In *Feminism and History*, edited by Joan Wallach Scott. Oxford: Oxford UP, 1999.

———. *Gender and the Politics of History*. New York: Columbia UP, 1988.

———. "Gender: A Useful Category of Historical Analysis." In *Feminism and History*, edited by Joan Wallach Scott, 152–80. Oxford: Oxford UP, 1999.

———. "Women's Studies on the Edge: Introduction." *A Journal of Feminist Cultural Studies: Differences — Women's Studies on the Edge* 9, no. 3 (1997): i–v.

Scribner, R. W. *Religion and Culture in Germany (1400–1800)*. Edited by Lyndal Roper. Leiden: Brill, 2001.

Scribner, Robert W. *For the Sake of Simple Folk: Popular Propaganda for the German Reformation*. Cambridge: Cambridge UP, 1981.

———. *Popular Culture and Popular Movements in Reformation Germany*. London: Hambledon, 1987.

Seelbach, Ulrich. "Fremde Federn. Die Quellen Johann Fischarts und die Prätexte seines idealen Lesers in der Forschung." *Daphnis* 29, no. 3–4 (2000): 465–583.

Selderhuis, H. J. *Marriage and Divorce in the Thought of Martin Bucer*. Translated by John Vriend and Lyle D. Bierma. Kirksville, MO: Thomas Jefferson UP, 1999.

Sommerhalder, Hugo. *Johann Fischarts Werk. Eine Einführung.* Berlin: Walter de Gruyter, 1960.

Spargo, Tamsin. "Introduction: Past, Present and Future Pasts." In *Reading the Past Literature and History,* edited by Tamsin Spargo, 1–17. Basingstoke: Palgrave, 2000.

Spengler, Walter Eckehart. *Johann Fischart, Gen. Müntzer. Studie zur Sprache und Literatur des ausgehenden 16. Jahrhunderts.* Ph.D. dissertation, Göppingen, 1969.

Spriewald, Ingeborg. "Jörg Wickram und die Anfänge der realistischen Prosaerzählung in Deutschland." Ph.D. dissertation, Potsdam, 1971.

———. *Vom Eulenspiegel zum Simplicissimus. Zur Genesis des Realismus in den Anfängen der deutschen Prosaerzählung.* Berlin: Akademie-Verlag, 1974.

Stede, Marga. "Ein Grausame unnd erschrockenliche History. Bemerkungen zum Ursprung und zur Erzählweise von Georg Wickrams Rollwagenbüchlein — Geschichte über einen Mord im Elsass." *Daphnis* 15 (1986): 124–34.

Stone, Lawrence. *The Past and the Present.* Boston: Routledge & Kegan, 1981.

Strasser, Ulrike. "Intime Antagonisten: Postmoderne Theorie, feministische Wissenschaft und die Geschichte der Frauen." *Traverse* 7, no. 1 (2000): 37–50.

———. "Jenseits von Essenzialismus und Dekonstruktion: feministische Geschichtswissenschaft nach der linguistischen Wende." *L'Homme. Zeitschrift für Feministische Geschichtswissenschaft* 11, no. 1 (2000): 124–29.

Strassner, Erich. *Schwank.* 2nd ed. Stuttgart: Metzler, 1978.

Text im Kontext: Anleitung zur Lektüre deutscher Texte der Frühen Neuzeit. Edited by Alexander Schwarz and Laure Abplanalp. Bern: Peter Lang, 1997.

Thomas, Norbert. *Handlungsstruktur und dominante Motivik im deutschen Prosaroman des 15. und Frühen 16. Jahrhunderts.* Nuremberg: Hans Carl, 1971.

Wagner, Berit. "Kultur, Geschlecht, Erzählen." *Geschlecht und Kultur. Beiträge zur historischen Sozialkunde* Sondernummer (2000).

Wahrig Deutsches Wörterbuch. Gütersloh: Bertelsmann, 1986.

Wailes, Stephen L. "Johann Fischart (1546 or 1547–1590 or 1591)." In *German Writers of the Renaissance and Reformation. Dictionary of Literary Biography, Vol. 179,* edited by James Hardin and Max Reinhart, 55–62. Detroit: Gale Research, 1997.

Walter, Tilmann. *Unkeuschheit und Werk der Liebe. Diskurse über Sexualität am Beginn der Neuzeit in Deutschland.* Berlin: De Gruyter, 1998.

Watt, Tessa. *Cheap Print and Popular Piety 1550–1560*. Cambridge: Cambridge UP, 1991.

Wåghäll, Elisabeth. *Dargestellte Welt — Reale Welt: Freundschaft: Liebe und Familie in den Prosawerken Georg Wickrams*. Bern: Peter Lang, 1996.

———. "Georg Wickram (Circa 1505–Circa 1561)." In *German Writers of the Renaissance and Reformation. Dictionary of Literary Biography, Vol. 179*, edited by James Hardin and Max Reinhart, 309–16. Detroit: Gale Research, 1997.

———. "Georg Wickram — Stand der Forschung." *Daphnis* 24, no. 2–3 (1995): 491–540.

———. "Jörg Wickram." In *The Encyclopedia of the Renaissance*, vol. 6, edited by F. Grendler. New York: Charles Scribner's Sons, 1999.

Weigel, Sigrid. "Geschlechterdifferenz und Literaturwissenschaft." In *The Graph of Sex and the German Text: Gendered Culture in Early Modern Germany 1500–1700*, edited by Lynne Tatlock, 7–26. Amsterdam: Rodopi, 1994.

Weinberg, Florence. "Fischart's Geschichtklitterung: A Questionable Reception of Gargantua." *Sixteenth-Century Journal* 3 (1982): 23–35.

———. *Gargantua in a Convex Mirror*. New York: Lang, 1986.

Wendel, Francois. *Le mariage a Strasbourg a l'epoque de la Réforme 1520–1692*. Strasbourg: Imprimerie Alsacienne, 1928.

White, Hayden. *The Content of the Form: Narrative Discourse and Historical Representation*. Baltimore: Johns Hopkins, 1987.

———. *Figural Realism: Studies in the Mimesis Effect*. Baltimore: Johns Hopkins UP, 1999.

Wiesner, Merry. *Christianity and Sexuality in the Early Modern World: Regulating Desire, Reforming Practise*. London: Routledge, 1999.

———. *Gender, Church and State in Early Modern Germany*. Harlow: Longman, 1998.

———. *Gender in History*. Oxford: Blackwell, 2001.

———. "The Hubris of Writing Surveys, or A Feminist Confronts the Textbook." In *Attending to Early Modern Women*, edited by Susan D. Amussen and Adele Seeff, 297–307. Newark: U of Delaware P, 1998.

———. *Women and Gender in Early Modern Europe*. Cambridge: Cambridge UP, 1993.

———. *Working Women in Renaissance Germany*. New Brunswick: Rutgers UP, 1986.

Wiesner, Merry E. "The Religious Dimensions of Guild Notions of Honor in Reformation Germany." In *Ehrkonzepte in der Frühen Neuzeit: Identitäten und Abgrenzungen,* edited by Sibylle Backmann, et al., 223–33. Berlin: Akademie Verlag, 1998.

Williams, Gerhild S. *Defining Dominion: The Discourses of Magic and Witchcraft in Early Modern France and Germany.* Ann Arbor: U of Michigan P, 1995.

———. "On Finding Words: Witchcraft and Discourses of Dissidence and Discovery." In *The Graph of Sex and the German Text. Gendered Culture in Early Modern Germany 1500–1700,* edited by Lynne Tatlock, 45–66. Amsterdam: Rodopi, 1994.

———. "Provokation und Antwort. Hans Blumenbergs Frühe Neuzeit." In *"Der Buchstab tödt — der Geist macht lebendig." Festschrift zum 60. Geburtstag von Hans-Gert Roloff von Freunden, Schülern und Kollegen. Band I,* edited by James Hardin and Jörg Jungmayr, 109–26. Bern: Peter Lang, 1992.

———. "Der Teufel und die Frau: Textformen und Aussagen." In *Text und Geschlecht. Mann und Frau in Eheschriften der Frühen Neuzeit,* edited by Rüdiger Schnell, 280–302. Frankfurt am Main: Suhrkamp, 1997.

Wiltenburg, Joy. *Disorderly Women and Female Power in the Street Literature of Early Modern England and Germany.* Charlottesville, VA: UP of Virginia, 1992.

———. "Family Murders: Gender, Reproduction, and the Discourse of Crime in Early Modern Germany." *Colloquia Germanica* 3–4 (1995): 357–74.

Winckelmann, Otto. *Das Fürsorgewesen der Stadt Straßburg vor und nach der Reformation bis zum Ausgang des sechzehnten Jahrhuderts.* 2 vols. Leipzig: M. Heinsius Nachfolger, 1922.

Wolfthal, Diane. "Women's Community and Male Spies: Erhard Schön's *How Seven Women Complain About Their Worthless Husbands.*" In *Attending to Early Modern Women,* edited by Susan D. Amussen and Adele Seeff, 117–54. Newark: U of Delaware P, 1998.

Women in Reformation and Counter-Reformation Europe: Public and Private Worlds. Edited by Sherrin Marshall. Bloomington: Indiana UP, 1989.

Women, Marriage, and Family in Medieval Christendom: Essays in Memory of Michael M. Sheenan. Edited by Constance M. Rousseau and Joel T. Rosenthal. Kalamazoo, MI: The Medieval Institute, 1998.

Wunder, Heide. *Der andere Blick auf die Frühe Neuzeit: Forschungen 1974–1995.* Edited by Barbara Hoffmann, et al. Königstein/Taunus: Ulrike Helmer Verlag, 1999.

———. "Geschlechtsidentitäten: Frauen und Männer im späten Mittelalter und am Beginn der Neuzeit." In *Frauengeschichte — Geschlechtergeschichte,* edited by Karin Hausen and Heide Wunder, 131–36. Frankfurt/New York: Campus, 1992.

———. *He Is the Sun, She Is the Moon: Women in Early Modern Germany.* Cambridge: Harvard UP, 1998.

———. "'Weibliche Kriminalität' in der Frühen Neuzeit. Überlegungen aus der Sicht der Geschlechtergeschichte." In *Von Huren und Rabenmüttern. Weibliche Kriminalität in der Frühen Neuzeit,* edited by Otto Ulbricht, 39–62. Cologne: Böhlau, 1995.

Zemon Davis, Natalie. "Displacing and Displeasing: Writing About Women in the Early Modern Period." In *Attending to Early Modern Women,* edited by Susan D. Amussen and Adele Seeff, 25–37. Newark: U of Delaware P, 1998.

———. *Fiction in the Archives: Pardon Tales and Their Tellers in Sixteenth-Century France.* Stanford: Stanford UP, 1987.

———. *Society and Culture in Early Modern France.* Stanford: Stanford UP, 1975.

———. "Women on Top." In *Feminism and Renaissance Studies,* edited by Lorna Hutson, 156–85. Oxford: Oxford UP, 1999.

———. "'Women's History' in Transition: The European Case." In *Feminism and History,* edited by Joan Wallach Scott, 79–104. Oxford: Oxford UP, 1999.

Zinsser, Judith P. "Theoretical Issues: 'Much More is at Stake Here': A Response to 'The Construction of History.'" *Journal of Women's History* 9, no. 3 (Autumn 1997): 133–39.

Index

Critics referred to or discussed only in the notes are not included in the index.

abuse, 34, 62, 90 n. 99–100, 176;
  sexual, 31, 42, 62
Adelphus, Johann, 43
adultery, 29, 32, 42, 49, 60, 142–
  43, 158, 161, 165–66, 168–70,
  176
age difference, 36–37, 50, 82 n. 32
apprentice, 114

Bakhtin, Mikhail, 55, 149 n. 11
Bebel, Heinrich, 43, 89 n. 92
Becker-Cantarino, Barbara, 7, 13–
  14
beguines/beguinage, 53–54,
  87 n. 79
Belsey, Catherine, 5
Bennewitz, Ingrid, 195
bigamy, 135
Boccaccio, 11, 58
Boccaccio, works by: *Decamerone*,
  11, 28, 58, 62, 66, 67
Bodin, Jean, 12
Bodin, Jean, works by:
  De Démonomanie de Sorcieres,
  12, 62, 131, 145
Bolte, Johannes, 43, 58, 88 n. 89,
  183 n. 15
Brandt, Sebastian, 34
Brandt, Sebastian, works by:
  Narrenschiff, 34, 95
Brauner, Sigrid, 192
brothel, 50, 67–68, 91 n. 110,
  162–164, 168
Brucker, Johann, 161–62
Bucer, Martin, 77 n. 78, 100,
  116, 143, 155 n. 55, 188 n. 59

canonical law, 173–74
capital punishment, 166, 176
castration, 48, 87, 91 n. 118
Catholic Church, 48, 174
celibacy, 5, 29, 32, 58, 66, 136,
  158, 165
censorship, 43, 70
chapbooks, 3, 27–29
chastity, 60, 62, 103, 115, 136,
  175
child/children, 8, 33–34, 36, 38,
  46–48, 52, 70–75, 92 n. 121,
  96–98, 104–9, 110–19, 140,
  142, 144–46, 165, 174, 195
childbirth, 53, 70, 104, 136
childlessness, 33, 51, 96, 104–5,
  144, 52
chivalry, 96
Chrisman, Miriam Usher, 11
city council, 33, 157, 159, 161,
  167–80
city ordinances, 3, 10, 165, 168,
  171, 180, 194–95
clandestine marriages, 173
clergy, 48, 50, 67, 69, 76,
  86 n. 71, 194
concubinage, 162, 165
convent, 53, 67–70, 188 n. 59
corporal punishment, 161, 164,
  177
court records, 36, 158
cultural turn, 4
culture, 4; definition of, 17 n. 12

death, 38, 63, 100, 107, 110,
  116–17, 170; death sentence,

6, 72, 72, 82 n. 33, 131, 166, 170, 176–77
decapitation, 166, 176
deployment of alliance/ sexuality, 8
desire, 8, 29, 141; female desire, 34–35, 43, 60, 64, 75, 103, 195; male desire, 31, 48, 62 52
devil, 72, 13, 45–46, 52, 73–74
discourse; definition, 2, 4 16 n. 9
discursive fields, 2, 7–8
dissidents, 6
divorce, 143, 155 n. 55, 158–60, 164, 172, 174, 177, 188 n. 59. *See also* separation
divorce tracts, 159
dowry, 177
drowning, 166, 176, 178, 185 n. 38

early modern period, 1, 4–6, 12, 14, 45
education, 11, 96, 113–14, 123, 27, 151 n. 23
Epochenschwelle, 17 n. 11
Erasmus of Rotterdam, 10, 116
Erasmus of Rotterdam, works by: *Colloquia familiara,* 116; "Virgo misogamus," 116; "Virgo poenitens," 116
Eschenbach, Wolfram von, 71
Eschenbach, Wolfram von, works by: *Parzival,* 71
Eve, 5, 19 n. 21, 103, 109, 137, 144, 179
exempla, 9
extramarital affairs/intercourse, 10, 61, 70, 141, 143–44, 191

fable, 9
facetiae, 27, 89 n. 92
female conduct, 151 n. 24, 164, 170
fertility/infertility, 48–50

fiction, 3, 9–10, 14 n. 3, 194–95; non-fiction, 3, 9–10
Fischart, Johann, 3, 7, 11, 13, 23 n. 47
Fischart, Johann, works by: *Ehezuchtbüchlein:* 12, 145; *Flöh, Hatz, Weiber Tratz,* 12, 132; *Geschichtklitterung,* 3, 131–156
fool (Narr), 32, 35, 43, 49, 51, 56, 86 n. 71, 87 n. 76, 146
Foucault, Michel, 7, 21 n. 32–33
fornication/fornicator, 29, 42, 50, 158–59, 166, 168, 173, 175, 177
Frey, Jakob, 3, 7, 11, 13, 23 n. 45
Frey, Jakob, works by: *Garten Gesellschaft,* 11, 28, 42–56, 57
friars, 31–32
friendship, 65, 66, 110, 128 n. 55
Fuchs, Joseph, 159

gender discourse, 8
gender hierarchy, 46, 76, 100, 194
gender identity, 6–7, 10, 52, 97, 141, 145–46, 195
gender roles, 2, 7, 10, 108, 112, 125 n. 38, 193
gender relations, 3, 28–29, 117, 133, 145, 158
gender studies, 6
genre, 8, 14 n. 3, 22 nn. 39–40, 41, 58, 70, 119 n. 2, 131, 151 n. 23
German law, 180 n. 3
Glowa, Josef K., 134, 148 n. 9
Goedeke, Karl, 58
guardian, 49, 62, 71, 98–99, 112, 118, 171, 173

Haushofer, Marlen, 42
Haushofer, Marlen, works by: *Die Wand,* 42
Heilsgeschichte, 5
heterosexuality, 29, 76, 97, 136–37, 142

homosexuality, 52, 142–43, 184 n. 33
honor, 33, 38, 54, 61–63, 66, 89 n. 98, 115, 140, 162, 173, 178
household, 31–32, 36, 41, 46, 50, 64, 108, 112, 114, 135, 138, 167; head of the household, 36–40, 65, 74, 76, 85 n. 63, 116, 177

illicit sex, 163, 165
incest, 188 n. 63
individuality, 7
Institoris, Heinrich, 12
Institoris, Heinrich, works by: Hammer of Witches, 12, 131; *Hexenhammer,* 12, 13, 131; *Malleus Maleficarum,* 62, 131
intercourse (sexual), 43, 48, 52–55, 59, 62, 67, 70, 119, 135, 140–43, 163, 170, 173, 175, 194
inwohner, 161

jealousy, 34–35, 81 nn. 30–31

kinship, 8

late medieval period, 2, 5
Latin, texts in, 12, 27, 43, 57
legislation, 10, 117, 159–60, 162–64, 173, 186 n. 46, 188 n. 59
legislative texts, 10, 160, 194
letter writing, 114, 126 n. 49–50, 127 n. 55
literacy, 22 n. 38, 43, 79 n. 10, 126 n. 50, 161
love, 7, 10, 38–39, 51, 62, 64, 66, 72, 92 n. 121, 106, 108, 110–11, 114, 116, 124 nn. 32, 36, 126 n. 49, 138, 142, 144; courtly love, 95, 122 n. 20
lover, 34, 38, 54, 60, 63, 114, 178, 191

lovesickness, 66
Lucretia, 116, 128 n. 59
Lugowski, Clemens, 150 n. 21
Luther, Martin, 85 n. 63, 98, 100, 116, 120 n. 11, 143, 158, 192–93
Lutheran, 160, 173

magic, 52, 60, 131, 148 n. 6
maid, 33, 49–52, 56, 108, 114, 119, 143, 156 n. 72, 177
Mandats et Reglements, ix, 159
marriage, 5, 8, 10, 12, 29, 32, 34–37, 40, 51, 53, 60, 66, 70, 71, 96–104, 110–11, 116, 118, 131–32, 134–37, 140–43, 158–61, 163, 171, 174–76, 192–95; age for marriage, 173–74; clandestine marriages, 173; marriage court, 172, 174, 188 n. 58; marriage proposal, 100, 102; marriage tracts, 12, 98, 116, 131, 149 n. 11
Mary, 5, 104, 109, 119, 179
masculinity, 33, 35, 47, 76, 140, 167
melancholy, 42, 84 n. 46
merchant/merchants, 11, 95, 99, 109
misogyny, 2, 5, 10, 27, 42, 57, 64, 102, 107, 131
Moi, Toril, x
monks, 32, 48, 56, 66–67, 69, 80 n. 20
Montanus, Martin, 3, 7, 11, 13, 23 n. 44
Montanus, Martin, works by: *Das ander theyl der Garten gesellschaft,* 11, 57–76; *Cymon und Iphigenia,* 58; *Guiscardus und Sigismunda,* 58; *Theobaldus und Ermilina,* 58; *Der Wegkürtzer,* 11
Morgengabe, 169–70
Moser-Rath, Elfriede, 29
motherhood, 144

Moxey, Keith, 28
murder (killings), 38, 46, 54, 62, 63, 65, 71–75

neighbors, 35, 47, 50, 76, 110, 113, 115–17, 128 n. 55, 136
nobility, 95, 103, 173
nuns, 53, 66–69, 164, 193

oikos, 112, 152 n. 28
order, 6, 33, 35–36, 66, 117, 119, 137, 147, 160; disorder, 142, 158; divine, 168, 172, 179; legal, 53, 171, 174, 179; social, 20 n. 30, 29, 41, 46, 49, 53–54, 60, 67, 70, 159, 168, 191

Panofsky, Erwin, 28
parable, 9, 96, 97
parenthood, 52, 70, 105, 111, 122 n. 22
passivity, 61, 101, 107
Pauli, Johannes, works by: *Schimpf und Ernst*, 27
peasants, 56
penalty/penalties, 158, 166, 168, 177, 185 n. 38
periodization, 21 n. 32
Poggio, Francesco, 43, 89 n. 92
polygamy, 135
pornography, 43, 69
poverty, 75, 105
power, 41, 70, 75, 81 n. 28, 102, 108; female, 36, 65, 191; male, 6, 40, 44, 66, 69, 146, 192, 195; physical, 65
pregnancy, 33–34, 38, 48, 53, 59, 62, 70, 73, 104–6, 119, 123 n. 23, 136, 141, 170, 174
priests/priesthood, 32, 48, 50, 56, 70, 165
procreation, 48, 51, 54, 59, 76, 136, 143, 158, 165, 173, 192
procuration, 162, 164, 169, 178, 187 n. 52

the prodigal son, 96, 106, 120 n. 5
prostitutes, 104, 119, 137, 142, 162–67, 171, 178, 183 n. 20, 185 n. 34
prostitution, 10, 48, 131, 146, 154 n. 52, 159, 160, 162–66, 171, 183 n. 19–20, 184 n. 31
puberty, 75, 162, 165, 177
punishment, 38–39, 48, 61, 107–8, 113–14, 123 140, 161, 164, 166–71, 176–77

Rabelais, Francois, 12
Rabelais, Francois, works by: *Gargantua*, 12, 132–34
rape, 31, 75, 168, 170, 177
Reformation, 5, 8, 10, 29, 53, 104, 131, 158, 160, 165–67, 171; Counter-Reformation, 132; reformation movements, 4; Reformation propaganda, 39, 98–99
Roman law, 173–74, 180 n. 3
Roper, Lyndal, 14
Rummel, Erika, 14

Scherer, Wilhelm, 58
Schmidt, Erich, 58
Schnell, Rüdiger, 9, 22 n. 40, 96
Schwank, 27–29
Scott, Joan, 2, 7
secrecy, 50, 62, 127 n. 51
self-control, 44, 116, 118, 163
separation, 143, 174–77. *See also* divorce
sermon, 9
sexuality, 8–9, 29, 31, 32, 51–53, 59, 69, 104, 141, 175; female, 43–44, 47, 55, 59, 70, 103, 119; male, 48, 55, 69, 135, 141, 163
sodomy, 136, 142
soldiers, 39, 54, 96
Spiegelliteratur, 9

Stepmother, 36, 74–75
Strasbourg, 3, 10–13, 22 n. 38; printers in S., 58, 68, 157–61, 163, 165, 179, 194–95
student, 54, 113
submissiveness, 35, 37, 66, 100–101, 115, 118
suicide, 38, 71, 116
syphilis, 142, 154 n. 52

Till Eulenspiegel, 44

violence, 35, 37, 56, 62, 64, 71, 117
virgin, 31, 62, 64, 104, 117, 147, 175–77, 195
virginity, 31, 59, 61, 104, 175, 178, 195; male virginity, 61
virility, 33, 50, 56, 68, 143, 188 n. 63
virtue, 35, 60–61, 102, 107, 115, 138, 140
Vives, Jean Luis, 139

wedding, 38, 53, 61, 64, 66, 96, 98, 100, 103, 110, 122 n. 17, 167, 174–75, 179, 181 n. 10
Western Church, 4
whore, 45, 54
Wickram, Georg, 1, 3, 7, 11, 13, 23 n. 46, 28, 30, 96
Wickram, Georg, works by: *Gabriotto und Reinhart*, 95, 123 n. 28; *Galmy*, 95, 122 n. 17; *Der jungen Knaben Spiegel*, 11, 96–109, 193–95; *Das Rollwagenbüchlein*, 11, 28–42, 98, 101, 167; *Von guten und bösen Nachbarn*, 1, 11, 96, 109–119, 134, 168, 174, 193–95
widow, 31, 36, 37, 39, 54, 56, 71, 72, 98–100, 103, 109, 185 n. 40
Wiesner-Hanks, Merry, 14, 114, 170

Williams, Gerhild S., 13
witch, 13, 19 n. 26, 34, 45–46, 62, 109, 144, 180, 192, 184
witch Sabbath, 13
witch tract, 6, 12, 62, 131, 145–46
witch trials, 6, 12, 131, 166
witchcraft, 6, 12–13, 60, 131
woman on top, 42, 83 n. 45
women's studies, 6
woodcuts, 28
world turned upside down, 39, 42, 46, 50, 70, 74, 95, 134, 146, 192
Wunder, Heide, 14, 114, 145, 170